ndows 10 for Seniors

Studio Visual Steps

Windows 10
for Seniors

Get started with Windows 10

www.visualsteps.com

This book has been written using the Visual Steps™ method.
Cover design by Studio Willemien Haagsma bNO

© 2015 Visual Steps
Author: Studio Visual Steps

First printing: August 2015
ISBN 978 90 5905 451 6

Do you have questions or suggestions?
Email: info@visualsteps.com

Would you like more information?
www.visualsteps.com

Website for this book:
www.visualsteps.com/windows10

Table of Contents

Foreword

In this book you will learn how to work with *Windows 10*. We assume that you already have some experience with computers. You may already have worked with *Windows 8.1* or *Windows 7*, for instance, and you already have some basic skills, such as typing text and surfing the Internet.

Windows 10 is the most recent version of the operating system manufactured by Microsoft. Possibly you have already turned on your computer or laptop with *Windows 10* and taken a look at your computer.
Then you will have noticed that some things have radically changed, while others have hardly changed at all, with respect to the version of *Windows* you previously used.

In this book you will become acquainted with the new and renewed programs and options of *Windows 10*. Step by step, and at your own pace, you will master the basic skills necessary for working with *Windows 10*. You will find that some operations are completely new to you. But you may also already know some of the other operations, and you can repeat them once more by following the instructions in this book.

We hope you will enjoy reading this book!

The Studio Visual Steps authors

P.S. Your comments and suggestions are most welcome. Our email address is: mail@visualsteps.com

Visual Steps Newsletter

All Visual Steps books follow the same methodology: clear and concise step-by-step instructions with screen shots to demonstrate each task.
A complete list of all our books can be found on our website **www.visualsteps.com**

You can also sign up to receive our **free Visual Steps Newsletter**.
In this Newsletter you will receive periodic information by email regarding:
- the latest titles and previously released books;
- special offers, supplemental chapters, tips and free informative booklets.
Also, our Newsletter subscribers may download any of the documents listed on the web page **www.visualsteps.com/info_downloads**
When you subscribe to our Newsletter you can be assured that we will never use your email address for any purpose other than sending you the information as previously described. We will not share this address with any third-party. Each Newsletter also contains a one-click link to unsubscribe.

Introduction to Visual Steps™

The Visual Steps handbooks and manuals are the best instructional materials available for learning how to work with the computer. Nowhere else can you find better support for getting to know your *Windows* computer or *Mac*, your iPad or iPhone, Samsung Galaxy Tab, the Internet and a variety of computer applications.

Properties of the Visual Steps books:

- **Comprehensible contents**
  Addresses the needs of the beginner or intermediate user for a manual written in simple, straight-forward English.
- **Clear structure**
  Precise, easy to follow instructions. The material is broken down into small enough segments to allow for easy absorption.
- **Screen shots of every step**
  Quickly compare what you see on your screen with the screen shots in the book. Pointers and tips guide you when new windows or alert boxes are opened so you always know what to do next.
- **Get started right away**
  All you have to do is turn on your computer or laptop and have your book at hand. Perform each operation as indicated on your own device.
- **Layout**
  The text is printed in a large size font and is clearly legible.

In short, I believe these manuals will be excellent guides for you.

dr. H. van der Meij
Faculty of Applied Education, Department of Instructional Technology, University of Twente, the Netherlands

What You Will Need

To be able to work through this book, you will need a number of things:

The primary requirement for working with this book is having the US or English version of *Windows 10* installed on your computer or laptop. *Windows* comes equipped with all the programs you need to work with this book. This book is not suitable for tablets.

Please note: The screen shots shown in this book have been made using a local user account. It is also possible to login with a *Microsoft* account. Since this is a book for beginning computer users, we have chosen to not to use this type of account. If you are working with a *Microsoft* account, you will sometimes see different windows and other options.

It's also important to work with an up-to-date computer. You will learn how to update in *section 7.5 Windows Update*.

A functioning Internet connection.

A computer mouse.
To perform the actions and exercises shown in this book, it is necessary to have a mouse installed.

Do you have a touchscreen? In *Bonus Chapter Working with a touchscreen* you will read how to operate *Windows* with a touchscreen. You can read how to open this chapter in *Appendix C Opening the Bonus Online Chapters*.

The following things are useful. But it is not a problem if you do not have them. You can read through the sections where these items are used.

A USB stick (also called a USB memory stick or memory stick). A USB stick with a storage capacity of 2 GB is more than enough.

A printer is required for some of the exercises.

You will need a digital camera to practice transferring photos from the camera to the computer.

A music CD.

Prior Computer Experience

In this book we assume you already have some computer skills and can work with *Windows 8.1* or *Windows 7*, for example. These are the basic skills you need to have:

- starting up and shutting down *Windows*;
- clicking the mouse;
- opening and closing programs;
- typing text;
- opening web pages;
- sending and receiving emails;
- adjusting settings on your computer.

In this book you will learn how to apply these operations in *Windows 10*. You will see that some of the operations have hardly changed, while others have indeed changed.

If you were previously using *Windows Vista* or *XP*, you can also use this book, but the differences will probably be a lot bigger.

If you do not have any experience whatsoever with the computer, it is better to start working with *Windows 10* by using another book, that is to say:

Windows 10 for Seniors for the Beginning Senior
ISBN 978 90 5905 461 5

On this web page you can find more information on this book:
www.visualsteps.com/windows10senior

How To Use This Book

This book has been written using the Visual Steps™ method. The method is simple: just place the book next to your computer or laptop and execute all the tasks step by step, directly on your own device. With the clear instructions and the multitude of screen shots, you will always know exactly what to do. This is the quickest way to become familiar with *Windows 10* and use the various programs and services it offers.

In this Visual Steps™ book, you will see various icons. This is what they mean:

Techniques
These icons indicate an action to be carried out:

⊕ᐟ The mouse icon means you need to do something with the mouse.

▦ The keyboard icon means you should type something on your keyboard.

☞ The hand icon means you should do something else, for example, turn on the computer or carry out a task previously learned.

In addition to these icons, in some areas of this book extra assistance is provided to help you successfully work through each chapter.

Help
These icons indicate that extra help is available:

➥ The arrow icon warns you about something.

 The bandage icon will help you if something has gone wrong.

1 Have you forgotten how to do something? The number next to the footsteps tells you where to look it up at the end of the book in the appendix *How Do I Do That Again?*

In this book you will also find a lot of general information, and tips. This information is displayed in separate boxes.

Extra information
Information boxes are denoted by these icons:

 The book icon gives you extra background information that you can read at your convenience. This extra information is not necessary for working through the book.

 The light bulb icon indicates an extra tip for using a program or service.

The Website Accompanying This Book

On the website that accompanies this book, you will find additional information about this book along with the Bonus Online Chapters and instructional videos. Please, take a look at the website from time to time. The website is **www.visualsteps.com/ windows10**

Instructional Videos

On the website that accompanies this book you will find instructional videos that illustrate some of the key concepts explained in the book. Each video refers to a specific section in the book. You will recognize a video to .
You can read how to view this videos in *Appendix D Opening the Instructional Videos*.

Test Your Knowledge

After you have worked through this book, you can test your knowledge online, on the **www.ccforseniors.com** website. By answering a number of multiple choice questions you will be able to test your knowledge. After you have finished the test, you will receive a *Computer Certificate*.
Participating in the test is **free of charge**. The computer certificate website is a free service from Visual Steps.

For Teachers

This book is designed as a self-study guide. It is also well suited for use in a group or a classroom setting. For this purpose, we offer a free teacher's manual containing information about how to prepare for the course (including didactic teaching methods) and testing materials. You can download the teacher's manual (PDF file) from the website which accompanies this book: **www.visualsteps.com/windows10**

The Screen Shots

The screen shots used in this book indicate which button, folder, file or hyperlink you need to click on your computer screen. In the instruction text (in **bold** letters) you will see a small image of the item you need to click. The line will point you to the right place on your screen.
The small screen shots that are printed in this book are not meant to be completely legible all the time. This is not necessary, as you will see these images on your own computer screen in real size and fully legible.

Here you see an example of an instruction text and a screen shot. The line indicates where to find this item on your own computer screen:

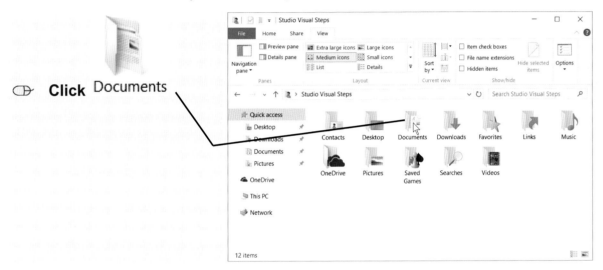

Sometimes the screen shot shows only a portion of a window. Here is an example:

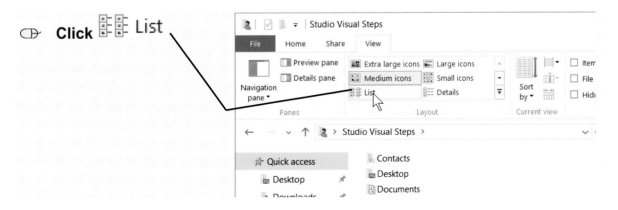

It really will **not be necessary** for you to read all the information in the screen shots in this book. Always use the screen shots in combination with the image you see on your own computer screen.

1. Starting Windows 10

Over the last thirty years *Microsoft*, the manufacturer of *Windows*, has issued various versions of *Windows*. *Windows 10* is the latest version.

In all the *Windows* versions prior to *Windows 8*, the *desktop* screen was the place where you started after logging on to your computer. This changed in *Windows 8*, and the new *Start screen* became the starting point. Many users were not happy with this. They missed their old, familiar desktop. So in *Windows 10* the desktop and the popular Start menu have returned. The new desktop also includes the taskbar, the system tray and icons for popular programs.

Another new feature in *Windows 8* were the *apps*. Originally, apps were programs for mobile devices, such as smartphones and tablets. But you can also use apps in *Windows 10*. The difference between apps and programs is less apparent in *Windows 10*. Both are opened up and used within a window.

The new *Task View* feature is a useful addition to *Windows 10*. It lets you quickly see which windows are open and you can easily switch to another window.

The search function is also a new addition to the taskbar. This function not only lets you search for a specific program, app or setting in *Windows,* you can also start a search on the Internet right away.

In this chapter you will learn how to:

- start *Windows 10*;
- use the desktop;
- open a program or app using the search function;
- use the ribbon;
- maximize and minimize windows;
- use the Start menu to open a program or app;
- restore a window with the taskbar button;
- use Task View;
- close a program or app;
- open a program or app from a tile;
- lock, sign out or turn off the computer.

1.1 Starting Windows 10

Windows 10 starts up automatically when you turn on your computer.

In a short while you will see a screen that looks like this:

This is called the *lock screen*.

Please note:

The images of the *Windows* screens and other windows displayed in this book may differ from those on your own screen. Every computer user can determine just how a *Windows* screen or window will look like by making adjustments to the settings. Computer manufacturers or suppliers also tend to adjust some of the screens sometimes, which can make them look different.

This will not affect the way in which you use the *Windows* program, so you can just continue working, in the case that your screen looks a little different.

⊕ **Click somewhere on the lock screen**

Once you have clicked, you will see the *Windows 10 login screen*. On this screen you will login to your user account. This is also called *signing in*.

Please note:

In this book we assume that you are using a mouse to operate your computer. A touchpad can be used to operate *Windows 10* on laptops and notebooks, and with other computers you may be able to use a touchscreen. We recommend that you use a mouse to perform the exercises in this book.

If you would you like to learn how to use a touchpad or touchscreen later on, you can read the *Bonus Chapters Working with a Touchpad* and *Working with a Touchscreen*. You can download these bonus chapters from the website that accompanies this book **www.visualsteps.com/windows10**. In *Appendix C Opening the Bonus Online Chapters* you can read how to open the bonus chapters.

You will see tiny images on the screen in this example. These images are called icons. You may see multiple icons on your screen, or just a single one. The icons may also look a little different or have another name. The color of the screen you see may be different as well. But none of this matters in learning how to work with *Windows 10*.

If necessary, click the icon with your name

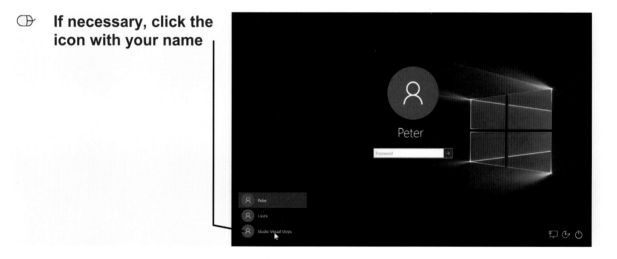

You will need to have a password in order to continue. If you do not know the password, ask the owner of the computer to log you in.

 **Type the password**

While you are typing, little black dots will appear in the box:

This is normal. This way, your password remains secret. Others will not be able to see what you are typing.

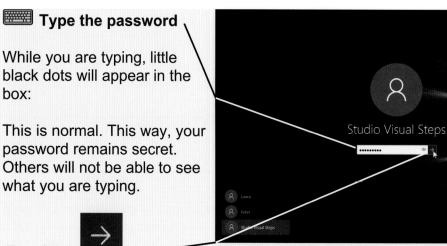

Studio Visual Steps

Click →

1.2 The Desktop

Now you see the desktop. You already know something about the desktop from previous versions of *Windows*. But in this version, a number of buttons and options have been added.

The desktop in this example is a uniform color. You may see a landscape image or something else on your own screen.

We will use a green screen in this book. This helps to make the screenshots very clear.

At the bottom of the desktop you see a horizontal bar across the full width of the screen: —————

This bar is called the *taskbar*.

The taskbar in this example is black, but it may have a different color on your own screen.

To the far left of the taskbar you will see this icon. This is the Start button: —————

You can use to open the search function: —————

With you can open the Task View: —————

In this example, there are three other buttons on the taskbar. These are called *taskbar buttons*. You can open programs and apps with these buttons.

On the right-hand side of the taskbar you see the system tray. Here you find the icons for programs, apps or settings, such as for the sound. The system tray is used by some programs, apps and devices, such as antivirus programs and printers, to display notifications and status information.

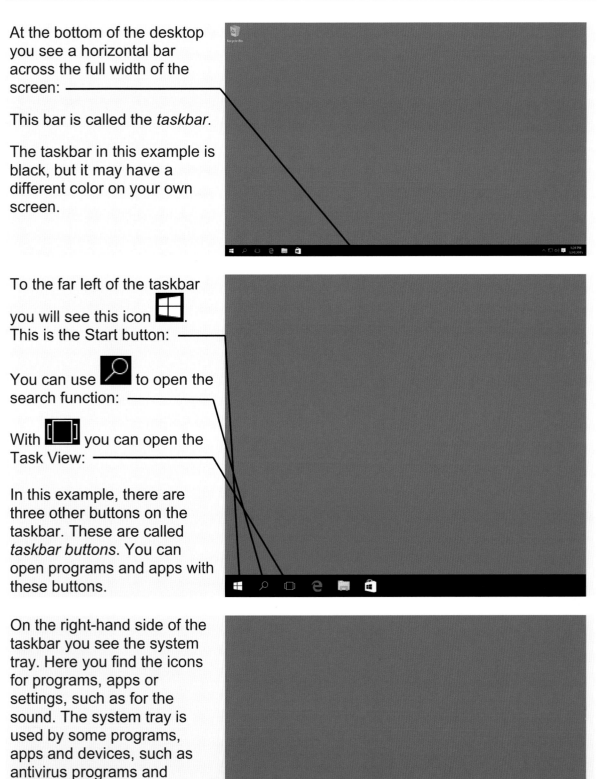

In *Chapter 7 Useful Settings and Security* you can read more about the system tray.

The way your desktop looks will not affect any of the actions you will be carrying out in this book. In *Chapter 7 Useful Settings and Security* you will learn how to adjust the desktop to suit your own needs or preferences.

1.3 Opening a Program or App Using the Search Function

Like you now, almost everything you do on a computer requires the use of a computer program. A computer program is usually just called a program, or an app. A computer program is a set of commands or instructions that tells the computer what to do in order to carry out certain tasks. There are many different kinds of programs and apps.

In this book you will come across two different names for a computer program: program and app. *App* is short for *application*, which actually means program. So an app is just another name for a program.

Sometimes, there is a distinction between a program and an app. Originally, an app was a program designed for use on a tablet or a smartphone. But in *Windows 10* you can also use apps on the computer. One of the main differences between the two, is that an app is often less extensive than a program, but not always. In this book you will be working with programs and apps.

You can open a program or app such as *WordPad* (a simple text editing program) using the search function:

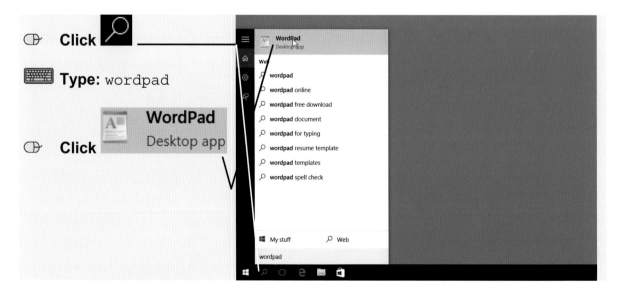

HELP! I see a search box.

If you see a search box instead of 🔍, then click the search box

Search Windows

WordPad will be opened on the desktop:

You will see the *WordPad* window:

On the taskbar you will see a

taskbar button ▯:

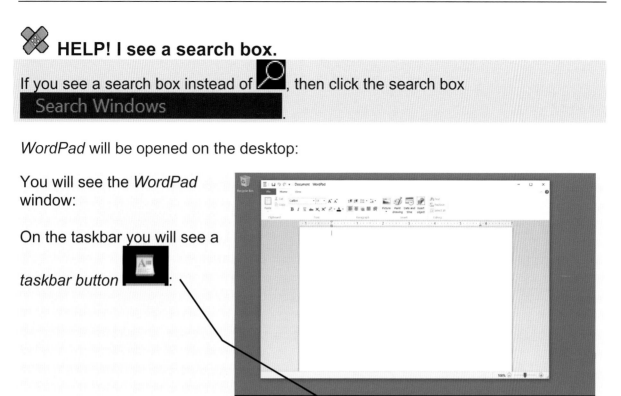

Just like in previous versions of *Windows*, you can use a taskbar button to perform various actions. You will learn more about this later on in this book.

You will see the *WordPad* window with a blank document in it:

At the top of the window you see the *title bar*.

This bar contains the name of the WordPad program.

In the right-hand corner of the window you see three buttons — ☐ ✕:

You can drag the edges and corners of a window. Then the size of the window will change.

The programs and apps that are included in *Windows 10*, all have the same buttons — ☐ ✕ on the title bar in the upper right corner of the window.

1.4 The Ribbon

Most programs and apps will show a menu or list of commands that you can click to carry out a certain task.

All the commands you use in *WordPad* are neatly arranged across the top of the window in what is known as the ribbon. The ribbon is designed to help you quickly find the commands you need while you are working on your document. The commands are arranged in tabs. Each tab is arranged in logical groups that refer to a certain kind of activity, such as writing and formatting a page. This is what the ribbon looks like in *WordPad*:

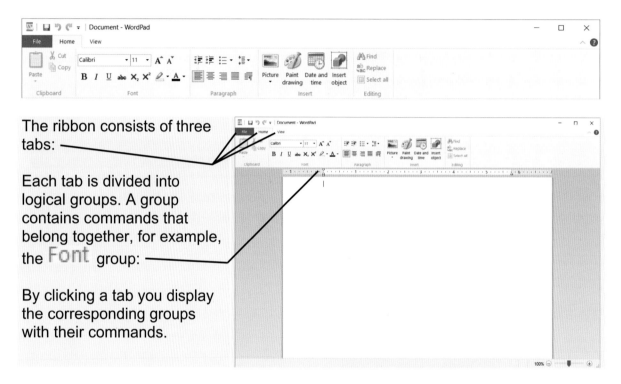

The ribbon consists of three tabs:

Each tab is divided into logical groups. A group contains commands that belong together, for example, the Font group:

By clicking a tab you display the corresponding groups with their commands.

Just take a look at the *View* tab:

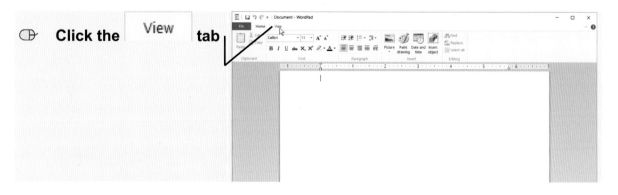

👆 **Click the** View **tab**

You will see the various options for viewing a page in the window:

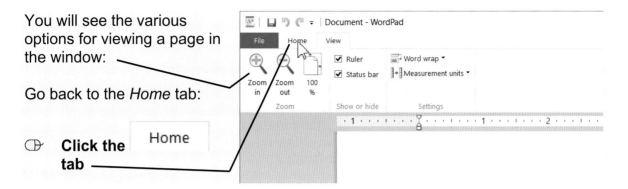

Go back to the *Home* tab:

⊕ **Click the** | Home
    tab

You will see the *Home* tab again. You can temporarily shrink the ribbon, if you need more work space:

⊕ **Click** ⌃

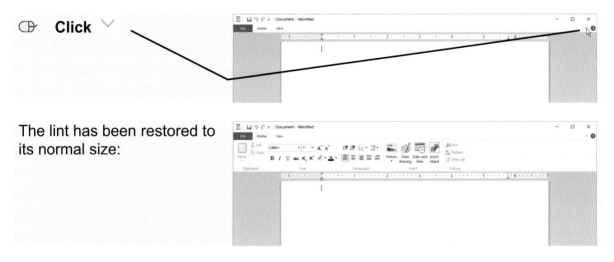

You see that the ribbon has almost disappeared:

Only the names of the tabs are displayed.

This is how you restore the ribbon:

⊕ **Click** ⌄

The lint has been restored to its normal size:

Other programs use the ribbon too. You will see this later on in this book when you begin using *File Explorer*.

1.5 Minimizing a Window

By *minimizing* a window, you can make a program or app disappear from the desktop without actually closing the program or app. This can be useful if you want to use another program or app for a while and need more space on the desktop. You will probably be familiar with the actions described in the next few sections, but it is still a good idea to practice using them, to find out how they work in combination with opening multiple programs or apps in *Windows 10*:

In order to minimize a window, you need to use the — button.

☞ **Click** —

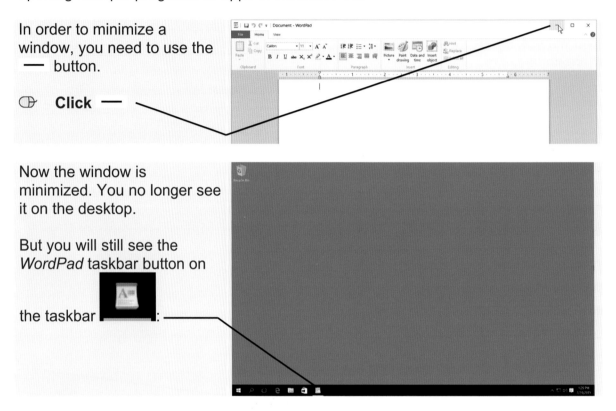

Now the window is minimized. You no longer see it on the desktop.

But you will still see the *WordPad* taskbar button on

the taskbar :

This tells you that the *WordPad* program is still open. You just cannot see the window on the desktop anymore.

1.6 Opening a Second Program or App from the Start Menu

You can have multiple programs and apps open in *Windows 10*. To open a second program or app you can practice using the Start menu in this section. The Start menu is a gateway to the programs, apps, folders, and settings on your computer. It is called a menu because it provides a list of options, just like a menu in a restaurant. It is the place where you start or open items.

In order to open the Start menu, you use the Start button:

In the bottom left corner of
the screen:

☞ **Click the Start button**

Once you have clicked the Start button you will see a window:

This window is called the
Start menu:

Just like in a restaurant
menu, you will see a list of
options in this menu:

The Start menu on your own computer may look a bit different from the menu in this
book. This will not affect the following exercises. Below you can see the Start menu
up close:

The pane on the left contains
a list of programs and apps.
This list of programs and
apps is subject to change.
This is because *Windows*
places the most frequently
used programs and apps in
this list. This way, you can
quickly find them.

On the right-hand side you
see square and rectangular
icons. They are called *tiles*.
You can open programs or
apps with these tiles too.

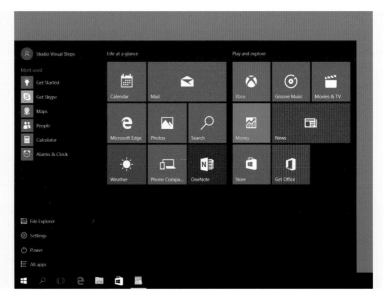

In the bottom left corner of the Start menu you see some other buttons:

When you click All apps, a full list of programs and apps will be displayed.

Click File Explorer to access the *Windows* folder window.

Click Settings to open the *Settings* app.

Click Power to turn the computer off, restart it, or switch to sleep mode.

Practice opening *Calculator* using the list with all programs and apps:

In the bottom left corner of the Start menu:

⊕ **Click** All apps

You will see a list of programs, apps and folders, for example, the *Windows Accessories* folder. You may already be familiar with this folder from a previous version of *Windows*.

☞ **Drag the scroll box downwards**

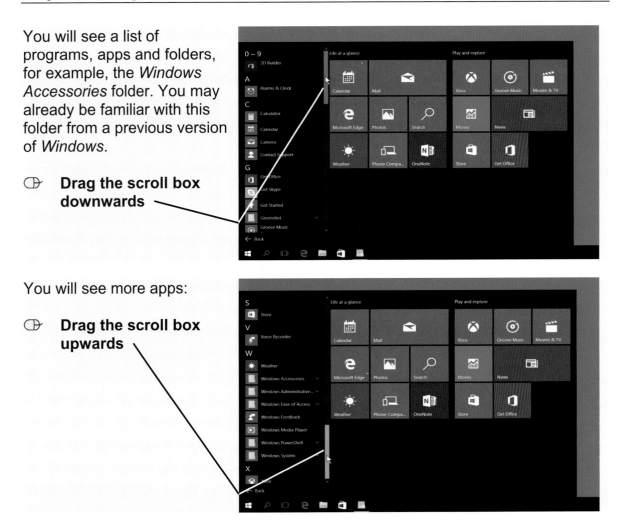

You will see more apps:

☞ **Drag the scroll box upwards**

This is how you open *Calculator*:

☞ **Drag the scroll box upwards until you see C**

☞ **Click** Calculator

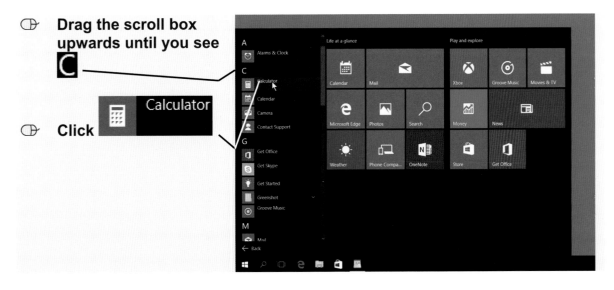

The *Calculator* window will be opened:

You will see a new taskbar
button added to the taskbar:

Now you see two active
taskbar buttons

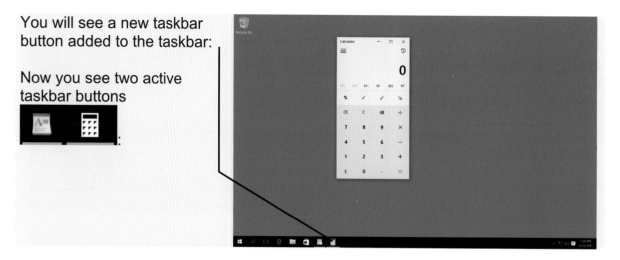

1.7 A Menu

Most programs and apps will contain a list of options or commands to perform certain
tasks. These commands are neatly arranged in menus. A menu is a list of options
that only becomes visible once you click a button. Just see how this works in
Calculator:

In the upper left corner of the
window:

☞ **Click** ☰

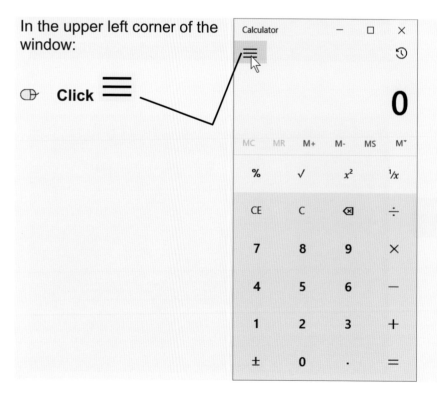

In this program, the menu appears on the left-hand side of the window:

Just look at one of the menu options:

⊕ **Click**

    ⚙ **Settings**

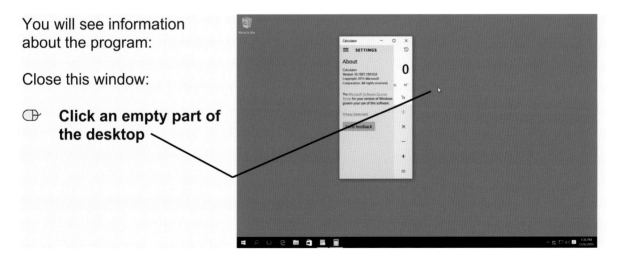

The left side of the window changes:

You will see information about the program:

Close this window:

⊕ **Click an empty part of the desktop**

1.8 Maximizing and Minimizing

The *Calculator* window can be displayed on a full screen, or on a part of the screen. You can decide how large the window needs to be. You can use window buttons to do this.

With this button ☐ you can maximize the window. This means the window will fill the entire screen.

In the upper right corner of the window you see this button:

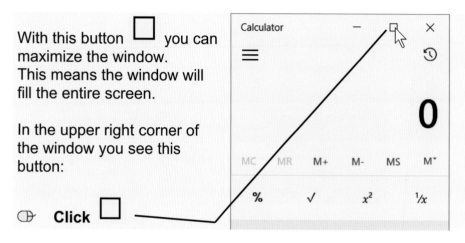

☞ **Click** ☐ ──

The window fills the entire screen. The window has been *maximized*.

The window can also be minimized, just like you did with the *WordPad* window. In order to do this, you use the *Minimize* window button:

☞ **Click** ──

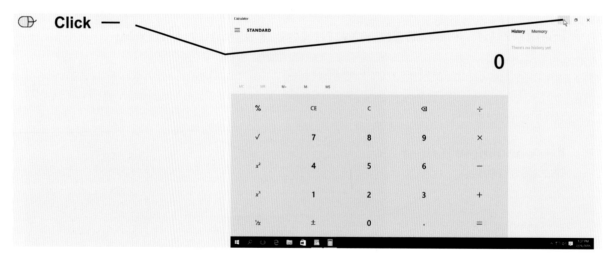

The window is minimized.

You have opened two programs: *WordPad* and *Calculator*. Both program windows have been minimized. This means you will not see any windows on the desktop. But the programs have not been closed.

You can tell by the two active taskbar buttons

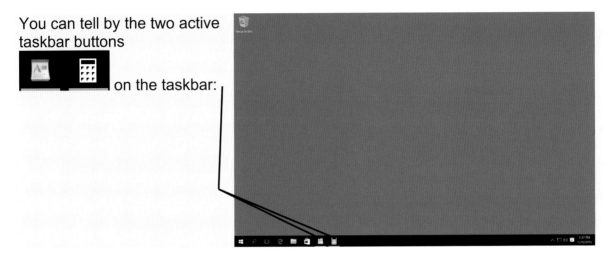

on the taskbar:

Just remember, you can always look at the taskbar buttons to see which programs have been opened on the desktop.

In case of an app, you will see a taskbar button for the minimized app on the taskbar as well.

1.9 Restoring a Window with the Taskbar Button

You can use the taskbar button to put the minimized window back on the desktop. Another handy feature is that you can also view a miniature (thumbnail) version of the window, to make sure you are using the correct button. Just give it a try:

☞ **Place the pointer on**

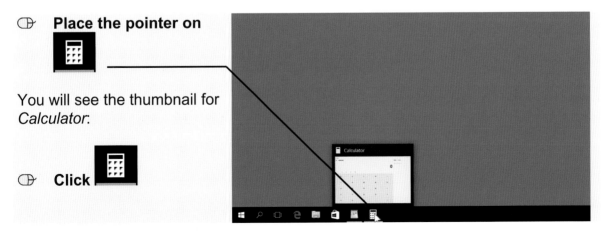

You will see the thumbnail for *Calculator*.

☞ **Click**

Now the *Calculator* window appears on the desktop again:

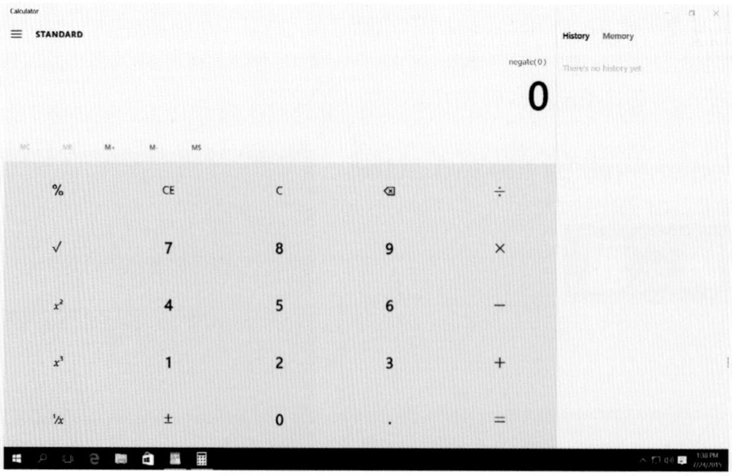

1.10 Reducing the Size of a Maximized Window

Previously, you had already maximized the *Calculator* window.
You can also make a maximized window smaller again and restore it to the size it was before you maximized it. You can use the ⧉ button to do this.

The ⧉ button is the middle of the three buttons in the

—   ⧉   ✕

window:

This button will appear instead of the ☐ button, if you have used that button to maximize a window.

⊕ **Click** ⧉

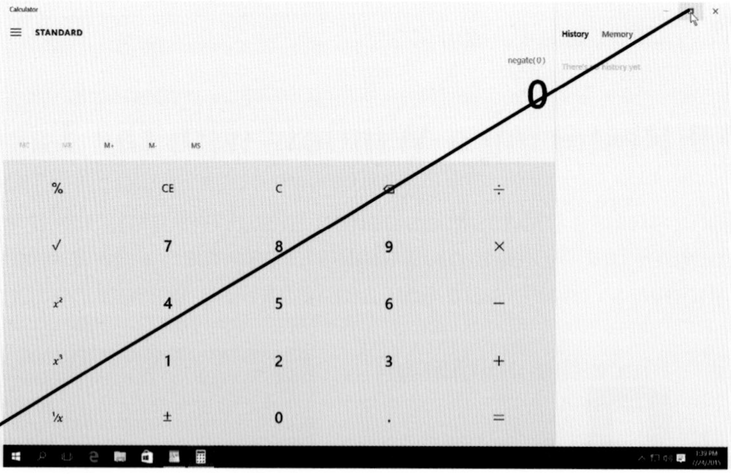

Now the window will be reduced to the previous size, that is to say, the size it had been before it was maximized.

1.11 Task View

Task View is a new and useful feature in *Windows 10*. It lets you see at a glance which windows are open, and lets you quickly switch to another window:

On the taskbar:

☞ **Click**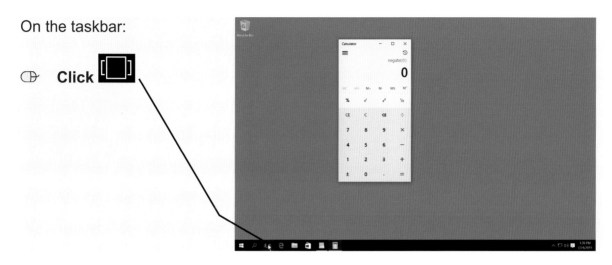

You will see the open windows. In this example, these are the *WordPad* and *Calculator* windows. If you want to quickly go to the *Calculator* window:

☞ **Click the *Calculator* window**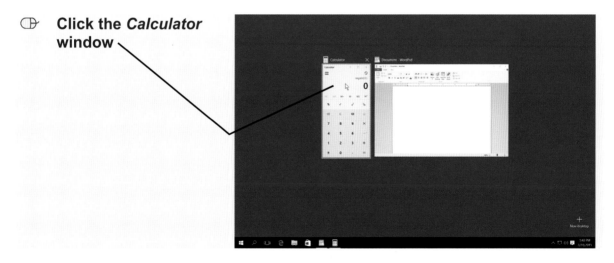

The window will be opened.

In the next section you will learn how to close a program or app.

Tip

Close Task View
When you click a window, the Task View window will automatically close. This is how you close the Task View, if you wish:

☞ **Click an empty part of the desktop**

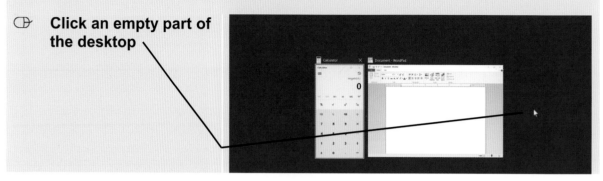

1.12 Closing a Program or app

A window can be permanently closed. This will also close the program or app itself.

To close a window on the desktop, you use the ✕ button.

You can find this button in the upper right corner of the program or app window:

☞ **Click** ✕

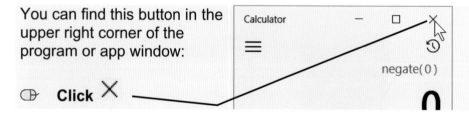

The window will be closed and *Calculator* is completely closed. The taskbar button for *Calculator* has also disappeared from the taskbar.

You can also close a minimized window directly:

☞ **Place the pointer on**

☞ **Place the pointer on the thumbnail**

☞ **Click**

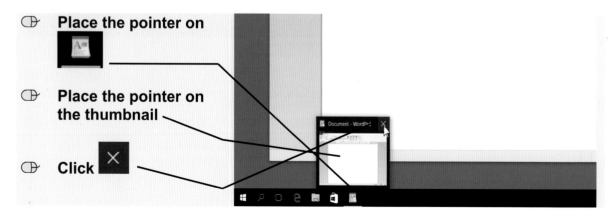

The corresponding taskbar button has disappeared from the taskbar. *WordPad* is closed. In the next section you will learn yet another method for opening a program.

1.13 Opening a Program or App from a Tile and Using it

You have just learned two methods for opening programs or apps in *Windows 10*.

In this section you will start working with the *Weather* app. You can open this app from one of the tiles in the Start menu. Tiles contain so-called 'live' content. A good example of this is the current weather forecast in the *Weather* app, or the latest news items in the *News* app. Most of the time the app or program needs to be opened at least one time before in order to see the 'live' content.

➥ Please note:

To work through the following section you need to have an active Internet connection. We assume this has already been set up. If necessary, contact your Internet provider, computer supplier or an experienced computer user for assistance.

This is how you open *Weather*:

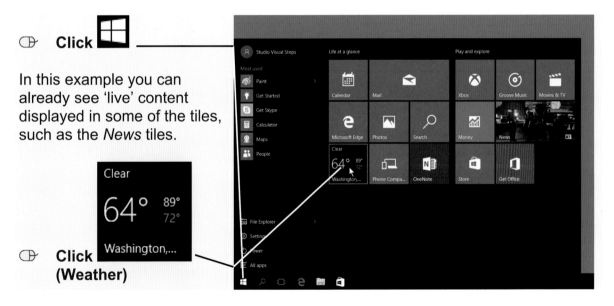

Click

In this example you can already see 'live' content displayed in some of the tiles, such as the *News* tiles.

Click (Weather)

The text and images displayed on a tile is constantly changing. In the *Weather* app you will see summaries of weather conditions in larger cities throughout the world.

✕ HELP! I do not see the Weather tile.

If you do not see *Weather*, you can open the app using the search function:

☞ **Click** 🔍

⌨ **Type:** `weather`

☀ **Weather**
Windows Store app

☞ **Click**

Weather will be opened. In this app you can display the weather conditions for your local area. You may already see your location. If you do not see your own location, you can add it, like this:

⌨ **Type the name of your location** ——

In this example we have used Boston.

☞ **Click the desired location, for example,**
Boston
Massachusetts, United States

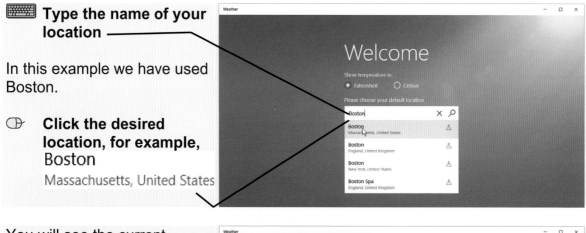

You will see the current weather and the weather forecast for your local area:

There is more data available:

☞ **Drag the scroll box downwards**

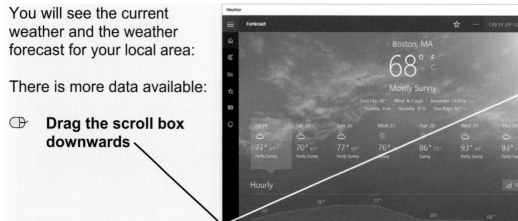

✕ HELP! My window looks different.

If your window looks different, you can drag the window borders. Then you will probably see a window similar to the one above.

You will see more data:

☞   **Drag the scroll box upwards**

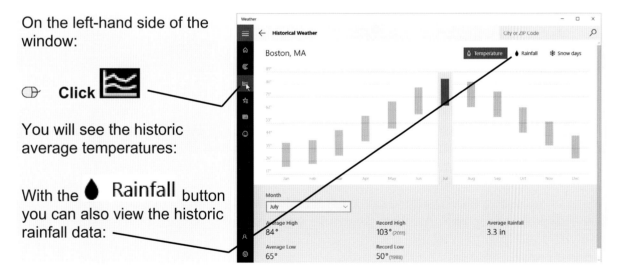

Tip

Look further ahead

By default, you will see the forecast for today and several days ahead. With the ▷ button (on the right-hand side of the window) you can display the weather forecast for the days to come.

You can also view historical data concerning the weather in your local area:

On the left-hand side of the window:

☞   **Click** 📈

You will see the historic average temperatures:

With the ● Rainfall button you can also view the historic rainfall data:

This is how you go back to
the weather forecast in your
local area:

⊕ **Click**

Now you will see the weather forecast for your own location again.

You have just been working with *Weather*. Have you noticed that this app works
slightly different than a program such as *WordPad*? Besides *Weather*, *Windows 10*
also contains other apps, for example *Mail*, *People*, *Maps*, and *Photos*. You will get
familiar with some of these apps later on in this book.

☞ **Close *Weather* ⚇¹**

1.14 Locking, Signing Off and Shutting Down

If you need to leave your computer for a short while, and you do not want others to
work with your user account, or view your data, you can lock your computer. You will
then need to sign in again in order to continue working. All documents, programs and
apps will be saved in the computer memory, and when you sign in again, you can
continue working right away.

If you or someone else wants to continue working with a different user account, you
will also need to sign off. All open programs and apps will be closed. After signing off
you will need to sign in again, with the same user name, or another one. Any
program or app that was opened earlier will need to be started up again.

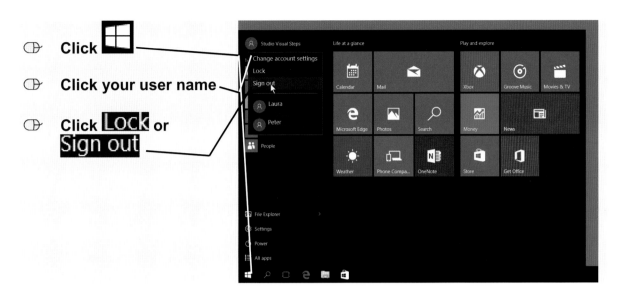

⊕   **Click** ⊞

⊕   **Click your user name**

⊕   **Click Lock or Sign out**

☞   **Sign in again** 👣²

💡   **Tip**

Working with multiple users
If you would like to continue working with another user account, you do not need to sign the current user off. You can sign in directly as another user. In this way you can alternate working with your business data and your personal data. In this case, two users are signed in, but just one of them is active. When the computer is shut down, both users need to be signed off individually, if you do not want to lose any data.

⊕   **Click your user name**

⊕   **Click the desired user**

☞   **Log in with the password for this user**

If you do not use the computer for a while, you can switch to sleep mode. The sleep mode puts the computer temporarily in a kind of 'stand-by' mode, so you can quickly resume working later on.

The computer uses a minimal amount of energy in sleep mode. Before activating the sleep mode, all open documents, programs and apps are automatically saved in *Windows 10*, so you can quickly wake up the computer when you resume working (usually within a few seconds).

When you enable sleep mode, your screen will turn dark right away. Now your computer is 'asleep'. In order to wake up your computer from sleep mode, you briefly press the power switch on the computer case, or you move the mouse.

➽ Please note:

This may work differently on your own computer. Read the documentation that came with your computer to find out how sleep mode works.
Some laptops will go into sleep mode by closing or opening the laptop cover. Read the documentation that came with your laptop to find out if this is the case for your own laptop.

With the restart option, you can restart *Windows* and the computer. Just remember that this option requires you to save your work and close programs and apps yourself. You can try the restart option if you feel your computer is not functioning properly. A restart can sometimes solve a problem right away. You will often need to restart after an update or a new program has been installed.

Usually you will want to completely shut down your computer if you do not intend to use it for longer periods of time. Keep in mind that you always need to save your work first and close any open programs or apps before you select the shut down option. For now, you can simply turn off the computer:

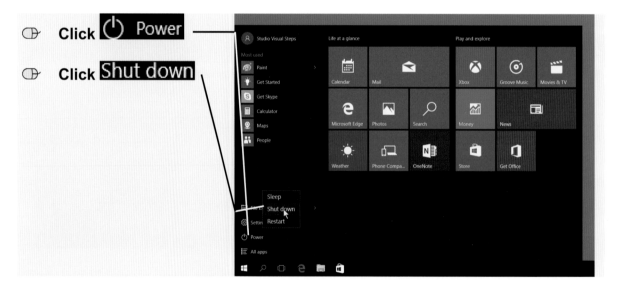

Now *Windows* and the computer will be completely shut down.

In this chapter you have learned how to open and close programs and apps. In the following exercises you can repeat these actions. This will help to reinforce what you have learned in this chapter.

1.15 Exercises

The following exercises will help you master what you have just learned. Have you forgotten how to do something? You can use the number beside the footsteps to look it up in the appendix *How Do I Do That Again?* at the end of this book.

Exercise 1: Opening and Closing

☞ Turn on your computer (and monitor) again and click the lock screen.

☞ If necessary, click your user account and log on with your password. $\mathcal{B}^2$

☞ Open *Calculator*. $\mathcal{B}^3$

☞ Minimize the *Calculator* window. $\mathcal{B}^4$

☞ Open *WordPad*. $\mathcal{B}^3$

☞ Maximize the *WordPad* window. $\mathcal{B}^5$

☞ Minimize the *WordPad* window. $\mathcal{B}^4$

☞ Display the *Calculator* window on the desktop again by using the taskbar button $\mathcal{B}^6$

☞ Close *Calculator*. $\mathcal{B}^1$

☞ Display the *WordPad* window on the desktop again by using the taskbar button. $\mathcal{B}^6$

☞ Minimize the *WordPad* window $\mathcal{B}^4$ and restore it back to its former size. $\mathcal{B}^6$

☞ Close *WordPad*. $\mathcal{B}^1$

Exercise 2: Using Maps

With *Maps* you can view maps and plan trips.

☞ Open *Maps*. &³

If you are asked to allow *Maps* to access your location:

☞ Click the desired option.

☞ Click the | Search | box.

☞ Type the place you want to find, for example: `Austin, Texas`

☞ Press **[Enter]**

You will see the place you have entered. In order to view another part of the map:

☞ Place the pointer on the map.

☞ Drag the map in the desired direction.

Plan a trip and get directions:

☞ Click **Directions**.

☞ By **A**, type the starting point.

☞ By **B**, type the destination.

☞ Click →.

☞ If necessary, click a destination or spot.

You will see the full route.

☞ Close *Maps*. &¹

If you have had enough practice, you can continue reading the *Background Information* and the *Tips* on the next few pages.

If you prefer to continue learning how to work on the computer in *Windows 10*, you can skip to *Chapter 2 Opening, Editing and Saving Documents*.

1.16 Background Information

Dictionary

App	Short for *application*, which means a program. Originally, an app was a program designed for use on a tablet or a smartphone. But in *Windows 10* you can also use apps on the computer.
Desktop	The work area on a computer screen, comparable to an actual desktop. When you open a program or app, it will appear on the desktop.
Icon	A small picture that indicates a file, folder, program or app.
Lock screen	The first screen you see when you turn on the computer. When you click this screen, you will go to the login screen.
Login screen	The screen that you use to log in with *Windows*. In this screen you can see all the user accounts on the computer.
Menu	A menu contains a list of program or app options. In order to keep the screen less cluttered, menus are often hidden until you click a specific button.
Program	A series of commands or coded instructions used by a computer to perform a certain task.
Ribbon	Extensive toolbar with tools and options arranged in tabs and logical groups. This ribbon replaces the menu bar in *WordPad* and many other *Microsoft* programs.
Start menu	The Start menu is a gateway to the programs, apps, folders and settings on your computer.
System tray	The system tray is located to the right of the taskbar and contains icons that display information and notifications, for example, concerning updates, and the network connection.
Taskbar	The taskbar is the horizontal bar at the bottom of the desktop. You can tell which programs and apps are opened, by looking at the taskbar buttons present on the taskbar.
Taskbar button	A button on the taskbar that indicates an open program or app. You can use it to switch between programs and apps.

- Continue on the next page -

Thumbnail	Miniature view of an opened window. Displayed when you click on the taskbar button.
Tile	Colored button that let you open a program or app from the Start menu.
Title bar	The horizontal bar at the top of a window that contains the name of the window. A title bar also contains buttons for closing the window and for changing its size.
User account	A collection of data that tells Windows which files and folders you are allowed to access, which computer settings you can change, and what your personal preferences are, for instance your desktop background.
Window	A rectangular area on a computer screen, in which programs, aps and other content are displayed.
Window buttons	Buttons on the title bar of a window, used for changing the size of the window, or for closing the window.
Windows 10	The computer program that manages all the other programs and apps on the computer. The operating system saves files, enables the use of programs and apps, and lets you use other devices, such as the keyboard, mouse and printer.

Source: Windows Help, Wikipedia

Windows 10 on different computers

Windows 10 is specifically designed for use on all kinds of computers. Apart from on a regular computer, the system also works on tablets, smartphones, the Xbox games computer, and other devices. The various versions of *Windows 10* are specifically adapted to the different types of computers, but the underlying engine is the same.

The big advantage of this is that different computers will be able to communicate and cooperate with each other. It is easy to connect the various *Windows* devices with each other, and actions such as exchanging files are usually quite easy to accomplish.

The high level of cooperation is also apparent when you look at the apps for mobile devices that can also be used on regular computers. The idea behind this is, that it should become more interesting to develop apps for *Windows 10*, which in turn will encourage users to buy a smartphone or a tablet with *Windows 10*.

By setting up a so-called *Microsoft* account on different devices, you can get the same views, files, and settings on both your computer and your tablet or smartphone. You can read more on this subject in the *Tip* at the back of *Chapter 5 Working with Mail*.

1.17 Tips

☿ Tip
Options of the taskbar button
You may have used a taskbar button in a previous version of *Windows* for more than just minimizing and restarting programs. This is still possible in *Windows 10*:

☞ **Right-click a taskbar button**

You will see a menu with various options:

By **Recent** you will see the names of recently opened documents:

If you click the name of a document, it will be opened.

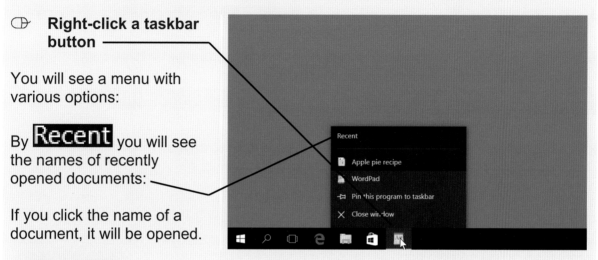

WordPad: with this option you can open a new *WordPad* window.

Pin this program to taskbar: with this option you can place a program button for this program on the taskbar. You can then open the program directly from the taskbar by clicking this button. You will not need to use the Start menu or the search function to open the program.

Close window: with this option you can close the program window.

☿ Tip
Circle

Has your mouse pointer ⬉ changed into a spinning circle with five dots ⟳ ?
This means your computer is busy doing something.

☞ **Just wait until the circle has disappeared**

Then you can proceed further.

💡 Tip

Screen saver

Has another image suddenly appeared on your screen?

A moving illustration, such as this perhaps: .

This means the *screen saver* on your computer has been activated. This may happen when you do not use your computer for a while.

You can stop a screen saver by pressing any key on the keyboard, or moving the mouse around a bit. Then you can resume working. Although you may need to sign in again.

In *Windows 10* you can adjust the settings for the screen saver to suit your own tastes. For example, you can set a period of time after which the screen saver kicks into action. You can also disable the screen saver.
You can read more about this in *Chapter 7 Useful Settings and Security*.

💡 Tip

Are you left-handed?

If you are left-handed, you should use the mouse with your left hand. You can set up the mouse in such a way that the function of the left and right mouse buttons are swapped. Then the mouse will be more suitable for lefthanders. In *section 7.21 Tips* you can read how to do this.

Please note: after you have swapped these mouse functions, you will need to think of the *Click* instruction in this book as an instruction to click the right mouse button. The *Right-click* instruction will mean you need to click the left mouse button.

💡 Tip

Setting up the Weather app

You can set multiple locations in *Weather*. This can be useful if you want to check the weather in your next vacation destination or if you want to see what the weather is like in the home town of one of your relatives.

☞ **Open** *Weather* 🦶³

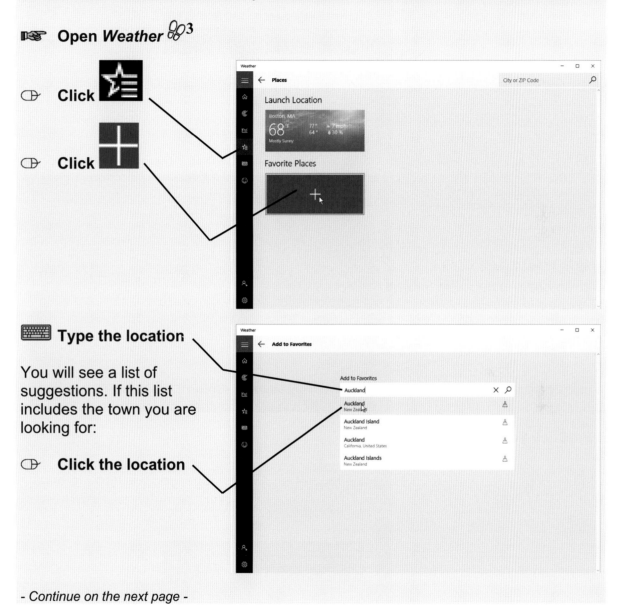

☞ **Click** [star/list icon]

☞ **Click** [plus icon]

⌨ **Type the location**

You will see a list of suggestions. If this list includes the town you are looking for:

☞ **Click the location**

- *Continue on the next page -*

The location has been added to the favorite locations:

☞ **Click**

You will see the current weather conditions and the weather forecast for this location:

This is how you go back to the weather in your local area:

☞ **Click** ⬅

☞ **Click your home town**

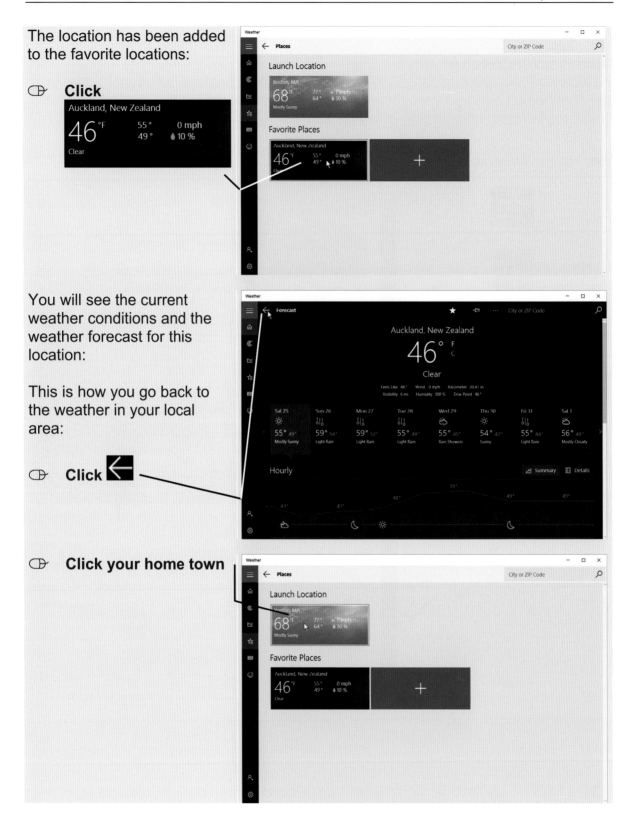

Tip

Games in Windows 10

Windows 10 also contains a number of games. These games have already been installed to the computer. You can open the games through the *Windows* search function on the taskbar:

☞ **Open *Microsoft Solitaire Collection*** 👣³

You may see some windows regarding the use of a *Microsoft* account, and Xbox. You can close these windows. It is possible to play these games as a guest, without these options.

You will see the games:

You may have played the *Solitaire* card game in a previous *Windows* version. This game is called *Klondike* in *Windows 10*:

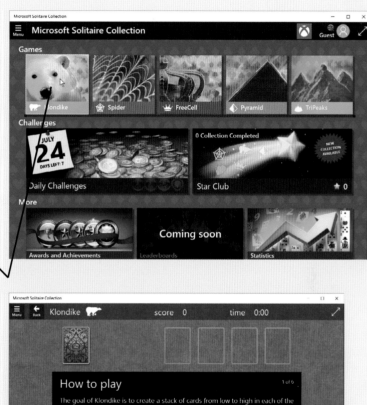

☞ **Click** Klondike

You will see the window of this game:

Before you can start playing, you will see some tips.

At the bottom of the games window, you will also see a number of games where the Xbox game computer is mentioned, for example, the Mahjong game. You can also play these games if you do not have an Xbox.

💡 Tip

Shortcuts

Windows contains various keyboard shortcuts to run certain commands without using the mouse:

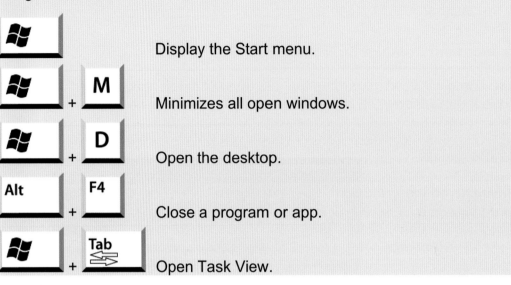

Display the Start menu.

Minimizes all open windows.

Open the desktop.

Close a program or app.

Open Task View.

2. Opening, Editing and Saving Documents

It is very easy to edit text on a computer. This is one of the reasons why computers have become so popular. No endless re-typing, no correction fluid or tape is needed; with a computer you can produce flawless letters, reports, and many other types of documents. You can make a few slight changes to a previously written text and use it over and over again. The newly edited text can then be sent to a large number of readers or recipients. You can also save an unfinished text if you want to stop working, and finish it later on. If you are satisfied with the changes made to a certain bit of text, you can choose to have it printed.

In this chapter you will compose a letter in *WordPad*, save this letter to your computer, and open it again. In this way you will learn all the actions needed for creating a file, saving it, and opening it on a *Windows 10* computer. You can use these skills later on with many other types of files.

In this chapter you will learn how to:

- adjust the font and the font size;
- undo an action;
- insert an image;
- save a document;
- re-open a document;
- print;
- save changes;
- open a new document;
- select and move text;
- edit text.

➠ Please note:

In this chapter we will use a practice file in one of the examples. You can select a different folder, or you can decide to copy the practice files to your computer's hard disk first. In *Appendix B Downloading the Practice Files* at the back of this book you can read how to do this.

2.1 Opening WordPad

In this step you will compose a letter in the *WordPad* text editing program. You start by opening *WordPad* with the search function:

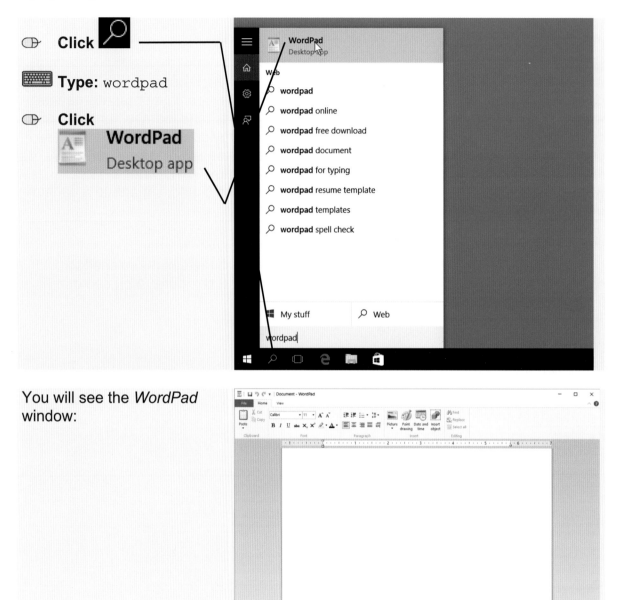

You will see the *WordPad* window:

2.2 A Larger and Different Font

The default font used in *WordPad* is called Calibri. Before you start typing, you can already select a different font. Here is how you do that:

On the ⬜ Home ⬜ tab:

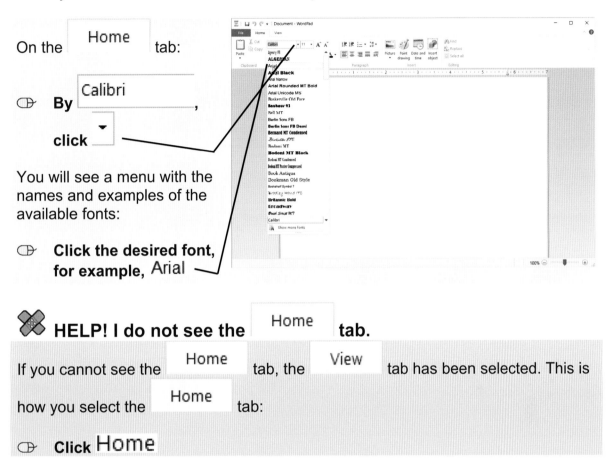

⬤ **By** ⬜ Calibri ⬜ ,

click ⬜▼⬜

You will see a menu with the names and examples of the available fonts:

⬤ **Click the desired font, for example,** Arial

✚ **HELP! I do not see the** Home **tab.**

If you cannot see the Home tab, the View tab has been selected. This is how you select the Home tab:

⬤ **Click** Home

The default font size used in *WordPad* is a bit small. It is better to select a larger font size when you start typing your letter. You can do that like this:

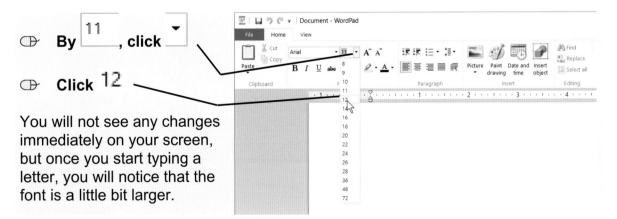

⬤ **By** ⬜ 11 ⬜ , **click** ⬜▼⬜

⬤ **Click** 12

You will not see any changes immediately on your screen, but once you start typing a letter, you will notice that the font is a little bit larger.

Now you can start composing your letter. You begin by typing your place of residence, and then the date. You do not need to type the date yourself. *WordPad* has a special command that will do this job for you.

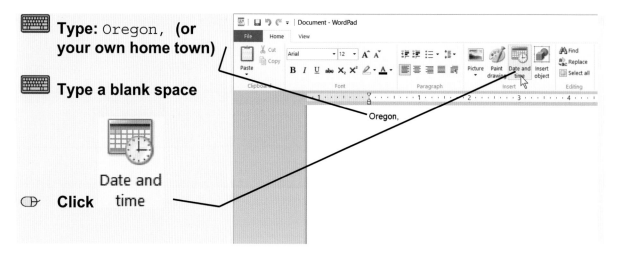

Type: Oregon, **(or your own home town)**

Type a blank space

Click Date and time

You will see a menu in which you can select the date format:

Click a date format

Please note: you will see a different date, of course.

Click OK

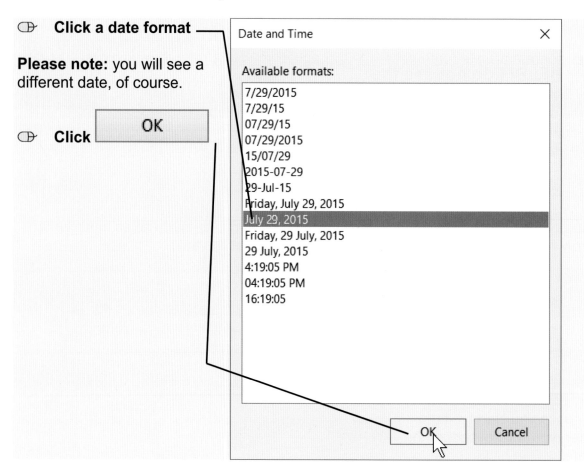

Date and Time   ✕

Available formats:

7/29/2015
7/29/15
07/29/15
07/29/2015
15/07/29
2015-07-29
29-Jul-15
Friday, July 29, 2015
July 29, 2015
Friday, 29 July, 2015
29 July, 2015
4:19:05 PM
04:19:05 PM
16:19:05

OK   Cancel

2.3 Undoing

If something goes wrong while you are writing, or if you accidentally press the wrong key, nearly every *Windows* program has a command that will *undo* a previous action. Just give it a try:

Press   Enter

Type: an error

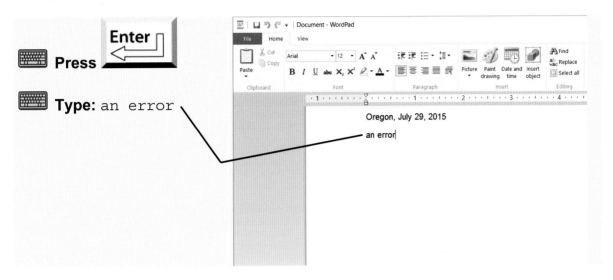

The program always remembers the last action you have performed. This is how you undo an action:

In the upper left corner of the window:

Click

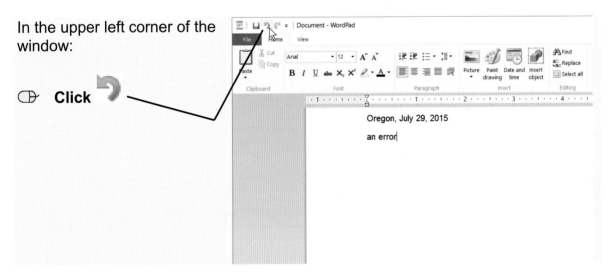

The line you just typed has been deleted. The same thing can be done by using the

 keys to delete or correct the text.

2.4 Typing a Letter

Now you can start typing the remainder of the letter:

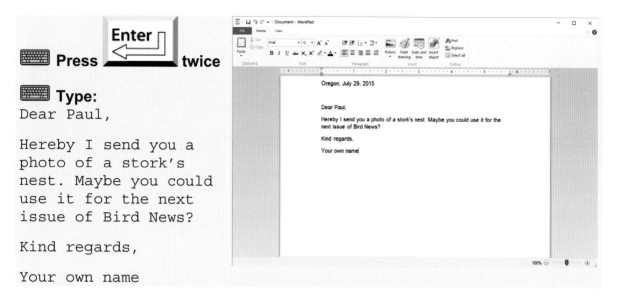

⌨ **Press** **Enter** **twice**

⌨ **Type:**
Dear Paul,

Hereby I send you a photo of a stork's nest. Maybe you could use it for the next issue of Bird News?

Kind regards,

Your own name

Instead of 'Your own name' you can also type some other name if desired.

2.5 Inserting an Image

In this step you will learn how to insert an image at the end of the letter. In the example shown, we have inserted and image from one of the practice files used in *Chapter 6 Introduction to Photos, Video and Music*. If you want, you can use one of your own photos instead:

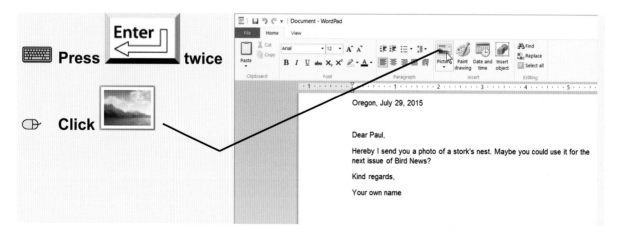

⌨ **Press** **Enter** **twice**

🖰 **Click**

You may see the content of the *Pictures* folder right away. Open the folder containing the images; in this case it is the practice files folder:

☞ **If necessary, click**
   🖻 Pictures

☞ **Double-click the desired folder**

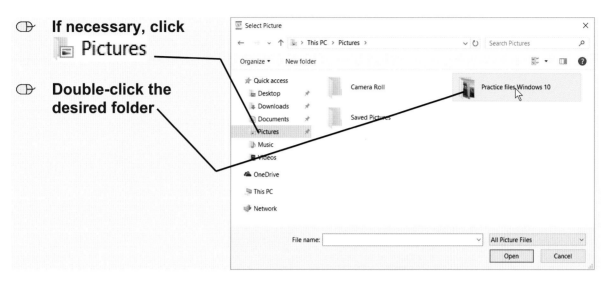

HELP! This folder looks different on my computer.

You can change the way in which files are displayed on your computer in the folder window. This is how you can get your window to look like the example in this book:

☞ **By 🖾, click ▼**

☞ **Click 🃏 Tiles**

In *Chapter 3 Folders, Files and Libraries* you can read more about this.

Select a photo:

☞ **Click a photo, for example**
   Photo10
   JPG File
   3.37 MB

☞ **Click** **Open**

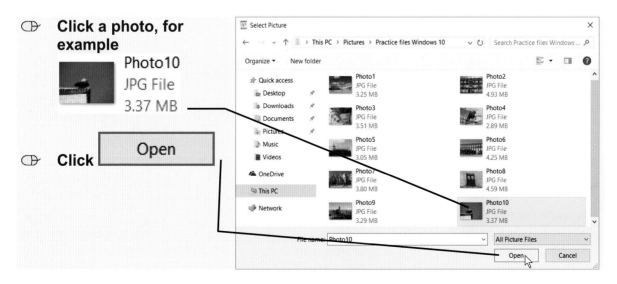

The photo has been inserted at the end of the letter:

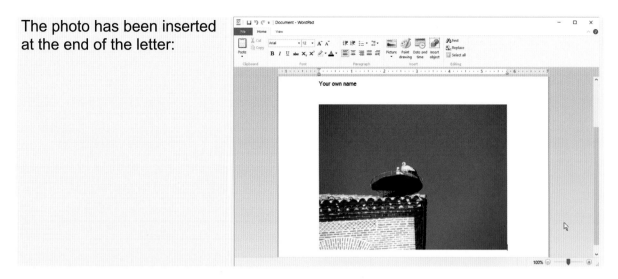

Now you can save the letter. You can continue working on it later on, if you wish.

2.6 Saving a Document

This is how you save a letter on the computer:

☞ **Click** File

You will see a menu:

☞ **Click** Save

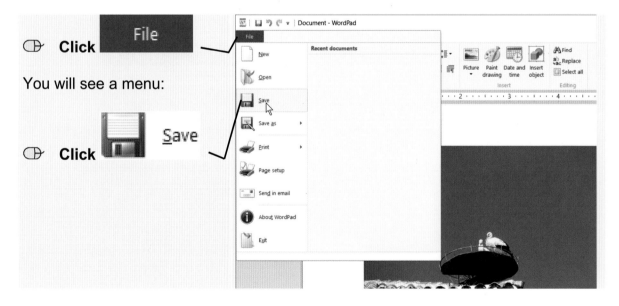

By default, *WordPad* will save a file in the *Documents* folder:

You can change the name of the letter:

⌨ **Type:** first document

⊕ **Click** | Save |

Now the letter is saved on your computer. You can open this letter later on and continue editing it. You will be doing that in the next section.

You will see the name of your letter in the title bar:

HELP! The file already exists.

Has this window appeared? If so, you (or someone else) has already saved a text with the name *first document*. In this example, you can replace it with the new document you have just created.

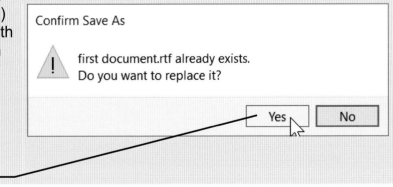

⊕ **Click** | Yes |

2.7 Closing WordPad

Now you can close *WordPad* for the time being. You do this in order to learn how to open the practice document once again, so that you can work on it another time:

☞ **Close** *WordPad* 🐾¹

Now you can open *WordPad* again:

☞ **Open** *WordPad* 🐾³

You will see an empty window, without your practice document.

The name *Document* is shown at the top:

Document is the default name for a new text. In order to get your practice document back on the screen, you need to open it first.

2.8 Opening an Existing Document

If you want to use a document that has been saved on your computer, you need to open it first. You can open a previously created document like this:

👆 **Click** `File`

👆 **Click** `Open`

You will see your letter in the window:

⊕ **Click**

A first document
Rich Text Document
82.1 MB

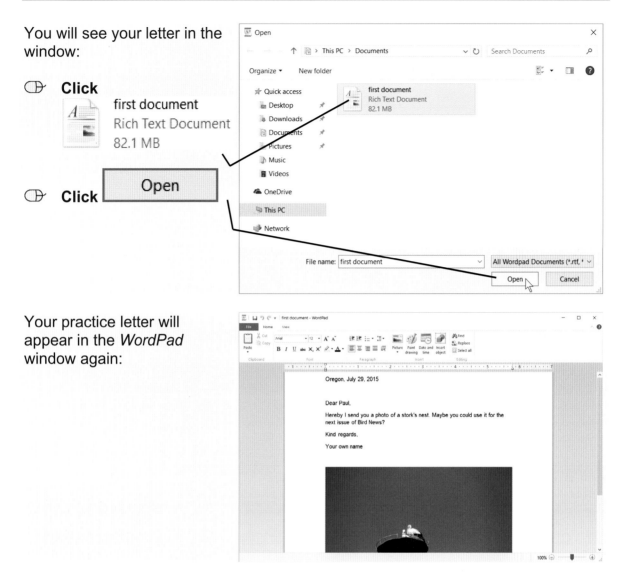

⊕ **Click** Open

Your practice letter will appear in the *WordPad* window again:

You can resume editing this document, if you want. But for now you do not need to do this. In the next section you will learn how to print the letter.

2.9 Printing the Document

When you compose a document such as a letter, most likely you will want to print it on paper.

 **HELP! No printer?**
If you do not have a printer, you can just skip this section.

Before you actually print a document, it is wise to look at a preview of what it will look like on paper. *WordPad* has a special command for this:

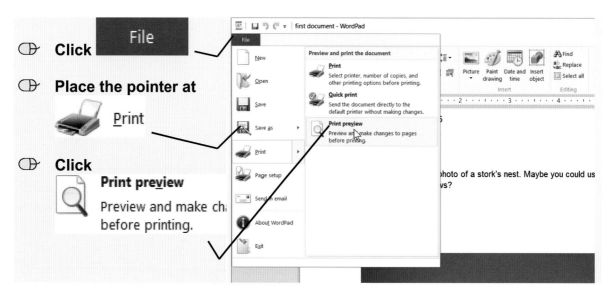

☞ **Click**   File

☞ **Place the pointer at**   Print

☞ **Click**
   Print preview
   Preview and make cha
   before printing.

You will see a window with a thumbnail image of the letter in the middle, just like it will look once it is printed on paper. The layout of the text is not very pretty. You can remedy this by inserting a few extra lines at the top. First, you need to close this window:

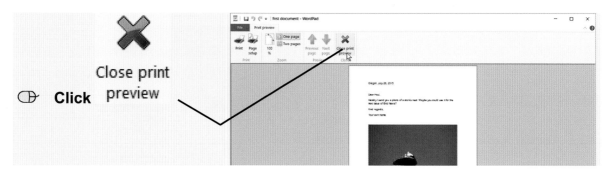

☞ **Click**   Close print preview

You will see your letter again.

☞ **Type two blank lines at the top of the letter** $\mathscr{O}\mathscr{O}$8

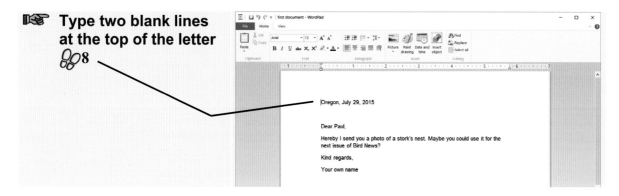

You can view the result in the print preview once again:

☞ **Open the print preview** 𝒪𝒪**9**

The letter has dropped down a bit lower on the page:

Close the print preview:

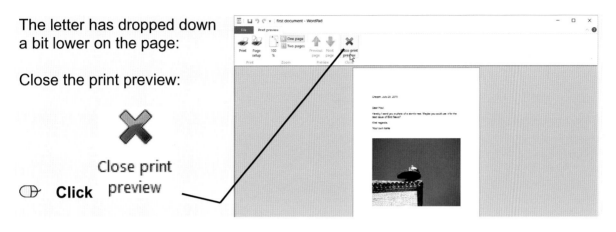

Close print
⊕ **Click** preview

Now you can print this letter.

☞ **Make sure the printer is turned on**

☞ **Make sure there is paper in the printer**

Is everything ready? Then you can tell the computer to print the document:

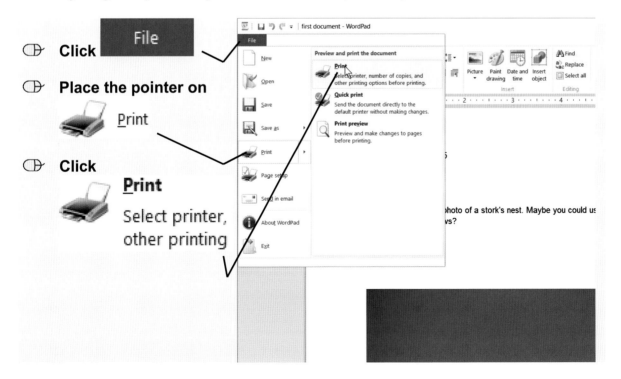

⊕ **Click** File

⊕ **Place the pointer on**

Print

⊕ **Click**

Print

Select printer,
other printing

Now you see a window in which you can choose various print settings:

☞ **Click** Print

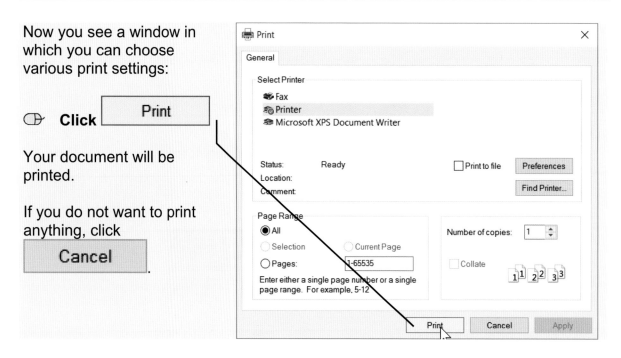

Your document will be printed.

If you do not want to print anything, click

Cancel .

2.10 Save Changes?

When you opened your practice letter, you made some changes. You added some extra lines at the top of the letter. You need to save the edited version of this letter first, if you want to keep the changes. It is very easy to forget about doing this. Fortunately, *WordPad* keeps an eye on these things and warns you if any changes will be lost. If you close *WordPad* without having saved the edited letter, the program will warn you. Just give it a try:

☞ **Click** ✕

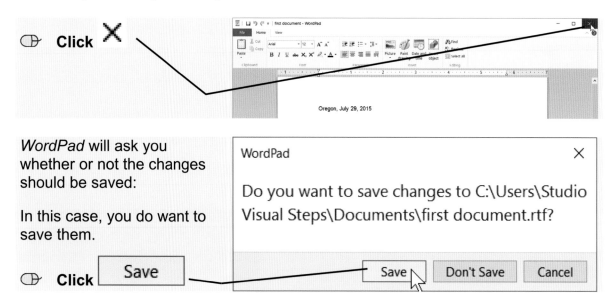

WordPad will ask you whether or not the changes should be saved:

In this case, you do want to save them.

☞ **Click** Save

The changes will be saved and *WordPad* will be closed.

 Tip

Saving
For many people, this window can be confusing. If you unexpectedly see this window, you apparently made at least one change. No matter how small, even if the change is simply one space, it is still regarded as a change in *WordPad*.

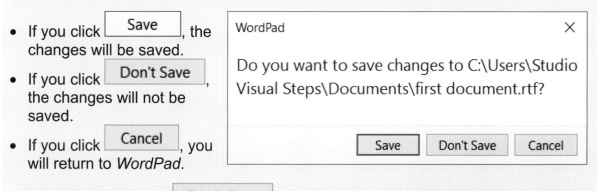

- If you click [Save], the changes will be saved.
- If you click [Don't Save], the changes will not be saved.
- If you click [Cancel], you will return to *WordPad*.

Please note: only click [Don't Save] if you do not want to save the text or the version of the text that you saved previously is better than the current version. In that case, you do not need to replace the new text.

Now you can open your practice document again to see what happens when you first save the changes yourself.

☞ **Open *WordPad*** ✇³

☞ **Open your practice letter**   first document
Rich Text Document
82.1 MB   ✇**10**

You will see the letter you have saved, including the three blank lines at the top. You can make a new small change to the letter:

⌨ **At the top of the letter, type:** test

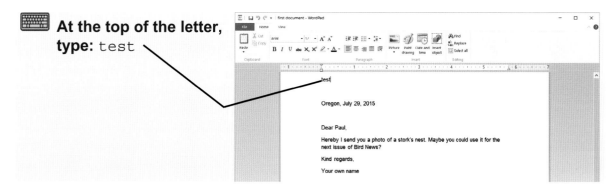

Now you can save this minor change:

This time you will not see the *Save* window. The document will be saved directly with the same name, which is *first letter*.

2.11 Opening a New Document

In this step you will be opening a new document. You do not need to close *WordPad* first in order to do that.

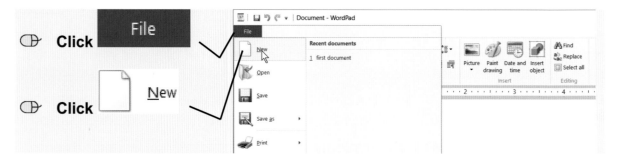

The document called *first document* will automatically be closed and a new, blank document will be opened. Here you will practice typing the words of a familiar nursery rhyme. You will type the words in the wrong order on purpose, and use an incorrect spelling somewhere in between:

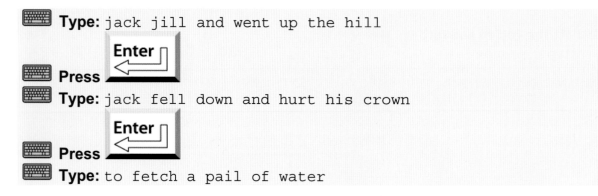

Type: jack jill and went up the hill

Press Enter

Type: jack fell down and hurt his crown

Press Enter

Type: to fetch a pail of water

2.12 Selecting and Moving Text

You have deliberately switched the order of the words in this nursery rhyme. This is a good way to practice selecting and moving text. First, you need to put the word 'and' in the right spot:

☞ **Double-click the word** and

The word 'and' turns blue:

This means the word has been *selected*.

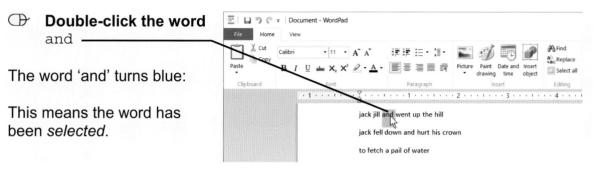

Drag the word to the correct spot:

☞ **Press the left mouse button and hold it down**

The pointer turns into 🔲:

This means you are dragging the word.

☞ **Drag the pointer to the right of the word** jack

☞ **Release the mouse button**

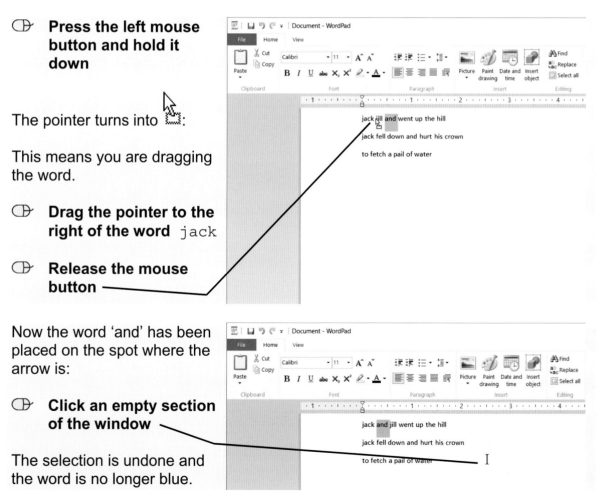

Now the word 'and' has been placed on the spot where the arrow is:

☞ **Click an empty section of the window**

The selection is undone and the word is no longer blue.

The word is in the right spot. You can do the same thing for the entire paragraph:

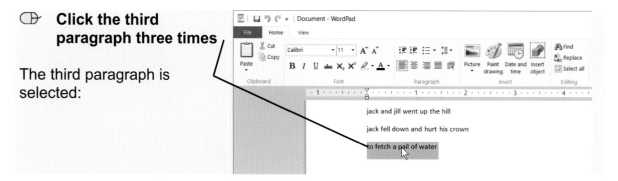

Click the third paragraph three times

The third paragraph is selected:

Dragging a paragraph works the same way as dragging a word.

You can place the pointer on the selected paragraph, and then drag it to the place you want it to be:

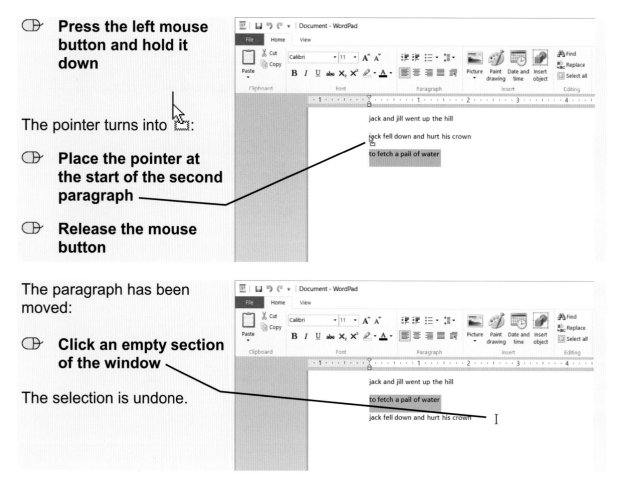

Press the left mouse button and hold it down

The pointer turns into ⏷:

Place the pointer at the start of the second paragraph

Release the mouse button

The paragraph has been moved:

Click an empty section of the window

The selection is undone.

2.13 Editing Text

If you have mistyped a word or part of a sentence, you can easily change it by selecting the text first, and then retyping it in the correct way:

☞ **Select the word** hurt ⁸⁸11

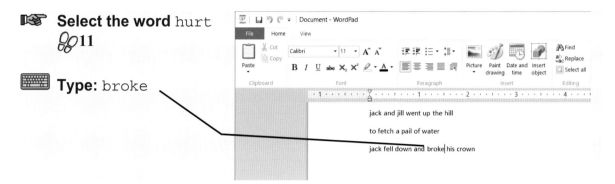

⌨ **Type:** broke

You will see that the word is immediately replaced by the word you type.
Close *WordPad* and save the document:

☞ **Close *WordPad* and save the document as a file called *Jack and Jill* ⁸⁸12**

In the next few exercises you can practice the things you have learned once more.

2.14 Exercises

The following exercises will help you master what you have just learned. Have you forgotten how to do something? You can use the number beside the footsteps 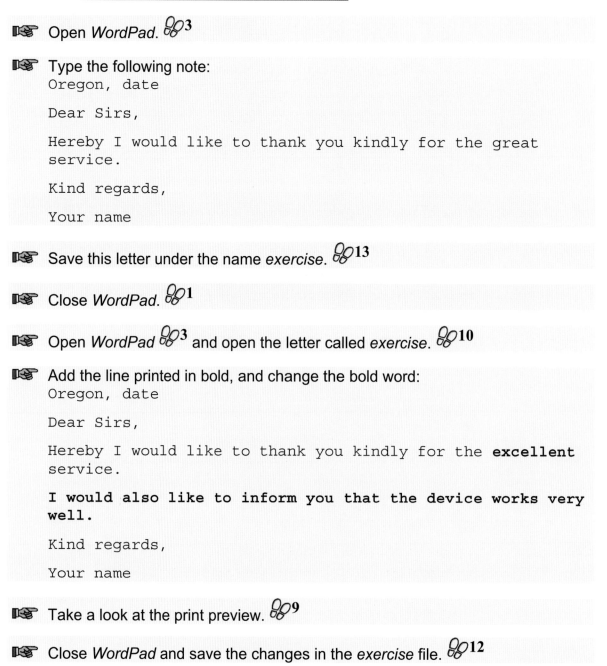 to look it up in the appendix *How Do I Do That Again?* at the end of this book.

Exercise 1: Save changes

☞ Open *WordPad*. $\mathscr{O}$3

☞ Type the following note:
```
Oregon, date

Dear Sirs,

Hereby I would like to thank you kindly for the great
service.

Kind regards,

Your name
```

☞ Save this letter under the name *exercise*. $\mathscr{O}$13

☞ Close *WordPad*. $\mathscr{O}$1

☞ Open *WordPad* $\mathscr{O}$3 and open the letter called *exercise*. $\mathscr{O}$10

☞ Add the line printed in bold, and change the bold word:
```
Oregon, date

Dear Sirs,

Hereby I would like to thank you kindly for the excellent
service.

I would also like to inform you that the device works very
well.

Kind regards,

Your name
```

☞ Take a look at the print preview. $\mathscr{O}$9

☞ Close *WordPad* and save the changes in the *exercise* file. $\mathscr{O}$12

2.15 Background Information

Dictionary

Bold	A font style that prints letters in bold.
Clipboard	A temporary storage area, used by *Windows*. Data can be copied to the *Clipboard* from a program or a location, and then pasted elsewhere. Every time you copy something to the *Clipboard*, the previous item will be replaced.
Copy	A command that copies (duplicates) a selected part of a document to the *Clipboard* in order to insert it somewhere else.
Cursor	Short blinking line that indicates where text will appear.
Cut	A command that copies (and removes) a selected part of a document to the *Clipboard* in order to insert it somewhere else.
Document	Text file, for example a letter.
Font	A complete set of characters in a particular size and style, including numerals, symbols, punctuation and the characters of the alphabet.
Format	The design of a document, including elements such as font size, font type, arrangement of headers, alignment, character spacing, and margins. Also called layout.
Italic	A font style where the letters are slanted to the right.
Open	Command to find and retrieve a document which has been saved on a computer, USB stick or other memory device.
Paragraph	A paragraph is a part of a text. A paragraph always begins on a new line and is concluded by pressing the Enter key.
Paste	A command that inserts a selected part of a text that has been previously cut or copied to the spot where the cursor is resting.
Print	Command to produce a copy of the document on paper with the help of a printer.

- Continue on the next page -

Print Preview	A feature that allows the user to view a document on a computer screen as it will appear on the printed page.
Save	Command to store a file on a computer, external hard drive, USB stick, SD card or other memory devices for future use.
Select	Action that marks a part of a document.
Underline	A font style that underlines a word or a letter.
Undo	Command to undo the last thing you did in a program.
WordPad	A text editing program that can be used to create and edit documents.

Source: Windows Help, Wikipedia

File types
Your computer will save a document in a file format associated with the program in which you created the document. Each program has its own unique set of file types (or file extensions). *WordPad* in *Windows 10* can open the following types of files: .rtf, .docx, .odt, .txt.

Printers

The printer most commonly used in the home is called an *inkjet* printer.
This type of printer prints characters by spraying very small, precise amounts of ink onto the paper.

Many of these printers can also create color prints. These printers do not only have a cartridge with black ink, but also another cartridge with at least three colors. Any color imaginable can be copied by mixing the various colored inks. Each type of printer has different cartridges.

Inkjet printer

Inkjet printers can print on regular paper as well as on special types of paper, depending on the quality of print you want. You can get special photo paper to print photos, for example.

Laser printers are often used in the office sector. They are a non-impact printing device which operates in similar fashion to a photocopier, in which a laser draws the image of a page on a photosensitive drum which then attracts *toner* (an extremely fine-grained powder) on to the paper, where it is subsequently bonded by heating.

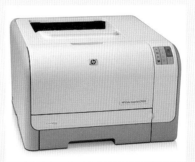

Laser printers are known for high quality prints, good print speed, and a low cost-per-copy. Laser printers are available in both color and monochrome varieties.

Laser printer

Photo printers use special photo paper to print digital photographs.

According to the manufacturers, these printers approach the professional quality of the photo printing services.

Photo printer

You can connect a printer to the computer, but there are also models that can print directly from a digital camera's memory card, through a Wi-Fi network or another network.

Storing files on the computer

The computer has a certain amount of *working memory*. This working memory consists of chips in which the information is temporarily saved.

When you turn the computer off, however, the memory is emptied. This is why you also need to be able to save information more permanently.

That type of memory exists in various types: the computer's *hard disk* or an external hard disk, but also USB sticks (USB memory sticks), SD cards, CD-recordable/-rewritable and DVD-recordable/-rewritable and Blu-ray disks.

Hard disk   *USB stick*   *External hard disk*

SD Card   *CD-r / CD-rw*   *DVD-r / DVD-rw*   *Blu ray disk*

The most important storage method uses the hard (disk) drive on your computer. The hard disk is a small, sealed box that has been built into your computer.

Hard disk   *Inside a computer case*   *Case (housing)*

In this box, a small disk rotates. The disk is magnetic, making it possible to save information on it.

You determine what is saved on the hard disk drive. You can save documents on it, or drawings, or computer programs. You can copy, move or delete files from the hard disk drive. In *Chapter 3 Folders, Files and Libraries* you will learn more about this subject.

Where do you save it?

Every computer has at least one hard disk drive and perhaps an additional CD and/or DVD drive that is capable of reading and writing to CD or DVD (this type of drive is also known as a 'burner'). Besides this, you can also connect external storage devices to a USB port on the computer. For example, a USB stick or an external hard drive.

In the *This PC* window you can see which components your computer contains. In this example you will see the following components:

Hard disk drive:

DVD-rw drive:

Removable disk:

External hard drive:

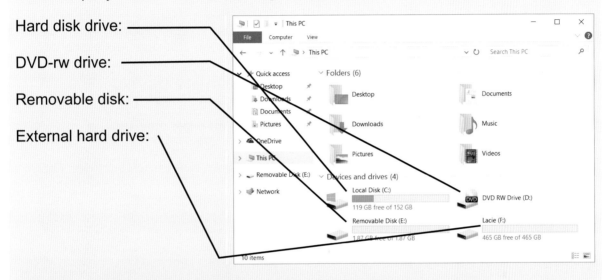

Windows assigns a letter to all the storage devices, by way of name:

- The hard disk drive is usually indicated by the letter C. If a second hard disk drive is present, it will be assigned the letter D.
- The CD or DVD drive will be assigned the next letter in the alphabet. In the example above, this is the letter D.
- Any device that comes next will be assigned the letter E, etc. In this example, there is a removable disk drive (often a USB stick) and an external hard drive. But these can also indicate the memory card of a digital camera (SD card).

Please note: there may be other devices or components installed on your own computer that are not present in this example. In this case, the letters will be different as well.

You will usually save your work on the computer's hard disk drive. But if you want to take your work to another computer, or create a safety copy of a file, you need to save your work on another type of memory device such as an external drive or a USB memory stick. Another option for saving your work is by burning it to a CD or a DVD, or saving it to an Internet location (also called 'in the cloud').

2.16 Tips

💡 **Tip**

More ways of selecting text by dragging
Besides clicking a word or part of a text, you can use other methods for selecting:

1. Selecting by dragging
You can select an entire word or sentence, but also a random piece of text:

- ⊕ **Place the cursor at the beginning of the section of text you want to select**
- ⊕ **Press and hold the left mouse button down while dragging the mouse over the desired text**
- ⊕ **Release the mouse button once you have selected the desired piece of text**

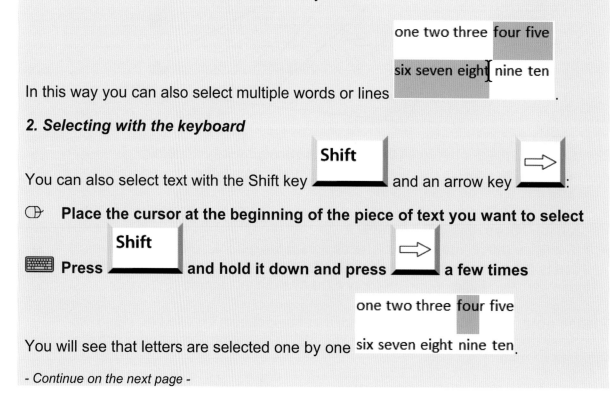

You will see that letters are selected one by one six seven eight nine ten.

In this way you can also select multiple words or lines.

2. Selecting with the keyboard

You can also select text with the Shift key **Shift** and an arrow key **⇒** :

- ⊕ **Place the cursor at the beginning of the piece of text you want to select**
- ⌨ **Press Shift and hold it down and press ⇒ a few times**

You will see that letters are selected one by one six seven eight nine ten.

- Continue on the next page -

In this way you can select multiple words, and by using 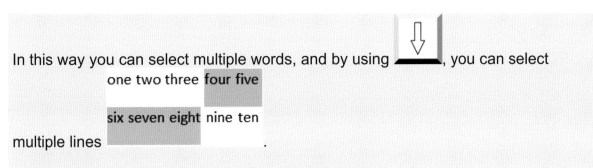, you can select

one two three four five

six seven eight nine ten

multiple lines .

3. Selecting lines by clicking and dragging

You can also select lines or paragraphs by clicking and dragging from the margin:

⊕ **Place the pointer on the left margin of the document** ———————

The pointer turns into 🖑:

⊕ **Press the left mouse button and hold it down**

⊕ **Drag the pointer downwards** ———————

The selected lines turn blue:

⊕ **Release the mouse button**

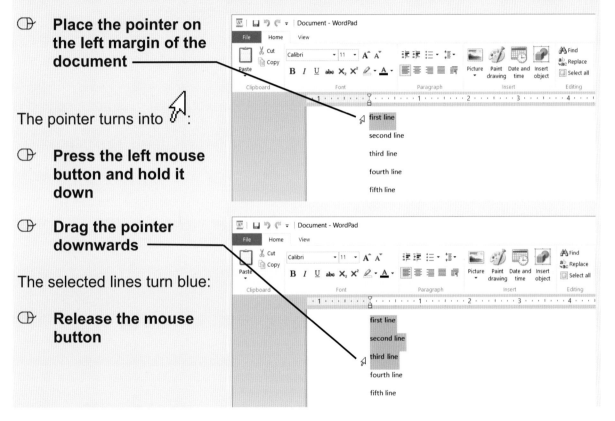

♀ Tip

Copy, cut, paste
Perhaps you have already cut, copied, and pasted a text before. Here is a brief reminder of how to do that:

☞ **Select the desired text**
*§§*11

⊕ **Click** 📋 Copy

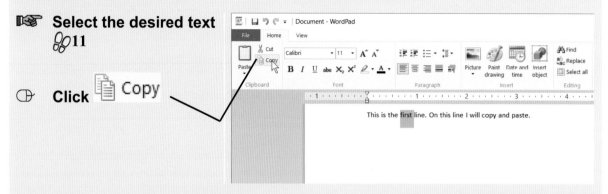

You will not see anything happen on the screen, but the word 'first' has been copied to the *Windows Clipboard*. The *Clipboard* is a temporary storage location.
Now the word can be pasted somewhere else in the document. It will be pasted on the spot where the cursor is resting.

⊕ **Place the pointer next to the word where you want to paste the copied word**

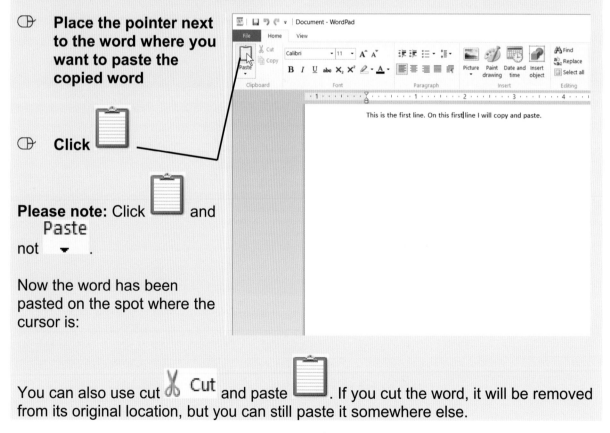

⊕ **Click** 📋

Please note: Click 📋 and
Paste
not ▼ .

Now the word has been pasted on the spot where the cursor is:

You can also use cut ✂ Cut and paste 📋 . If you cut the word, it will be removed from its original location, but you can still paste it somewhere else.

💡 Tip

Formatting text

In *WordPad* there are a number of tools for formatting text. You can find these tools in the Font font, on the ribbon:

In order to format a word or a piece of text, you need to select it first:

👉 **Select the desired text** 👣11

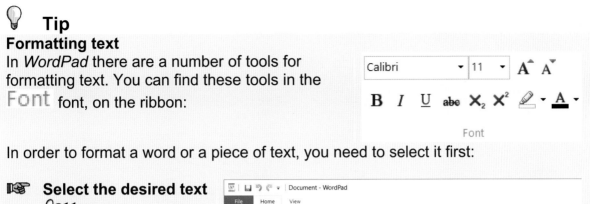

☞ **Click B**

Now the word has become bold:

These are the functions of the other buttons in the Font group:

Calibri ▾	Select font.
11 ▾	Select font size.
A A	Display selected text larger or smaller.
I	Display selected text in *italics*. The letter *I* on this button stands for *Italic*.
U	Underline selected text. The letter *U* on this button stands for *Underlined*.
abe	Strike through selected text.
X₂	Format selected text in subscript, such as the 2 in H_2O.
X²	Format selected text as superscript, such as the 2 in 4^2.
✏ ▾	Add a marker color to the selected text, just like marking a text with a colored felt pen. Use the ▾ button to select the desired color.
A ▾	Adjust the text color of the selected text, as with text color. Use the ▾ button to select the desired color.

💡 Tip

Line Spacing

In *WordPad* the default line spacing is 1.15. This means there is always some space between the text lines. You can change the line space as follows:

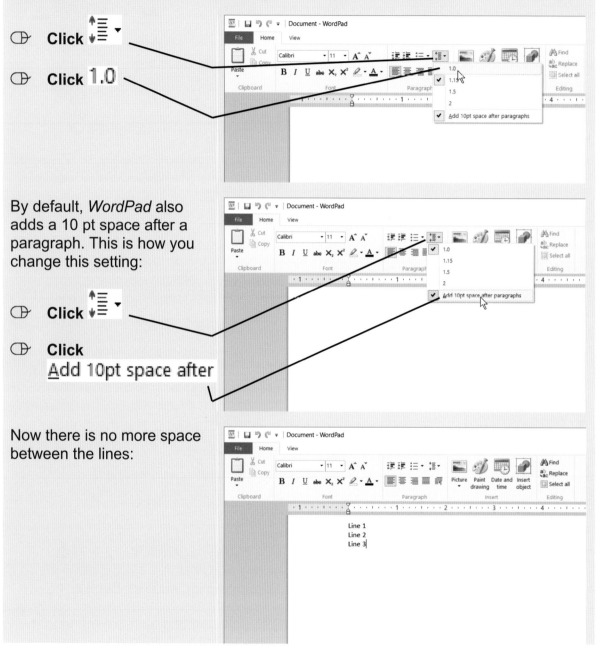

☞ **Click** ▲☰ ▾

☞ **Click 1.0**

By default, *WordPad* also adds a 10 pt space after a paragraph. This is how you change this setting:

☞ **Click** ▲☰ ▾

☞ **Click** Add 10pt space after

Now there is no more space between the lines:

Tip

Quick Access Toolbar

At the top of the window, you will see various buttons. This area is called the *Quick Access Toolbar*. You can use the buttons to enter a command with a single mouse click: .

These buttons have the following functions:

Save a document

Undo

Redo

When you click ▼ next to the Quick Access buttons, you will see more commands:
 	
When you click one of the commands, it will be added to the Quick Access Toolbar.
	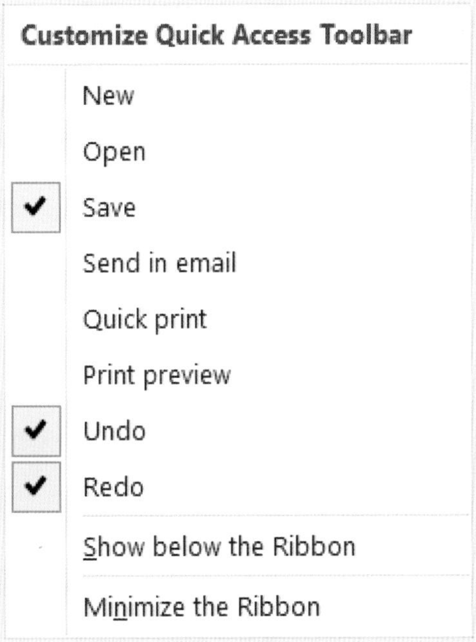 **Customize Quick Access Toolbar**
	
	   New
	   Open
	✔ Save
	   Send in email
	   Quick print
	   Print preview
	✔ Undo
	✔ Redo
	   Show below the Ribbon
	   Minimize the Ribbon

For example:

Create a new document

Open a document

Print the text

See the Print Preview

💡 Tip

Printing in black and white

If you have a printer that prints both in color and in black or white, usually it is set to print in color. If you do not want your color cartridges to empty prematurely and you are just printing text, you can choose to print in black and white. You do that like this:

☞ **Click** [File], [Print],

Print
Select printer, number of copies, and other printing options before printing.

You see the *Print* window, where you can set a number of different options.
The option to print in black and white can be found in another window.

☞ **Click** [Preferences]

You will see a new window with the specific settings allowable for your own printer. This window may look different on your own computer.

☞ **Click the** [Printing Shortcuts] **tab**

You will see the options for printing in black or color:

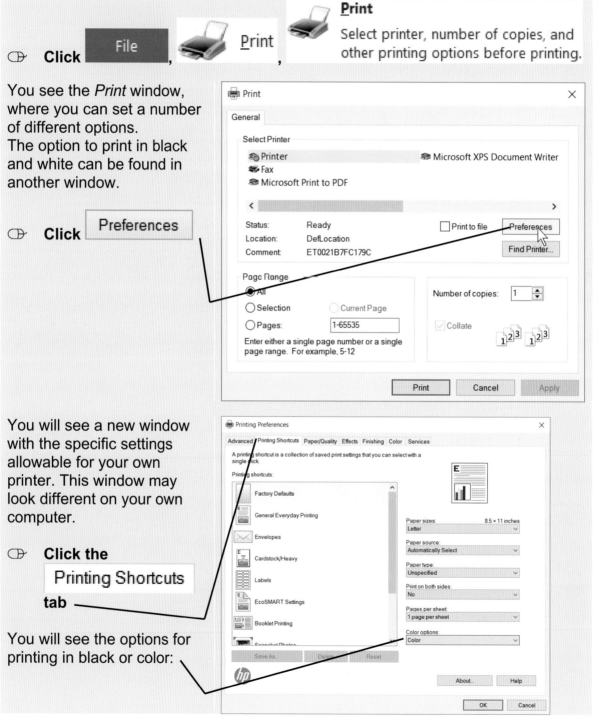

3. Folders, Files and Libraries

The window of *File Explorer* has changed in *Windows 10*. Depending on the *Windows* version you were previously using, you will notice this to a certain extent. Starting with *Windows 8*, the ribbon was a new feature in *File Explorer*, which meant that the commands and functions were distributed among the tabs. This is the same in *Windows 10*.

Besides working with the folders and files on your computer, you will also work with *libraries*. In a library, you can link folders and files. Then these folders and files will be displayed in the library. In this way you can easily find your files.

Just like in previous *Windows* versions, a number of default folders and libraries have already been created in *Windows 10* too. These are the following folders, among others: *Documents, Pictures, Music, Videos*, and *Downloads*. The default libraries are: *Documents, Pictures, Camera Roll, Saved Pictures, Music*, and *Videos*. You can use these folders and libraries to arrange your files.

In this chapter you will learn where to find the well-known commands for creating a new folder, for example, for moving documents, deleting files, and changing the view of the window. You will also get to know the option for creating a library.

In this chapter you will learn how to:

- use the window of *File Explorer*;
- change the display of the window;
- create a new folder and a new file;
- move a file, copy it to another folder, and delete it;
- change the name of a folder or file;
- empty the *Recycle Bin*;
- copy a file to a USB memory stick;
- create and delete a library.

➥ Please note:

In this chapter we will use the practice files folder in one of the examples. You can select a different folder, or you can decide to copy the practice files to your computer's hard disk first. In *Appendix B Downloading the Practice Files* at the back of this book you can read how to do this.

3.1 Opening Your Personal Folder

First you are going to open *File Explorer*. The button that opens the *Explorer* is located at the bottom of the desktop, on the left-hand side of the taskbar:

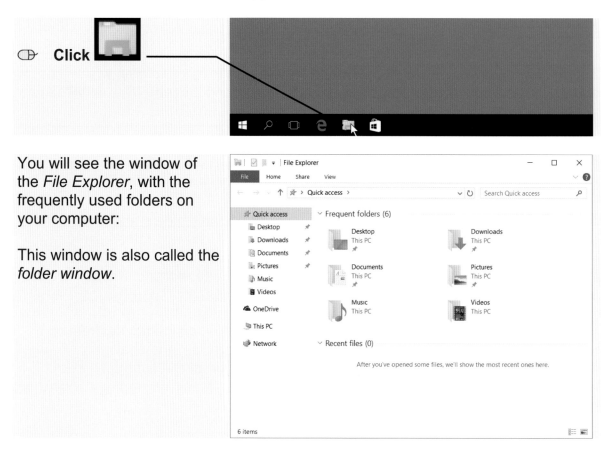

You will see the window of the *File Explorer*, with the frequently used folders on your computer:

This window is also called the *folder window*.

You will start by working in your *Personal folder*. Your *Personal folder* is the folder that contains the *Documents*, *Pictures*, *Music*, and *Videos* folders, among several others. The *Personal folder* has the same name as the name of your user account when you sign on with your computer.

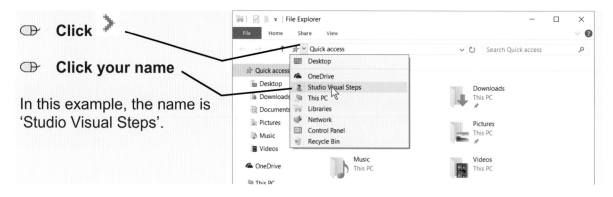

☞ **Click**

☞ **Click your name**

In this example, the name is 'Studio Visual Steps'.

You will see a window with the content of your *Personal folder*. Here you find the folders that have already been created for you:

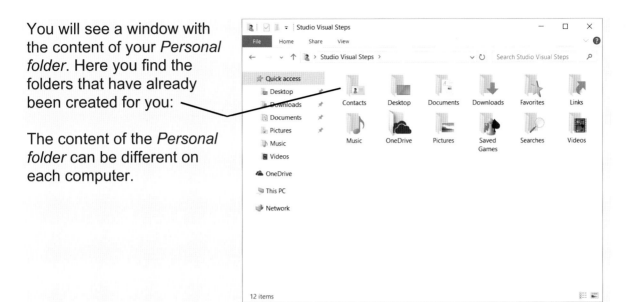

The content of the *Personal folder* can be different on each computer.

3.2 The Ribbon

Just as in *WordPad*, you will be working in a window with the ribbon. You can think of the ribbon as a very extensive taskbar containing all of the operations and commands you need to manage your files and folders. You cannot see all of these options at once. That is why the ribbon is organized into tabs.

The window consists of a number of tabs:

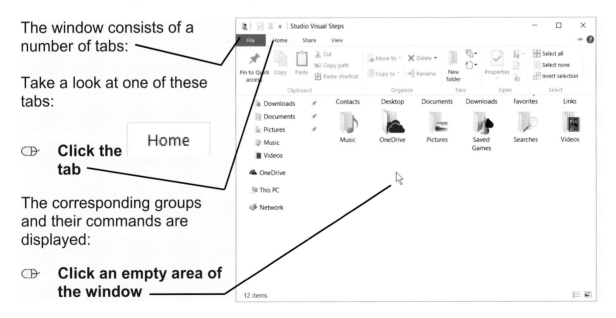

Take a look at one of these tabs:

☞ **Click the** Home **tab**

The corresponding groups and their commands are displayed:

☞ **Click an empty area of the window**

The ribbon will disappear. It is also possible to show the ribbon permanently:

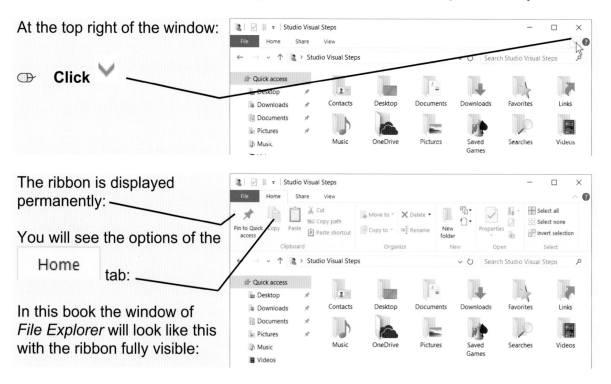

At the top right of the window:

☞ **Click** ⌄

The ribbon is displayed permanently:

You will see the options of the

    Home

tab:

In this book the window of *File Explorer* will look like this with the ribbon fully visible:

3.3 Changing the Display of the Window

There are several ways to view your folders in the window of *File Explorer*. Take a look at the display settings of your window:

☞ **Click the** View **tab**

☞ **Place the pointer on**
    ▤▤ List

Immediately you will see an example of this display:

☞ **Click** ▤▤ List

The display for this window is set to List. A blue frame appears round the option ▤▤ List. This means that this option is active.

Just take a look at another view:

☞ **Click**

▣ Large icons

The icons are displayed in a large size:

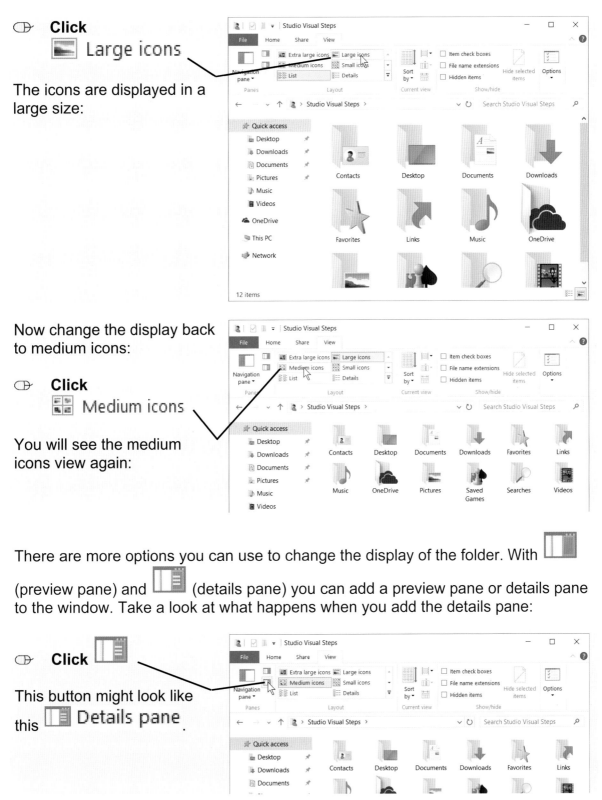

Now change the display back to medium icons:

☞ **Click**

▦ Medium icons

You will see the medium icons view again:

There are more options you can use to change the display of the folder. With ▯ (preview pane) and ▯▯ (details pane) you can add a preview pane or details pane to the window. Take a look at what happens when you add the details pane:

☞ **Click** ▯▯

This button might look like this ▯▯ **Details pane** .

The details pane will appear at the right-hand side of the window. A blue frame appears round the option [icon]. This means that this option is active.

The details pane:

When you select a file, you can see information about it in the details pane:

Now you are going to hide the details pane:

☞ **Click** [icon]

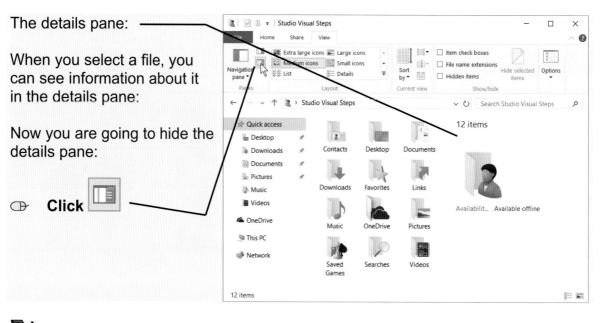

➽ Please note:

Don't click [icon] when there's no blue frame round this option. Click it only when you see a blue frame [icon].

The window on your computer should look the same as the window below:

You are going to open a folder. This is how you do it:

☞ **Double-click**

Documents

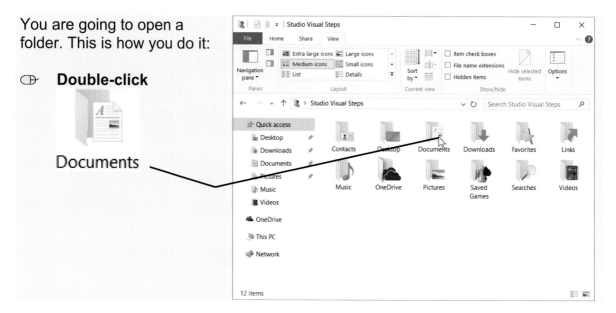

3.4 The Different Parts of the File Explorer Window

In addition to showing the contents of the folder, a window has specific areas that are designed to help you navigate to the files and folders on your computer and work with them more easily. Take a look now:

In the navigation pane you will see a number of folders that are present on your computer: ____

The Quick access list is new in *Windows 10*. This is a list of frequent folders that is always visible: ____

The address bar indicates which folder is open: ____

All the files in this folder are displayed in the file list: ____

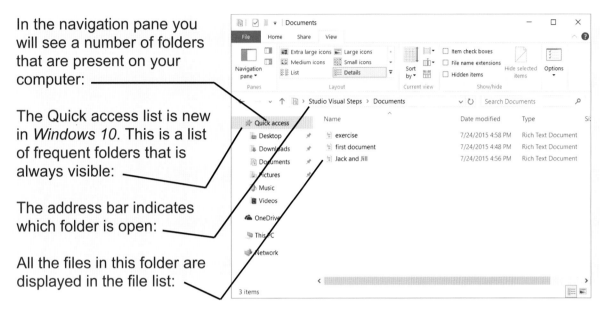

By using the navigation pane on the left side, you can quickly navigate to any folder on your computer. When you click an item or folder in the navigation pane, you will see the contents of that item or folder you clicked displayed in the file list, the main portion of the window.

In the previous section, you changed the display of your *Personal folder*. Now you have opened the *Documents* folder and you see that the contents are displayed differently. In *File Explorer*, you can change the view of how the files look in any window. For example if you set the view to medium icons, your files will become more easily recognizable:

Click
Medium icons

The display of the window will be changed:

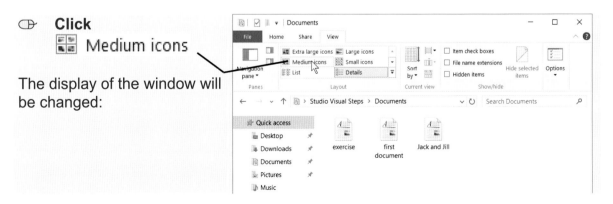

The *Documents* folder contains at least three files. These are the practice text files you have previously created in this book with *WordPad*, and have saved.

3.5 Creating a New Folder

A folder is a container that helps you organize your files. Every file on your computer is stored in a folder, and folders can also hold other folders. Folders located inside other folders are often called *subfolders*.
You can add new folders yourself. This can be handy, for example, to keep your letters separate from all your other documents. In following exercise, you will create a new folder inside the *Documents* folder.

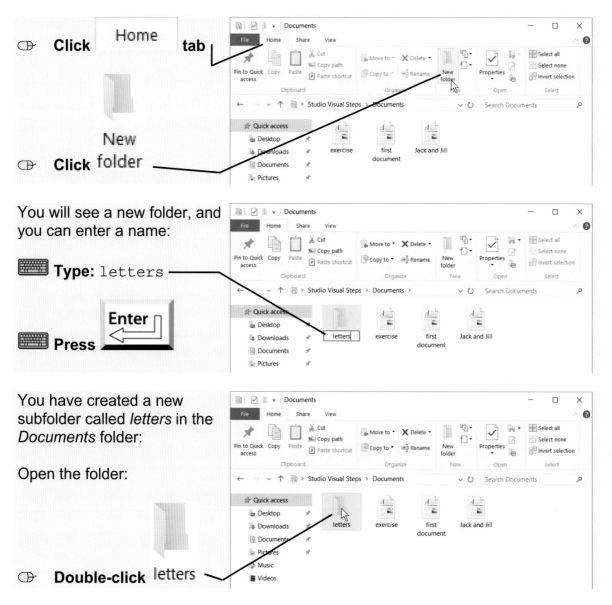

Click Home **tab**

Click New folder

You will see a new folder, and you can enter a name:

Type: letters

Press Enter

You have created a new subfolder called *letters* in the *Documents* folder:

Open the folder:

Double-click letters

3.6 Creating a New File

You can use this *letters* folder to save a letter, for instance.
But you can also create a new file through *File Explorer*. In this example you are going to create a new text file:

☞ **Click**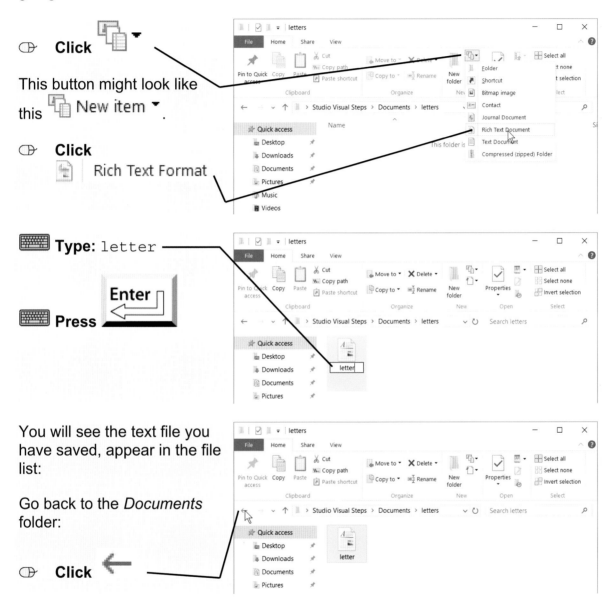

This button might look like this New item ▾.

☞ **Click**
  Rich Text Format

⌨ **Type:** letter

⌨ **Press** Enter

You will see the text file you have saved, appear in the file list:

Go back to the *Documents* folder:

☞ **Click** ←

Please note:

If the file icons of the files in this window look a lot bigger or indeed smaller on your own computer, you can adjust the view of the icons. In *section 3.3 Changing the Display of the Window* you can read how to do this.

3.7 Copying Files

You can also copy files. For example, if you want to have a second copy of a letter, in which you can change something. By way of practice you can copy your practice text. In order to do this, you select the file first, by clicking the icon or the file name:

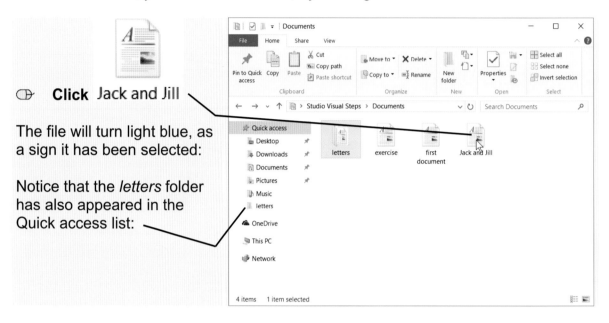

☞ **Click** Jack and Jill

The file will turn light blue, as a sign it has been selected:

Notice that the *letters* folder has also appeared in the Quick access list:

The Quick access list displays the folders you frequently use. If you prefer not to display these folders, you can read the *Tips* at the back of this chapter and find out how to disable this view.

 HELP! There is a blue box around the name.

Do you see a light blue box around the name? Has the pointer changed into I? For example: [Jack and Jill]

☞ **Click somewhere else in the window**
☞ **Try again**

 HELP! I see another window.

Do you unexpectedly see the window for *WordPad* or *Microsoft Word*? If so, you have double-clicked the file name, and opened the program. To close the program:
☞ **Click** ✕
☞ **Try again**

Tip

Selecting multiple files
You can also select multiple files at once. In order to select files that are not adjacent to one another:

☞ **Click the first file (or folder)**

⌨ **Keep** **Ctrl** **depressed**
☞ **Click the other file (or folder)**

In this way you can select a series of files (or folders) that are arranged in a row, one beside the other:

☞ **Click the first file (or folder) of the row**

⌨ **Keep** **Shift** **depressed**
☞ **Click the last file (or folder) of the row**

This is how you select all the files at once (or all the folders, if you are working with folders):

☞ **Click the** **Home** **tab**
☞ **Click** **Select all**

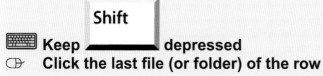

☞ **Click Copy**

Windows now knows you want to copy the file. The next step is pasting the copied file into the *letters* folder:

This is how you open the
letters folder:

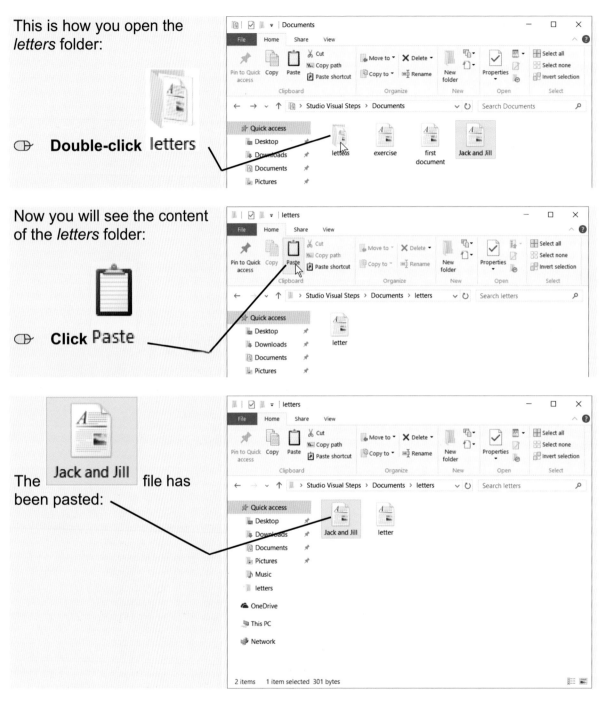

☞ **Double-click** letters

Now you will see the content
of the *letters* folder:

☞ **Click** Paste

The **Jack and Jill** file has
been pasted:

There are more ways to copy a file. For example, you can use the right mouse button. Try that now:

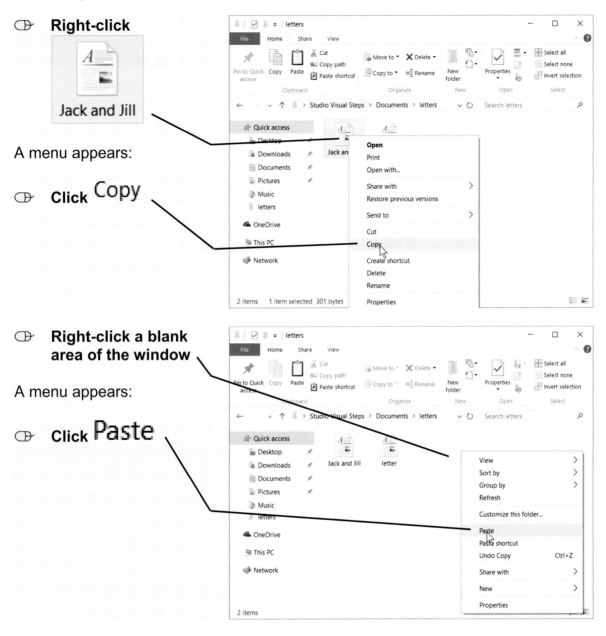

☞ **Right-click**

Jack and Jill

A menu appears:

☞ **Click** Copy

☞ **Right-click a blank area of the window**

A menu appears:

☞ **Click** Paste

                                        Jack and Jill
Now there is a copy of the file named   - Copy   in the same folder. Notice that the word 'Copy' has been automatically added to the name. This is because files with duplicate names are not allowed inside the same folder. Even though the content of the file is the same, the name of the file has to be different if it is located in the same folder.

You are going to open the *Documents* folder. Earlier in this chapter you learned how to go back to a previously viewed folder by using the ← button. You can also use the ↑ button to go up one level, to an item's parent folder. In this example you will be going up one level to the *Documents* folder. You can see that in the address bar

▊ > Studio Visual Steps > Documents > letters

To go back to the *Documents* folder:

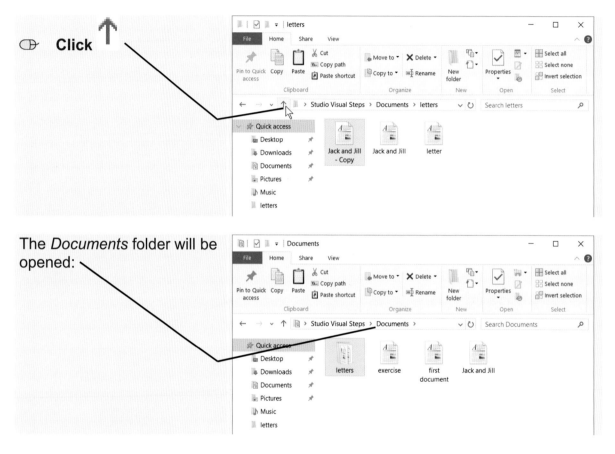

⊕ **Click** ↑

The *Documents* folder will be opened:

Remember: in the address bar of the window you can see which folder is opened:

▊ > Studio Visual Steps > Documents >

3.8 Moving a File

It is also possible to use the Cut command to paste a file into another folder. This means the file will be moved from one folder to another folder. This action is very similar to copying and pasting files:

- use the ✂ Cut and Paste buttons on the ribbon;
- right-click an empty part of the window and then choose Cut and Paste.

There is also another option available on the ribbon:

first

☞ **Click** document

The file is selected:

☞ **Click** ⬅ Move to ▾

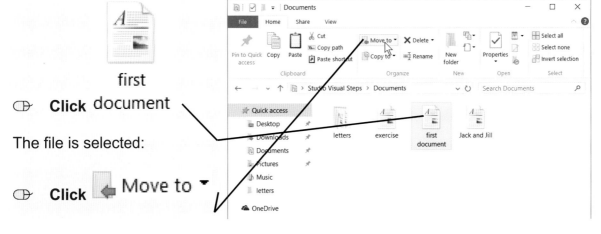

You are going to move the file into the *letters* folder:

In the menu you will see folders which you have recently opened. Including the folder *letters*:

☞ **Click** letters

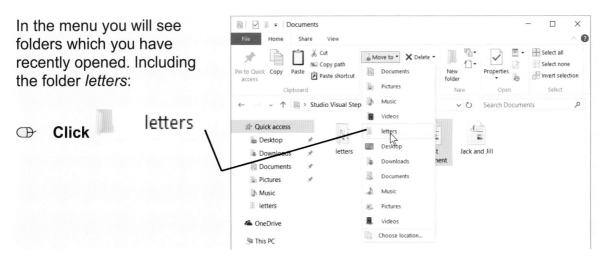

In the *Documents* folder
the *first document* file has
disappeared:

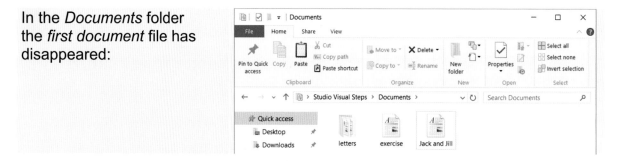

You can check if the file has moved to the *letters* folder:

☞ **Open the *letters* folder** ⬭⬭**16**

The file has been added to
the *letters* folder:

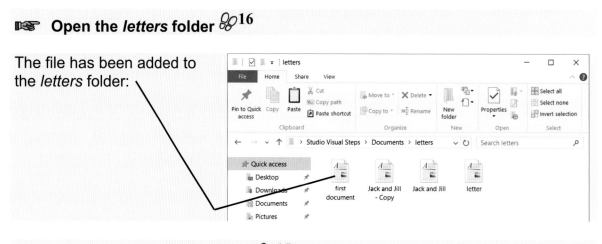

☞ **Open the *Documents* folder** ⬭⬭**15**

3.9 Dragging and Dropping Files

The easiest way to move files to another folder is by *dragging and dropping*.
Try it:

➱ **Drag *exercise* to the
letters folder**

When you see this box

→ Move to letters

appear:

➱ **Release the mouse
button**

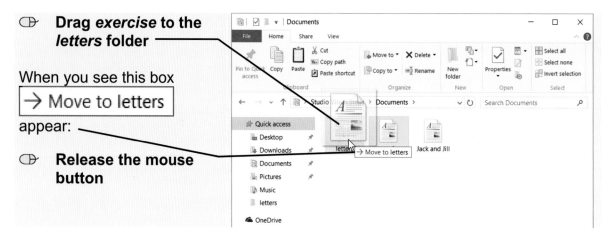

☞ **Open the *letters* folder** ✇14

You will now see the *exercise* file appear in the *letters* folder.

3.10 Changing the File Name

Sometimes you may want to give a file a different name. Perhaps you have several documents about the same subject, for example, and you want to be able to clearly distinguish one document from another:

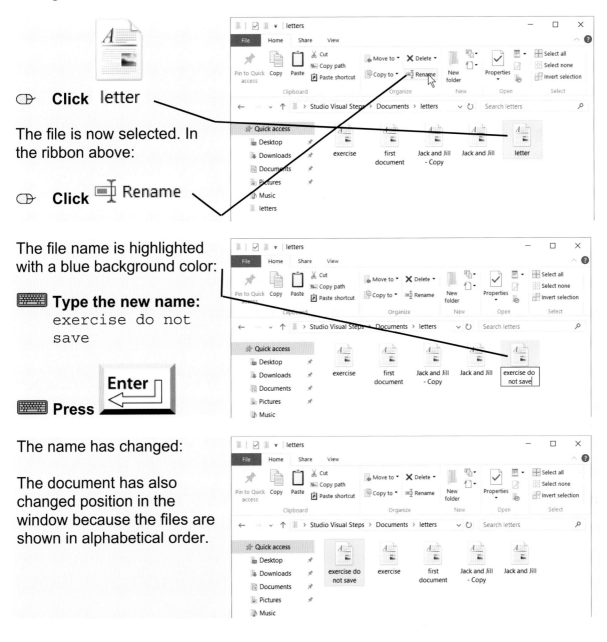

☞ **Click** letter

The file is now selected. In the ribbon above:

☞ **Click** ▭ Rename

The file name is highlighted with a blue background color:

⌨ **Type the new name:**
exercise do not save

⌨ **Press** Enter

The name has changed:

The document has also changed position in the window because the files are shown in alphabetical order.

HELP! I see another window.

You cannot save more than one file with the same name to a folder.
If you try to give a file a name that already exists, you will see:

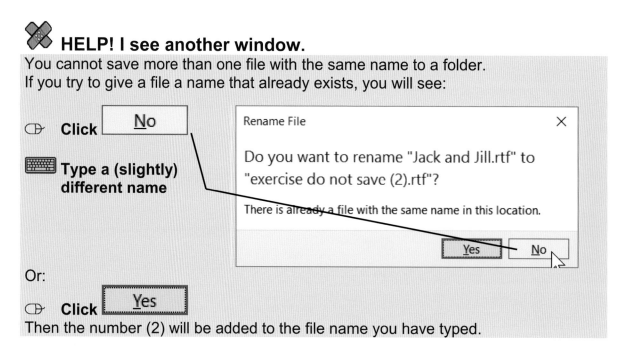

☞ **Click** | No |

⌨ **Type a (slightly) different name**

Rename File   ✕

Do you want to rename "Jack and Jill.rtf" to "exercise do not save (2).rtf"?

There is already a file with the same name in this location.

Yes   No

Or:

☞ **Click** | Yes |

Then the number (2) will be added to the file name you have typed.

3.11 Deleting Files

It is a good idea, every now and then, to do a regular 'spring cleaning' of your computer. To keep your computer manageable, you can delete files you no longer need. To practice, you can delete the *Jack and Jill - Copy* file in the *letters* folder, because this is a copy that you do not really need.

It is important to select the file carefully, so you will not delete the wrong files.

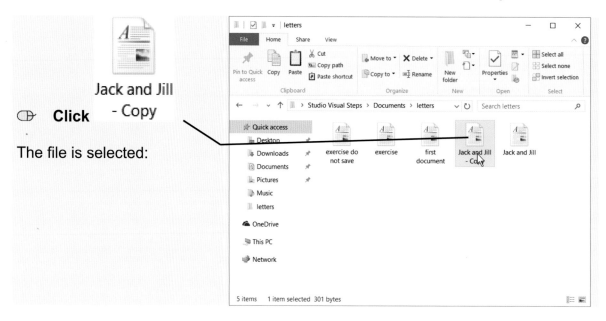

Jack and Jill - Copy

☞ **Click**

The file is selected:

Now you can delete the file. It will be 'tossed' into the *Recycle Bin*.

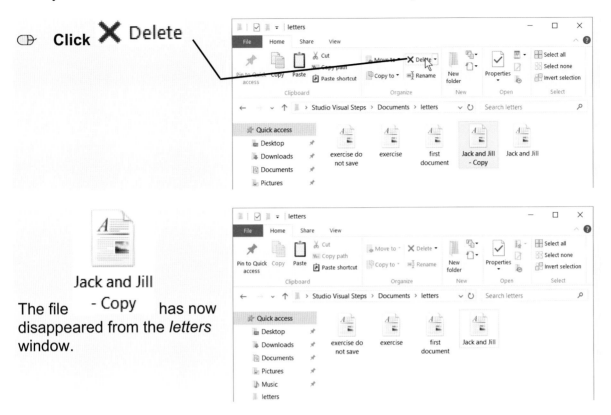

The file **Jack and Jill - Copy** has now disappeared from the *letters* window.

Files that have been deleted are not gone forever. As a kind of safety measure, they are moved to the *Recycle Bin* first. They are not really gone forever until you empty the *Recycle Bin*. As long as a file is in the *Recycle Bin*, you can retrieve it later if you need it.

You also have the option to remove a file directly. You do this by clicking ▾ next to ✖ Delete, and then ✖ Permanently delete. Be careful however if you use this option, for it means that the item is gone forever and will not be able to be recovered.

💡 Tip
Selecting an entire folder

You can also select an entire folder you want to delete. You can select a folder by clicking it, then you can delete it.

Please note:

Be careful when deleting files. Only delete files that you yourself have made. If you did not create the file, you might not be able to delete it.
Also, you cannot delete a file (or the folder that contains it) if the file is currently opened in a program or an app. Make sure that the file is not opened in any program or app, and then try to delete the file or folder again.
Never delete files or folders for programs or apps that you do not use. Program anda app files have to be deleted in a different way.

3.12 The Recycle Bin

All the files that you delete from your computer end up in the *Recycle Bin*. You can open the *Recycle Bin* to see its contents. It will contain all the files you have deleted.

You can open the *Recycle Bin* with its own icon on the desktop . You can also do this from within a *File Explorer* window:

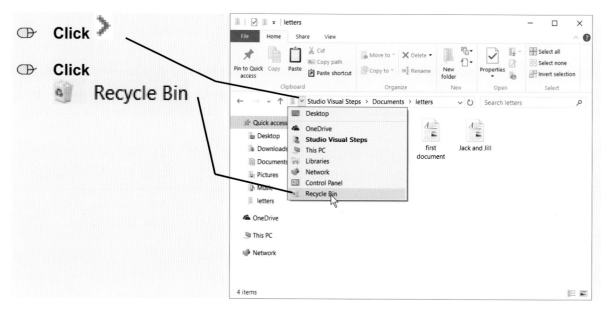

Now you will see the *Recycle Bin* window containing the *Jack and Jill- copy* file that you have deleted:

There is also a new tab especially for files in the *Recycle Bin*. You are going to use this tab to empty the *Recycle Bin*:

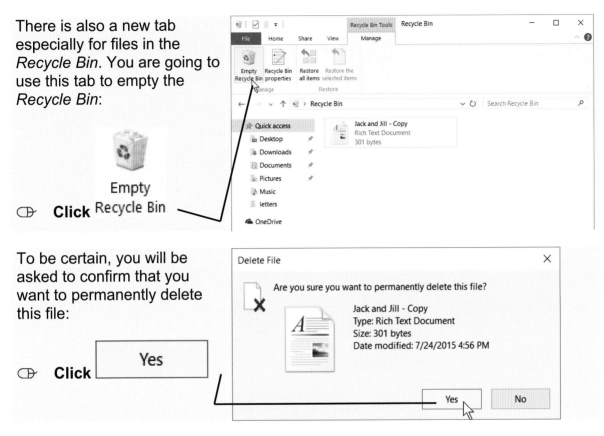

☞ **Click** Empty Recycle Bin

To be certain, you will be asked to confirm that you want to permanently delete this file:

☞ **Click** [Yes]

Now the file has been permanently deleted and cannot be retrieved.

💡 Tip
When should you empty the Recycle Bin?
You do not need to empty the *Recycle Bin* every time you delete a file. You only need to empty it when you want to permanently delete a file. It is better to collect your deleted files in the *Recycle Bin* and to wait until you do your 'spring cleaning'; then you can empty the whole bin at once.

💡 Tip
Is there anything in the Recycle Bin?
You can tell by the icon for the *Recycle Bin* on the desktop whether there is anything in it. The icon changes its appearance:

 not empty   empty

Tip

Restore an item from the Recycle Bin

Did you perhaps delete the wrong file, or on second thought want to restore a

Restore

deleted item? To restore all items all at once, you can use this button: all items.
If you would like to restore one or more selected items, you will need to select it and

Restore the

use this button: selected items. The file will be restored to the folder where it was removed.

☞ **Open the *letters* folder** 🐾16

3.13 Copying to a USB Stick

You may sometimes need to copy something to a USB stick. For example, you might want to transfer a file to another PC or store a backup copy of the file away from the computer. Try this now by copying the *Jack and Jill* file to a USB memory stick.

➥ Please note:

In order to work through this section, you will need a USB stick. A USB stick is a small, portable device that plugs into a computer's USB port. Just like your computer's hard drive, a USB stick stores information. A USB stick makes it very easy to transfer information from one computer to another.

If you do not have a USB stick, you can just read through this section.
If you have an external hard disk, you can execute the operations with this disk as well. An external hard disk is actually a bigger brother of the USB stick. You can store many times more information on such a disk.

First you have to insert the USB stick into the computer.

☞ **Locate the USB port on your computer**

A USB port can be situated on the front or the back of the computer, or both. On a laptop, a USB port could also be located on one of its sides.

🖝 **Insert the USB stick into the USB port and gently push it in**

Having trouble?

🖝 **Then turn the stick over and try again**

When you connect a USB stick to the computer, you will probably see this message in the bottom right-hand corner of the screen:

You can ignore this message.

Open the folder on the USB stick in *File Explorer*:

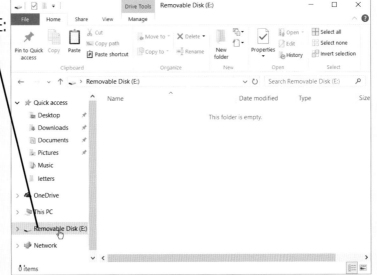

👉 **Click**
🖴 **Removable Disk (E:**

In this example, the USB stick is called Removable disk. This may be a different name on your own computer.

You will see the content of the USB stick. In this example, there are not yet stored any files on the USB stick.

You can copy the *Jack and Jill* file from the letters folder to the USB stick.

☞ **Open the *letters* folder** ⌘¹⁶

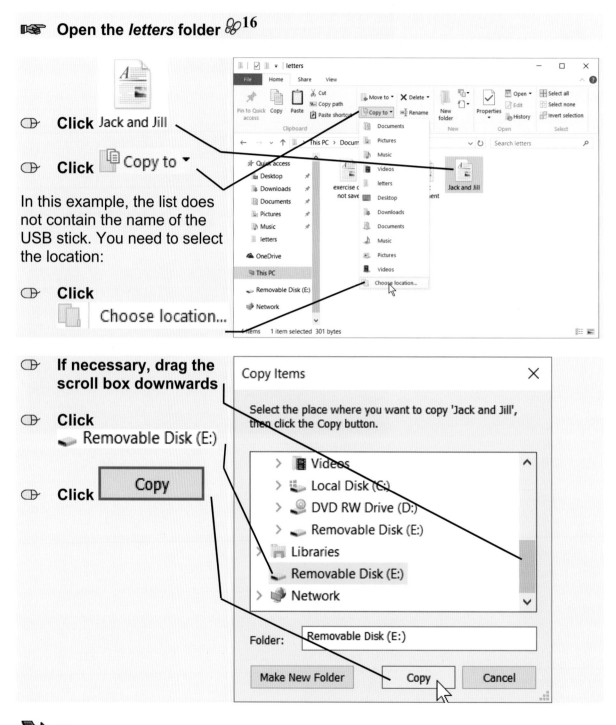

⊕ **Click** Jack and Jill

⊕ **Click** 📋 Copy to ▾

In this example, the list does not contain the name of the USB stick. You need to select the location:

⊕ **Click** 📁 Choose location...

⊕ **If necessary, drag the scroll box downwards**

⊕ **Click** 💾 Removable Disk (E:)

⊕ **Click** Copy

➥ Please note:

If multiple USB sticks are inserted, you also see the names of the other USB sticks. Then choose the one at the bottom. That will be the device you connected last.

The file will now be copied to the USB stick. You may see a message indicating this. In general, a message will appear only with larger files. The *Jack and Jill* file is small.

Now you can check to see if the file has been added to the USB stick. You can do this in the navigation pane on the left-side of the window.

☞ **Click**

⬤ Removable Disk (E:)

You will see the *Jack and Jill* file on the USB stick:

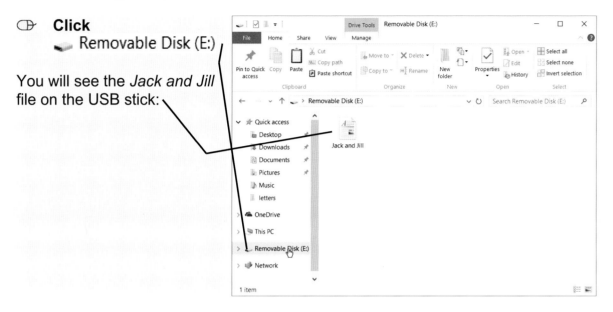

☞ **Close the window** 🐾¹

💡 Tip
Moving
If you want to move a file (or folder) to a different folder you will need to use

⬅ Move to ▾.

3.14 Safely Removing a USB Stick

Before removing storage devices, such as USB sticks, you need to make sure that the computer has finished saving any information to the device. If the device has an activity light flashing, wait for a few seconds until the light has finished flashing before removing it. You also need to do the following.

If you click 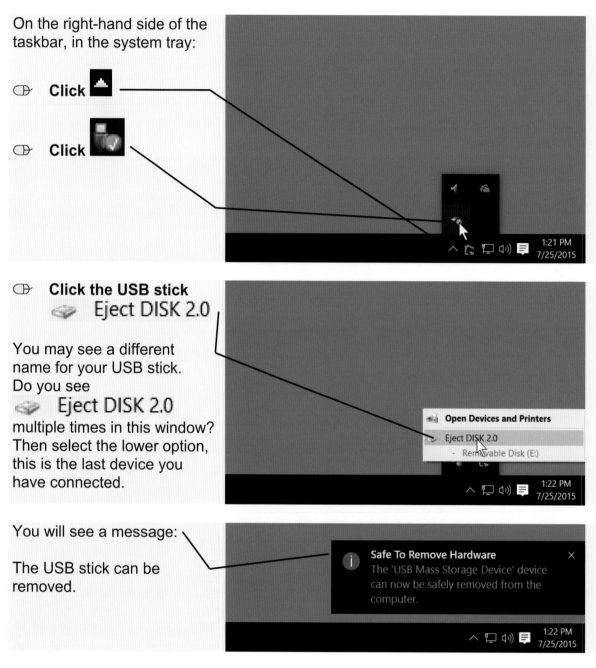 on the taskbar in the bottom right-hand corner, you will see ▨. With this you can check whether the USB stick can be safely removed:

On the right-hand side of the taskbar, in the system tray:

☞ **Click** ▲

☞ **Click** ▨

☞ **Click the USB stick**
   ⬦ Eject DISK 2.0

You may see a different name for your USB stick. Do you see
   ⬦ Eject DISK 2.0
multiple times in this window? Then select the lower option, this is the last device you have connected.

Open Devices and Printers
Eject DISK 2.0
   - Removable Disk (E:)

You will see a message:

The USB stick can be removed.

Safe To Remove Hardware ✕
The 'USB Mass Storage Device' device can now be safely removed from the computer.

☞ **Remove the USB stick from the computer**

In the next section you are going to work with libraries.

3.15 Libraries

In *Windows 10* you can link folders to a library. Libraries have been introduced in *Windows 7*. If you have previously used this *Windows* version, you might already be familiar with libraries.

Windows 10 has created a number of default libraries for you:

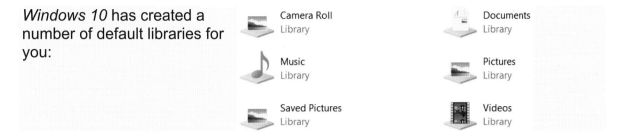

A library looks like a folder, but the difference is, that the files in a folder are actually only stored in that folder. A library does not contain files, but only links to folders. A library displays files that are actually stored in various folders, located all over the computer.
You can quickly and easily find your own files and folders in such a library. For example, the *Documents* library contains all the files from the *Documents* folder in your *Personal folder*.

Working with files and folders in libraries works the same way as working with files and folders in a regular folder.

First you will need to open the libraries. You open them in *File Explorer*:

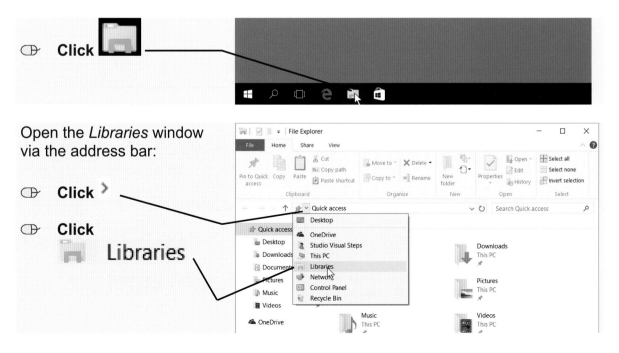

Now you will see the six default libraries on your computer:

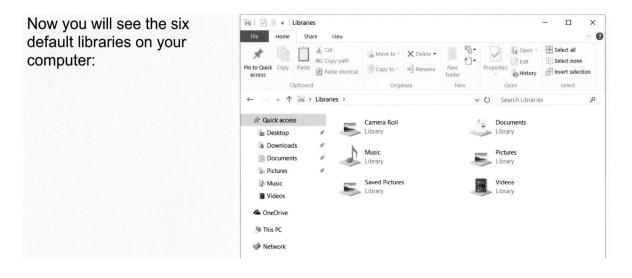

3.16 Creating a Library

In *Windows 10* you can create a new library yourself, in order to manage specific folders on your computer and maintain a good overview. In this example you are going to create a library with the following folders:
- the *letters* folder;
- the *Pictures* folder.

By adding these folders to a library, you will see how easy it is to collect files from different locations on your computer and bring them together in a single library.

💡 Tip
Library with vacation photos and stories
You could create your own library later on, for example, with your vacation photos and the stories that go with them.

In order to create a new library:

☞ **Click**

This button might look like this 🗂 **New item** ▾.

☞ **Click   Library**

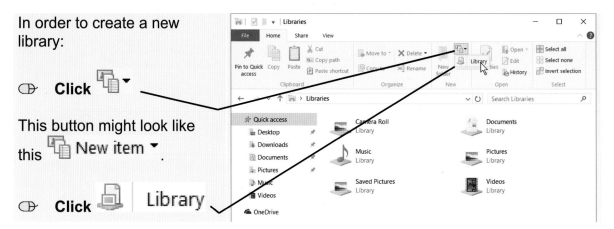

You will see a new library:

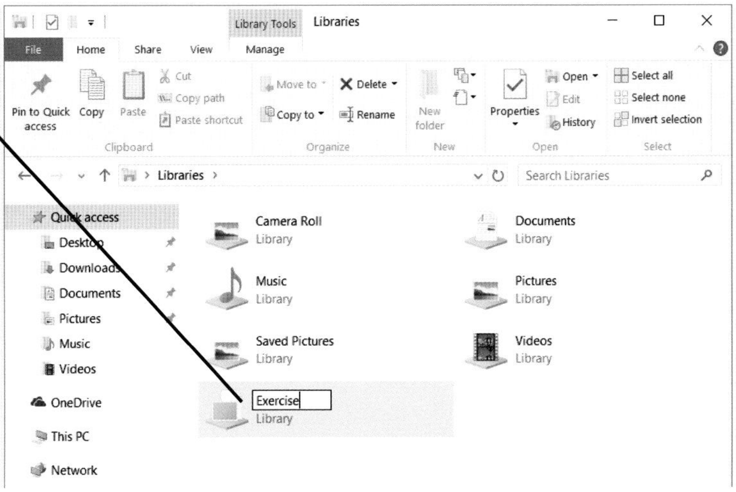

⌨ **Type:** `Exercise`

⌨ **Press** Enter

You have just created a new library. Now you can add folders to this library right away:

🖱 **Double-click**

Exercise
Library

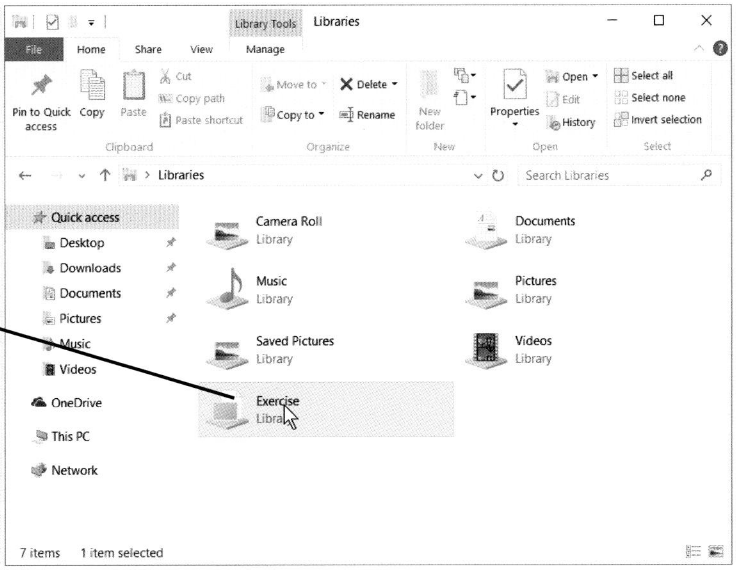

You can see that this library is still empty. Add a folder:

🖱 **Click**

Include a folder

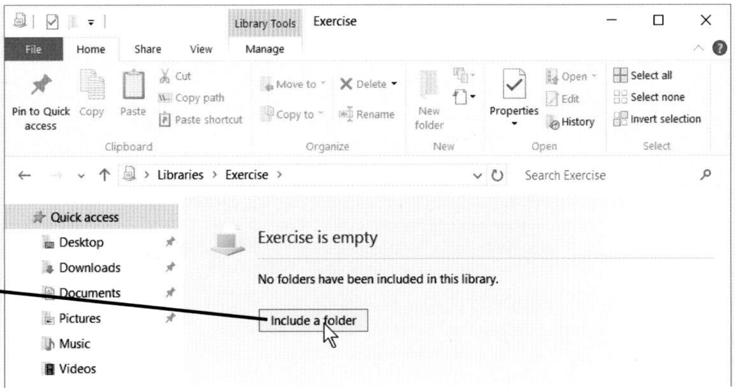

First, you are going to add the *letters* folder. Open the *Documents* folder:

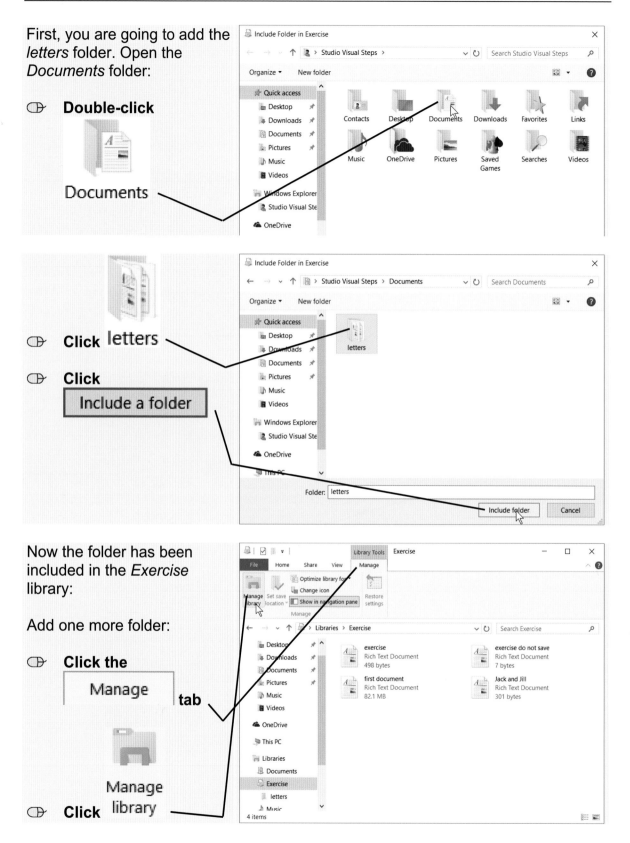

☞ **Double-click**

Documents

☞ **Click** letters

☞ **Click**

Include a folder

Now the folder has been included in the *Exercise* library:

Add one more folder:

☞ **Click the**

Manage tab

☞ **Click** **Manage library**

A new window is opened:

Here you see the *letters* folder:

In order to add a new folder:

☞ **Click** Add...

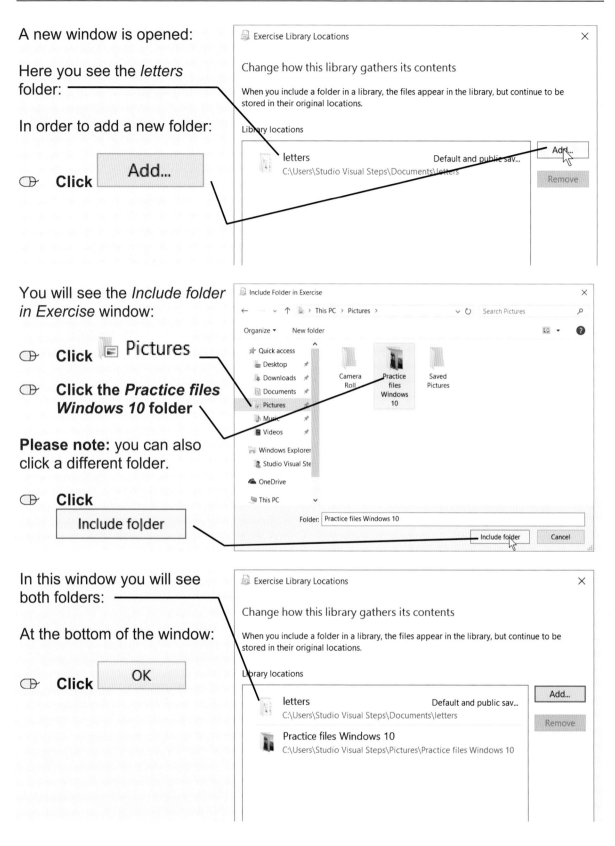

You will see the *Include folder in Exercise* window:

☞ **Click** Pictures

☞ **Click the *Practice files Windows 10* folder**

Please note: you can also click a different folder.

☞ **Click** Include folder

In this window you will see both folders:

At the bottom of the window:

☞ **Click** OK

You will see the files in the library:

To go back to the libraries window:

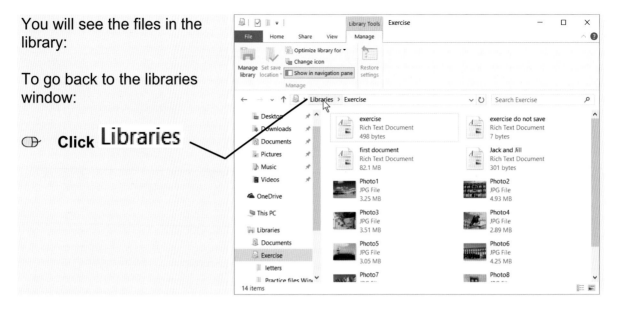

⊕ **Click** Libraries

You are going to delete the *Exercise* library. By doing this, you will only delete the library. The *letters* folder and the *Practice files Windows 10* folder will be saved on your computer's hard disk.

⊕ **Click**

Exercise
Library

⊕ **Click the** Home **tab**

⊕ **Click** ✖ Delete

Now the *Exercise* library has been deleted.

☞ **Close the window** 👣¹

In this chapter you have become acquainted with the *File Explorer* window in *Windows 10*. In the next couple of exercises you are going to repeat these operations.

3.17 Exercises

The following exercises will help you master what you have just learned. Have you forgotten how to do something? Use the number beside the footsteps to look it up in the appendix *How Do I Do That Again?*

Exercise 1: Opening File Explorer Windows

☞ Open *File Explorer*. $\mathcal{C}\!\mathcal{O}$[17]

☞ Open your *Personal folder*. $\mathcal{C}\!\mathcal{O}$[18]

☞ Open the *Documents* folder. $\mathcal{C}\!\mathcal{O}$[14]

☞ Open the *letters* folder. $\mathcal{C}\!\mathcal{O}$[14]

☞ Go back to the *Documents* folder using the Back button. $\mathcal{C}\!\mathcal{O}$[19]

☞ Go to the *letters* folder using the Forward button. $\mathcal{C}\!\mathcal{O}$[19]

Exercise 2: Creating a New Folder

☞ Open the *Documents* folder. $\mathcal{C}\!\mathcal{O}$[15]

☞ Create a new folder with the name *practice*. $\mathcal{C}\!\mathcal{O}$[20]

☞ Open the new *practice* folder. $\mathcal{C}\!\mathcal{O}$[14]

Exercise 3: Copying Files

Please note: in order to do this exercise, you need to do the exercise above first.

☞ Go back to the *Documents* folder using the Back button. $\mathcal{C}\!\mathcal{O}$[19]

☞ Copy the *Jack and Jill* file to the *practice* folder. $\mathcal{C}\!\mathcal{O}$[21]

Exercise 4: Renaming a File

Please note: in order to do this exercise, you need to do the exercises above first.

☞ Open the *practice* folder. $\mathscr{C}^{14}$

☞ Change the name of the *Jack and Jill* file to *poem*. $\mathscr{C}^{22}$

Exercise 5: Creating a Library

☞ Open *File Explorer*. $\mathscr{C}^{17}$

☞ Open the libraries window. $\mathscr{C}^{23}$

☞ Create a new library and call it *Exercise*. $\mathscr{C}^{24}$

☞ Include the *letters* folder and the *Practice files Windows 10* folder in the *Exercise* library. $\mathscr{C}^{25}$

☞ Go back to the window with the libraries by using the Back button. $\mathscr{C}^{19}$

☞ Delete the *Exercise* library. $\mathscr{C}^{26}$

☞ Close the window. $\mathscr{C}^{1}$

3.18 Background Information

Dictionary

Address bar	The address bar appears at the top of every *File Explorer* window displays your current location as a series of links separated by arrows. By using the address bar, you can see which folder is opened.
File	The generic name for everything saved on the computer. A file can be a program, an app, a data file with names, text you have written, a photo, a video or a piece of music. Actually, everything located on the hard drive of your computer is called a *file*.
File Explorer	The program that allows you to access, save and manage your files and folders.
File list	This is where the content of the current folder is displayed.
Folder	A folder is a container that helps you organize your files. Every file on your computer is stored in a folder, and folders can also hold other folders.
Folder list	List of folders in the navigation pane. By using the folder list in the navigation pane, you can navigate directly to the folder or library you are interested in by clicking on this folder.
Folder window	The window of *File Explorer*.
Frequent folders	Through Quick access you can directly access frequently used folders. This way, you can quickly access the folders you often use.
Hard drive	The primary storage device located inside a computer. Also called a hard disk or hard disk drive, it is the place where your files, programs and apps are typically stored.
Library	A library looks like a folder, but the difference is that in a folder, the files are actually stored in the folder only. There are no files stored in a library, but only the links to various folders. A library displays files that are actually stored in several different folders, distributed all over the computer.

- Continue on the next page -

Navigation pane	Shows a list of folders that can be opened in the *File Explorer* window. Displayed in the top left-hand corner in *File Explorer*.
Quick access	A list of folders displayed in the top left-hand corner in *File Explorer*. If you often use a specific folder, it can be useful to add this folder to the Quick access list.
Recent files	Through Quick access you can directly access your recent files. You can use these in order to quickly resume working with a file you frequently use, for example.
Recycle Bin	When you delete a file or folder, it goes to the *Recycle Bin*. You can retrieve a file from the *Recycle Bin*. But if you empty the *Recycle Bin*, all of its contents are permanently gone.
Search box	A box you find in the *File Explorer* window. If you type something in the search box, the contents of the folder are immediately filtered to show only those files that match what you have typed. It searches the current folder and any of its subfolders, but it can also search your entire computer.
USB port	A narrow, rectangular connection point on a computer where you can connect a universal serial bus (USB) device such as a USB stick.
USB stick	A small portable device, to store files and folders. Plugs into a computer's USB port. *Windows* will show a USB stick as a removable disk.

Source: Windows Help, Wikipedia

USB sticks, external hard drives, SD cards, CDs and DVDs

USB sticks, CDs and DVDs are storage media often used to store files outside the computer. For example, you can use them to transfer files to another computer or to save a *backup* copy. Software manufacturers often provide their products on a CD-ROM or DVD-ROM.

USB stick

A USB stick is a small storage medium with a large storage capacity. You can insert it directly into your PC's USB port. The storage capacity can vary up to 64 GB or more, with steady improvements in size and price per capacity expected. You can write files directly to a USB stick.

External hard drive

An external hard disk is also a kind of portable storage device, but with more storage capacity. Nowadays, external hard disks have a storage capacity of up to four terabytes (approximately 4000 GB).

SD card

Memory card for use in a digital camera, smartphone, tablet or eReader. The capacity varies from 4GB to 512 GB.

CD and DVD

Some software manufacturers deliver their software packages on CD or DVD. Recently however, many software manufacturers are delivering their programs through direct Internet download.
Large files, like movies can be distributed on DVD as well.

Writable CDs and DVDs

If your computer includes a CD or DVD recorder, you can copy files to a writable disc.

3.19 Tips

Tip
The folder list in the navigation pane
When you use the folder list in the navigation pane, you can navigate directly to the folder that contains the folders, subfolders or files you are interested in:

All you have to do is click a folder or library name and the content will be displayed in the file list. ———

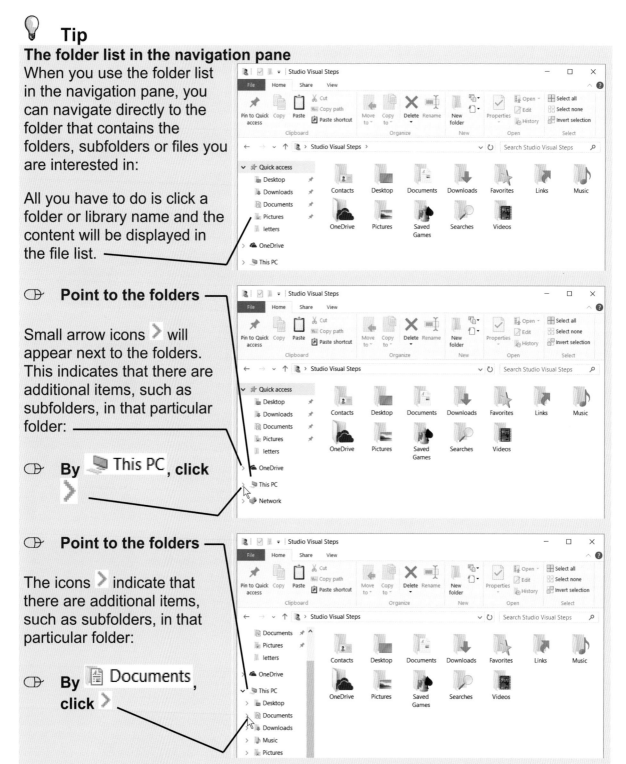

Point to the folders ———

Small arrow icons ❯ will appear next to the folders. This indicates that there are additional items, such as subfolders, in that particular folder: ———

By 🖥 This PC, click ❯

Point to the folders ———

The icons ❯ indicate that there are additional items, such as subfolders, in that particular folder:

By 📄 Documents, click ❯

- Continue on the next page -

You can see that in this example there is one subfolders stored in this folder:

Now the arrow ❯ has changed into ❯:

❯ indicates the folder is expanded to show the entire contents. Every folder with a the arrow ❯ contains one or more folders or subfolders.

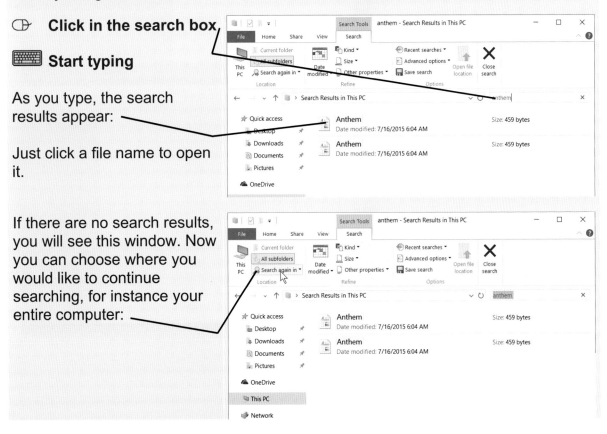

💡 Tip

Searching files in a folder

There are many ways to find your files on your computer. Most of the time, you will start by using the search box that is available within any *File Explorer* window.

⊕ **Click in the search box**

⌨ **Start typing**

As you type, the search results appear:

Just click a file name to open it.

If there are no search results, you will see this window. Now you can choose where you would like to continue searching, for instance your entire computer:

💡 Tip

Finding a file using the Search function on the taskbar

Along with the options to search for a file within a *File Explorer* window, you can also perform a search from the search function on the taskbar:

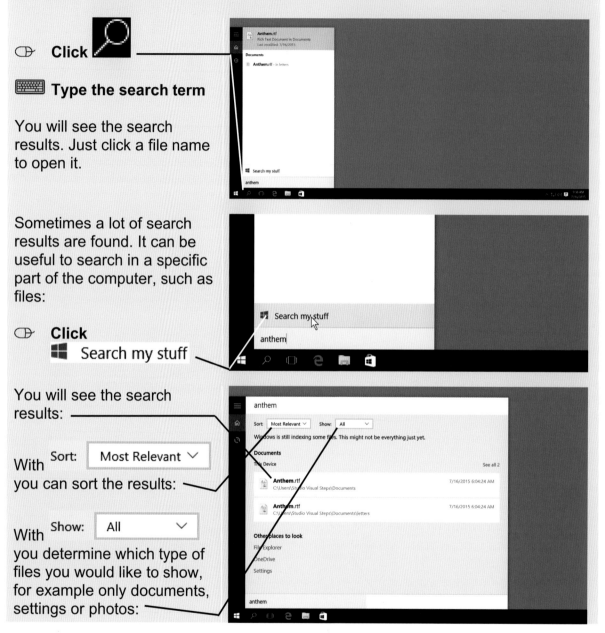

☞ **Click** 🔍

⌨ **Type the search term**

You will see the search results. Just click a file name to open it.

Sometimes a lot of search results are found. It can be useful to search in a specific part of the computer, such as files:

☞ **Click**
   ⊞ Search my stuff

You will see the search results:

With Sort: [Most Relevant ∨] you can sort the results:

With Show: [All ∨] you determine which type of files you would like to show, for example only documents, settings or photos:

🔅 Tip
Quick access
One of the new functions in *File Explorer* is called *Quick access*. This is a list of frequently used folders. By default, this list contains the *Desktop*, *Downloads*, *Documents*, *Pictures* folders, and mostly the *Music*, and *Videos* folders too. Besides, this list can be supplemented with the folders you often use. If you often use a specific folder, it can be handy to add this folder to Quick access. This is how you do it:

☞ **Click the desired folder**

☞ **Click** 📌 Pin to Quick access

The folder has been added to the list by ⭐ Quick access:

☞ **Click the folder**

The folder is opened.

To delete a folder from the ⭐ Quick access list:

☞ **Right-click the folder**

☞ **Click** Unpin from Quick access

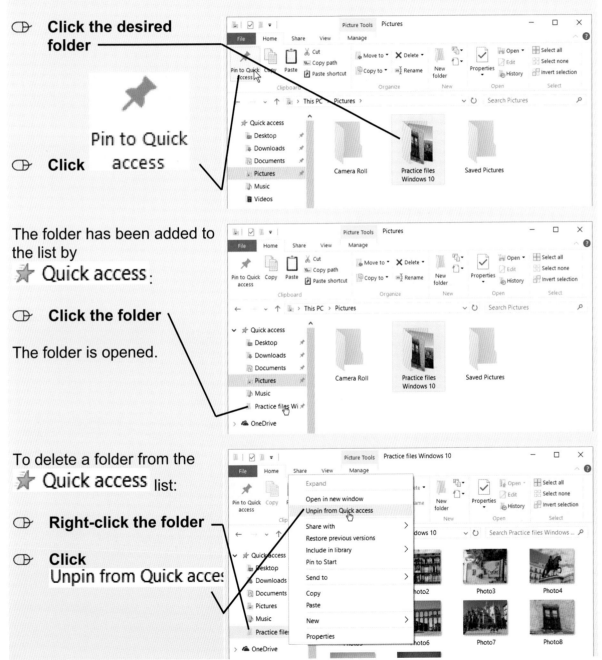

💡 Tip

Recent files and frequent folders

One of the new functions in *File Explorer* is the display of recent files and frequently used folders. You can use this function to quickly resume working on frequently used files:

If you want to view the frequently used folders and recent files, you click ⭐ *Quick access*:

Frequent folders:

Probably you will see more or different folders.

The recently opened files:

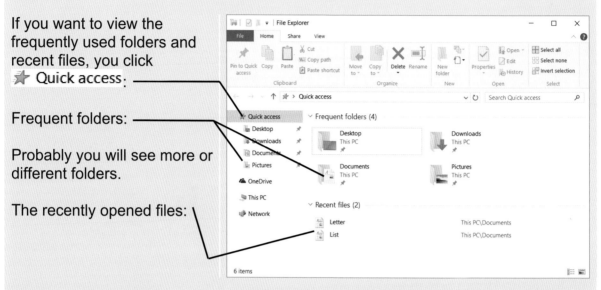

You can also disable the view of recent files and frequent folders. This is how you do it:

☞ **Click** File, Change folder and search options

At the bottom of the *General* tab you will find these options:

Uncheck the boxes if you do not want to display the files or folders anymore:

Only clear the current recent files and frequent folders and do not display them:

Privacy

☑ Show recently used files in Quick access

☑ Show frequently used folders in Quick access

Clear File Explorer history   [Clear]

[Restore Defaults]

[OK]   [Cancel]   [Apply]

4. Surfing the Internet

For many years, *Internet Explorer* was the default Internet browser that came with the *Windows* operating system. This is no longer the case in *Windows 10. Internet Explorer* has been replaced by a new browser called *Edge*. The main reason for this replacement is that *Internet Explorer* is outdated and cannot compete with the more recent Internet browsers any longer. *Edge* is a faster browser than *Internet Explorer*.

Internet Explorer is still available *Windows 10*, but will probably not be supported by Microsoft after a while. This means there will be no more updates, which may lead to security issues when using this browser.

In this chapter you will learn how to work with *Edge*. Some options and functions will look familiar to you because they are similar to *Internet Explorer* while others may need to be reviewed once more. There are also several new options available.

In this chapter you will learn how to:

- open *Edge*;
- open a website;
- zoom in and zoom out;
- save a web address;
- arrange your favorites;
- print a web page;
- work with tabs;
- use the reading list;
- use the reading view;
- take notes;
- set a home page;
- view the browser history;
- delete the browser history;
- use the security and privacy settings in *Edge*.

➥ Please note:

In order to work through this section you need to have an active Internet connection, and we assume your Internet connection has already been set up on your computer. If necessary, contact your Internet provider or computer supplier for further information. Or ask an experienced computer user to help you.

4.1 Opening Edge

In *Windows 10* you can access the program that allows you to view web pages directly from the Start menu: *Edge*. You can also launch *Edge* by clicking the taskbar button ![e]. But for now you will learn how to open the program using the search function:

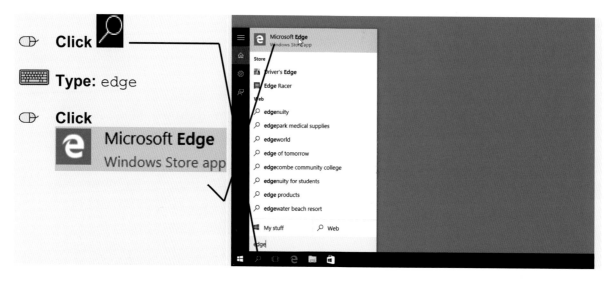

☞ **Click** 🔍

⌨ **Type:** edge

☞ **Click**
     Microsoft Edge
     Windows Store app

The program will be opened and automatically connects to the Internet. Your window is filled with a *home page*:

This is usually a page with information about *Edge*, or with news items. If you see news items, you may also see some advertisements on this page.

At the top you see one or two tabs:

If you see two tabs, you can close one of them:

☞ **Click** ✕

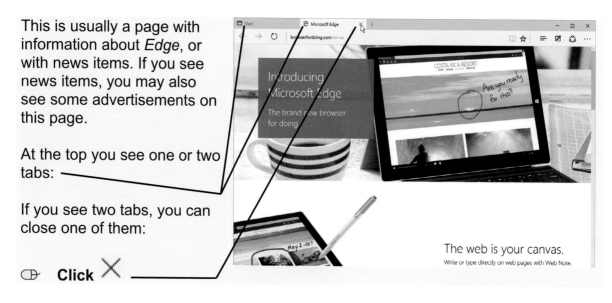

Please note:

The home page displayed above may look a little different from the one shown on your own computer. You may see a home page that was set up by someone else or yourself earlier on. Even if you do see the same web page, the content may differ. Many Internet pages are edited and updated on a daily basis.

4.2 Opening a Website

You now can practice opening another website. In this example you will be opening the website accompanying this book. You do this via the address bar at the top of the window:

In the address bar, type:
`www.visualsteps.com/windows10`

Press Enter

You may see some suggestions while you are typing:

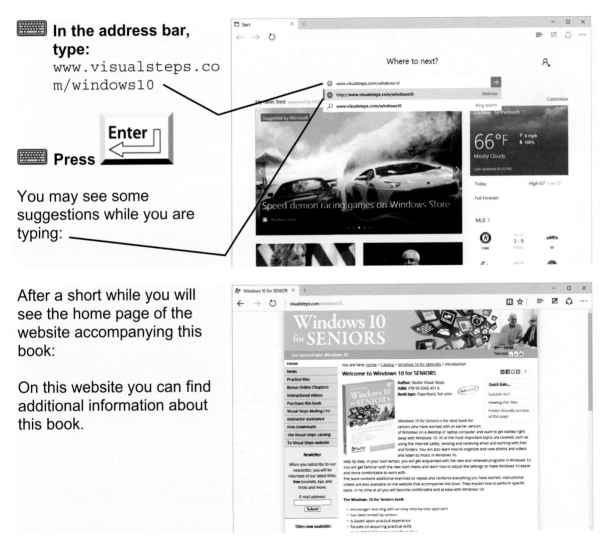

After a short while you will see the home page of the website accompanying this book:

On this website you can find additional information about this book.

If you want to see a previously visited website, you use the ⬅ button in the upper left corner of the window. You can also browse (navigate) 'the other way'. For this

you need to use the ➡ button instead.

With these buttons you can easily go from a previously visited website to another website. This is called 'surfing' the Internet.

Sometimes, a web page is not correctly displayed in the window. You can tell *Edge* to

load the page again. You do this by clicking the ↻ button. The web page will be refreshed. This button is also very useful when you are viewing web pages with news items. This way, you will always see the most recently updated news.

4.3 Zooming In and Out

Sometimes the content of a web page is difficult to read. In that case, you can try to zoom in on a web page. Zooming in will enlarge everything on a page, including the text and the images:

In the upper right corner of the window:

☞ **Click** `* * *`

☞ **By** Zoom, **click** ✛ **twice**

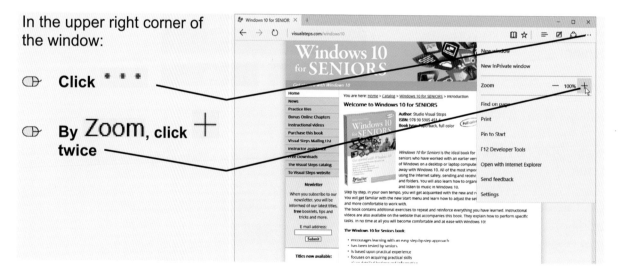

The entire page has been enlarged, including the images and buttons:

This is how you zoom out again:

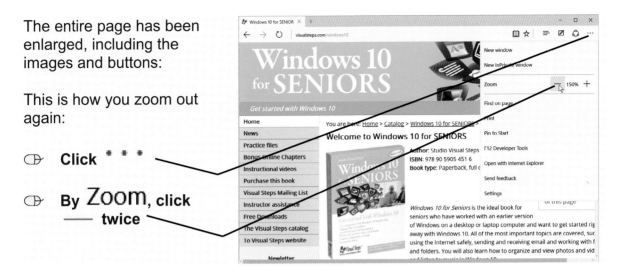

⊖ **Click** * * *

⊖ **By Zoom, click**
       —— **twice**

The page has become smaller again.

💡 **Tip**

Zooming with the mouse or keyboard
If you have a mouse with a scroll wheel, you can zoom in and out by pressing the

Ctrl

Ctrl key ▭ and rolling the scroll wheel.
You can also use the keyboard to zoom. You do this by pressing the Ctrl key

Ctrl

▭ and then pressing **+** or **-** .

4.4 Saving a Web Address

If you have found an interesting website, you can save its web address. Then you can quickly open the website without having to retype the web address again. Websites that are saved this way are called *favorites* in *Edge*. You can only save a web address as a favorite if the corresponding website is opened. You can try this with the Visual Steps website:

☞ **Open the www.visualsteps.com web page** ⬡⬡²⁷

In the upper right corner of the window:

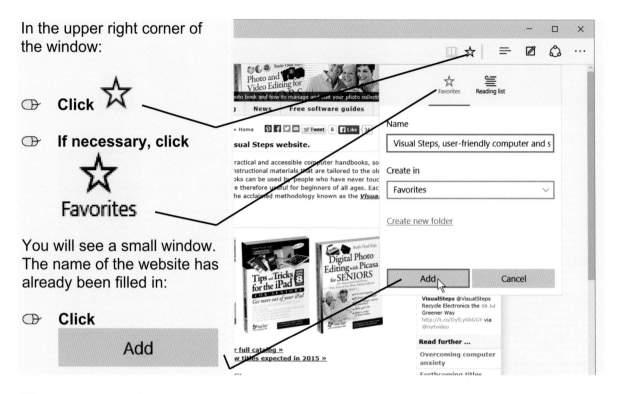

☞ **Click** ☆

☞ **If necessary, click**

☆
Favorites

You will see a small window. The name of the website has already been filled in:

☞ **Click**

Add

The website has been added to your favorites.

Now you can check and see how a favorite works. First, you need to open another website:

☞ **Open the web page www.cnn.com** $\mathcal{Q}\!\mathcal{Q}^{27}$

You will see the news website cnn.com. Now you can quickly open one of your favorite websites:

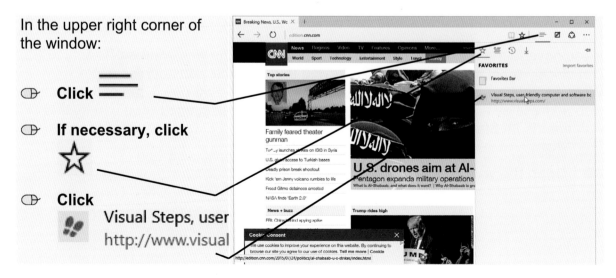

In the upper right corner of the window:

☞ **Click** ≡

☞ **If necessary, click**

☆

☞ **Click**

👣 **Visual Steps, user**
http://www.visual

The favorite website you just saved will be displayed:

Edge remembers all your favorites, even after you have closed the program. You can collect a lot of your favorite websites in the same manner, and access them quickly at any given time.

4.5 Arranging Your Favorites

You can assemble all your favorite websites in a single long list. But this is not very practical if you have a lot of favorites. It is better to arrange your favorites in separate folders. You can save the favorites ordered by subject, for example.
You can also use these folders to separate your own favorites from those of the other users on your computer.

To practice a little, you can create a folder for the website that accompanies this book.

☞ **Open the web page www.visualsteps.com/windows10** ✂²⁷

You will save this web page and create the folder all at once.

In the upper right corner of the window:

⊕ **Click** ☆

⊕ **Click**
Create new folder

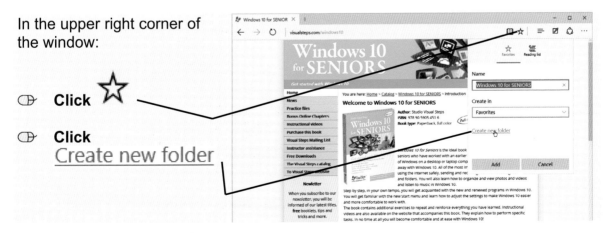

Add a name for the folder:

☞ **Click the box by Folder name**

⌨ **Type:** Computer books

☞ **Click**

Add

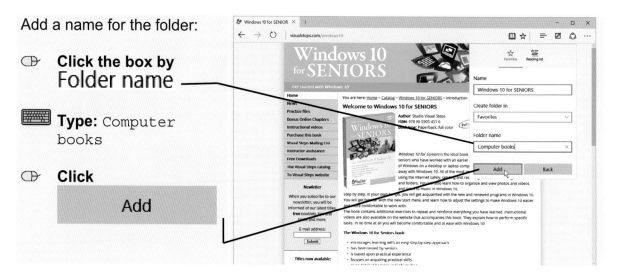

The folder has been created, and the web page has been added to the folder. You can check this right away:

☞ **Click** ≡

In the favorites list, you see the Computer books folder:

☞ **Click** Computer books

You will see the web page on the right-hand side of the window:

☞ **Click an empty spot of the window**

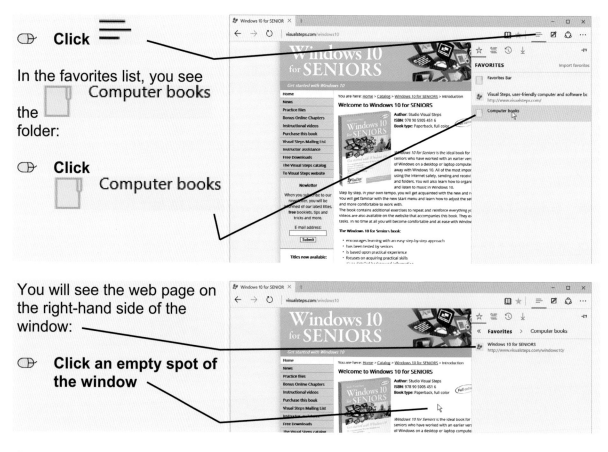

In the next section you will learn how to save web pages in a previously created folder.

4.6 Saving a Favorite in a Folder

It is very easy to save a web address in the new folder.

Please note:

You can only save a web address as a favorite, if the website in question is displayed in the *Edge* window.

- Click **The Visual Steps catalog**

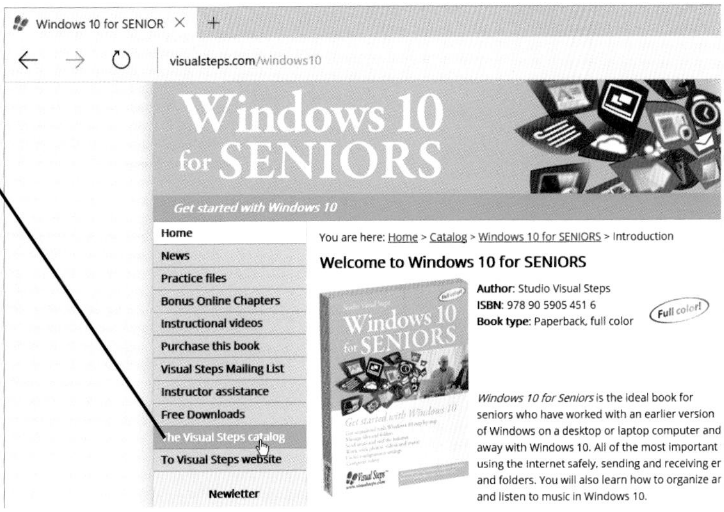

You will see an overview of the books published by Visual Steps. You will save this website in the new *Computer books* folder. Here is how you do that:

- Click ☆
- By Create in, click ∨

Select the folder you have just created:

- Click Computer books

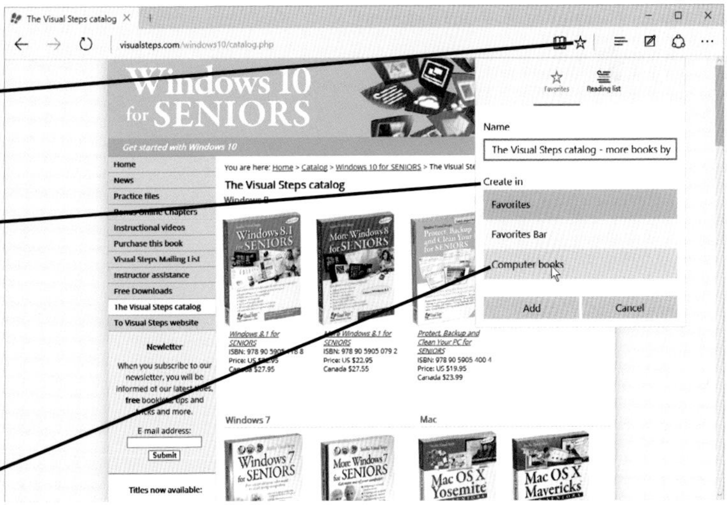

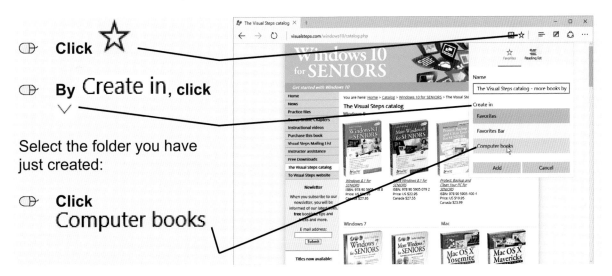

The correct folder has been selected:

☞ **Click**

Add

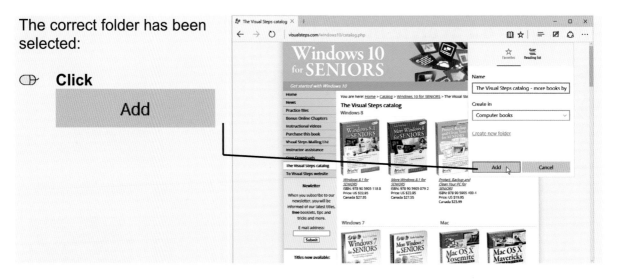

Now you can check to see if the favorite has been saved in the correct folder. First you open another website, for example, the Wikipedia website:

☞ **Open the web page www.wikipedia.com** ✂²⁷

You will see the Wikipedia home page:

☞ **Click** ☰

The *Computer books* folder is still open, and the favorite has been added:

☞ **Click**

The Visual Steps ca
http://www.visualst

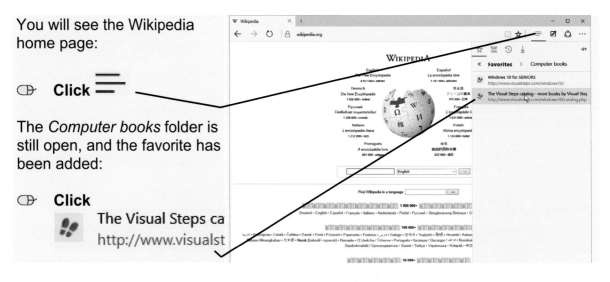

Now you will see the catalog web page with the overview of Visual Steps books again.

4.7 Printing a Web Page

It is not always easy to read a web page on a screen, especially if the page contains a lot of text. You may want to print the web page first, and read it later.

You do not have a printer?
If you do not have a printer, you can skip this section.

☞ **Check if the printer is turned on**

This is how you print a web page:

In the upper right corner of the window:

⊕ **Click** ⠿

⊕ **Click** Print

A window will be opened. On the right-hand side of the window you will see a print preview of the web page:

You can also select the number of prints, and the page orientation, if you wish.

If you want to print the page:

⊕ **Click**

Print

If you do not want to print the page, click

Cancel

The page will be printed.

4.8 Opening a Link in a New Tab

If you click a hyperlink, the new web page will replace the old web page in the tab you are working on. *Edge* also has an option that will open a link directly in a new tab. Just try this with one of the links on the Visual Steps web page:

☞ **Open the www.visualsteps.com web page** ✂²⁷

The page where you can subscribe to the newsletter of Visual Steps is opened in a new tab. This tab is hidden behind the first tab. You can open the second tab by clicking it:

☞ **Click the second tab**

You will see the new tab:

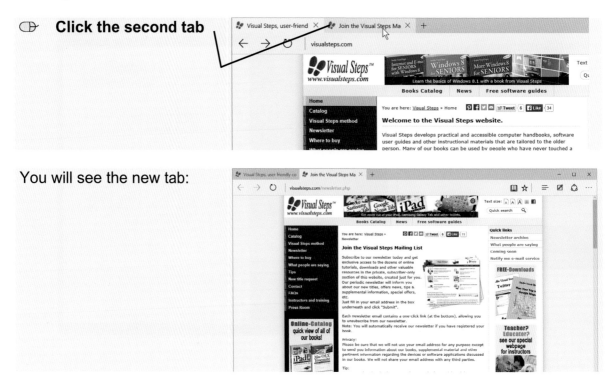

💡 **Tip**

Open a new tab
Of course, you can also open a new tab yourself, and then open a website in this new tab. To do that:

☞ **Click** ➕

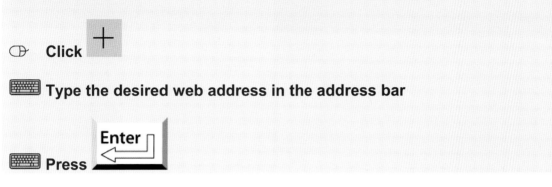

⌨ **Type the desired web address in the address bar**

⌨ **Press** Enter ⏎

4.9 Closing Tabs

If you do not want to use a tab anymore, you can close it. Just try to close the first tab:

☞ **Click the first tab**

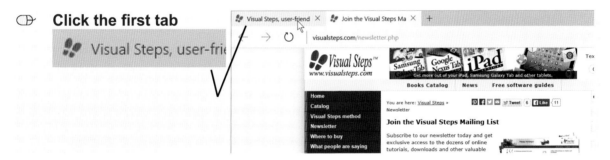

You will see the Visual Steps web page again. On the active

👣 Visual Steps, user-friend ✕ tab you will see a little button ✕ when you place the pointer on the tab; click this button to close the tab.

☞ **Click** ✕

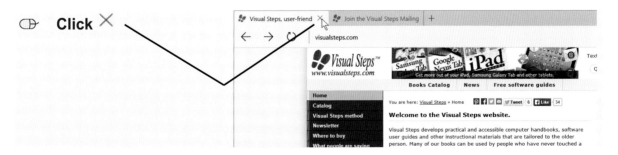

The first tab has disappeared:

4.10 Using the Reading List

The *reading list* is a useful feature in *Edge*. You can add pages to this list and read them later on offline without being connected to the Internet:

☞ **Open the www.grandmagazine.com website** $\mathcal{G}\mathcal{G}$27

☞ **Click an article**

Click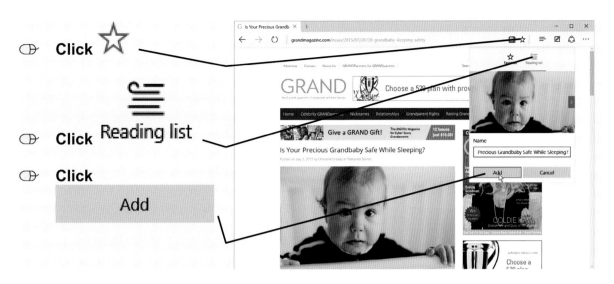

Click Reading list

Click

Add

The web page has been added to your reading list. Now you can check to see if you can quickly open the page. To do this, you need to go back to the previous website:

Click

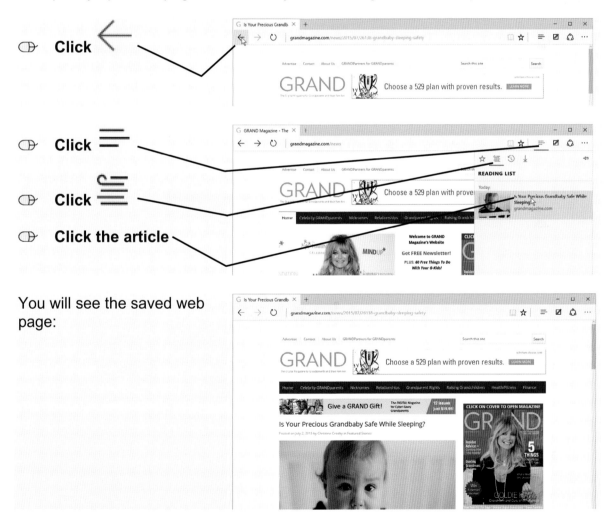

Click

Click

Click the article

You will see the saved web page:

4.11 Reading View

Many web pages not only contain text, but lots of other elements as well, such as advertisements and animated images. This can be very distracting if you just want to read the text. On some web pages, you can use the *reading view* to display only the text and any relevant images. Here is how you do that:

☞ **Open the www.washingtonpost.com website** 𝒫𝒫²⁷

⊕ **Click an article**

If an article can be viewed in the reading view, you will see

the 📖 icon in the upper right corner of the window:

⊕ **Click 📖**

You will see the article in the
reading view:

To go back to the regular
view:

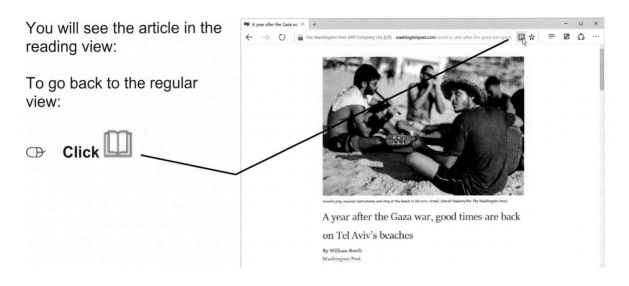

☞ **Click** 📖

4.12 Taking Notes

The new *Web notes* function will let you add notes to a web page. In this way you
can add some reminders or other additional information to a page. You can also
highlight a piece of text.

☞ **Open the www.visualsteps.com website** 🦶27

Add a note:

☞ **Click** 🖊

The web notes toolbar appears:

Markers:

Erase:

Type a note:

Select a part of a page:

Save notes:

Share notes:

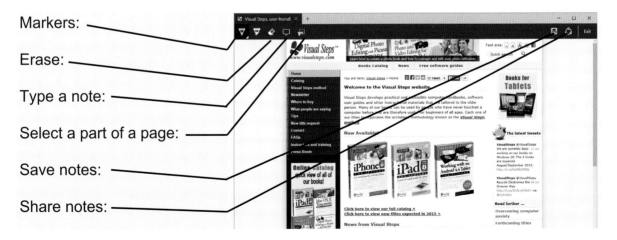

First, you can experiment with highlighting a piece of text:

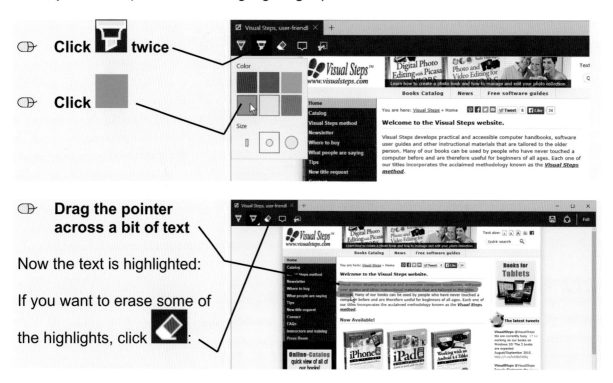

⊕ **Click** twice

⊕ **Click**

⊕ **Drag the pointer across a bit of text**

Now the text is highlighted:

If you want to erase some of

the highlights, click   :

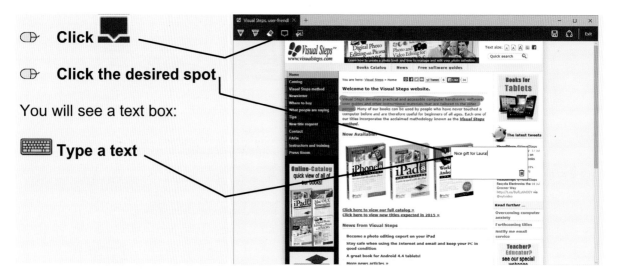

You can also type a note on the page:

⊕ **Click**

⊕ **Click the desired spot**

You will see a text box:

⌨ **Type a text**

You can minimize a note:

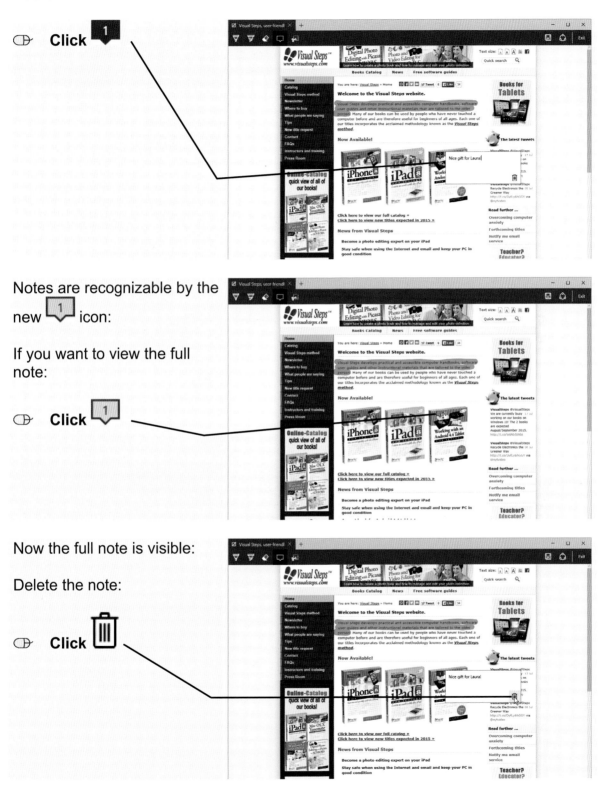

$\oplus$ **Click**

Notes are recognizable by the new icon:

If you want to view the full note:

$\oplus$ **Click**

Now the full note is visible:

Delete the note:

$\oplus$ **Click**

Along with the options for highlighting and taking notes, you can also copy a selected part of the page with ✂ :

For now, you can save the text that is still highlighted as a web note:

⊕ **Click** 💾

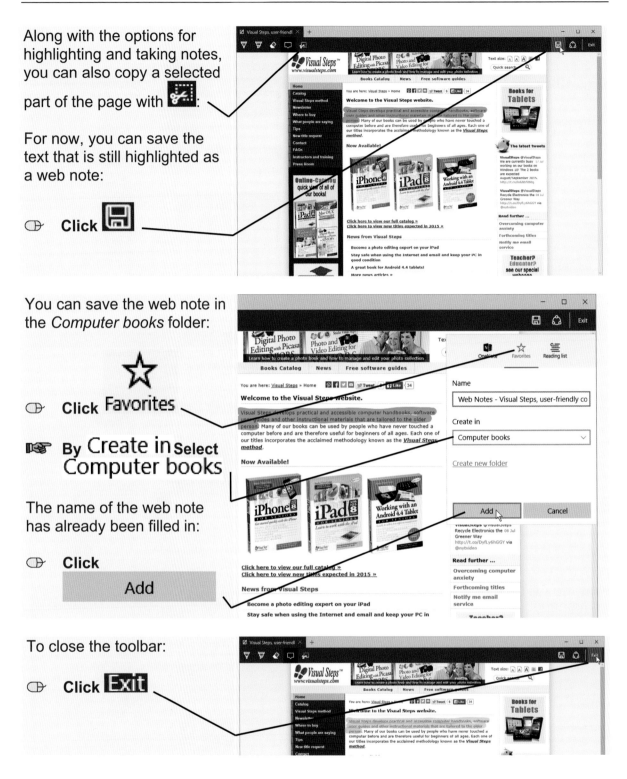

You can save the web note in the *Computer books* folder:

⊕ **Click** Favorites ☆

☞ **By** Create in **Select** Computer books

The name of the web note has already been filled in:

⊕ **Click**

    Add

To close the toolbar:

⊕ **Click** Exit

This is how you open the web note:

☞ **Click** ≡

☞ **Click** ☆

☞ **If necessary, click** Computer books

Now the *Computer books* folder is opened:

☞ **Click the web note**

The web page with the web note will be opened.

4.13 Setting the Home Page

When you open *Edge*, the program will display a specific web page. This is called the *home page*. You can replace the current home page with a page you have chosen yourself. To illustrate how to do this, you can set up the Visual Steps website as your home page.

In the upper right corner of the window:

☞ **Click** • • •

☞ **Click** Settings

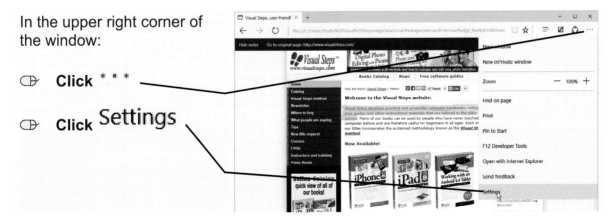

You will see the *Settings* window on the right-hand side:

☞ **Click the radio button ⊙ by**
A specific page or pag

☞ **Click** MSN

☞ **Click** Custom

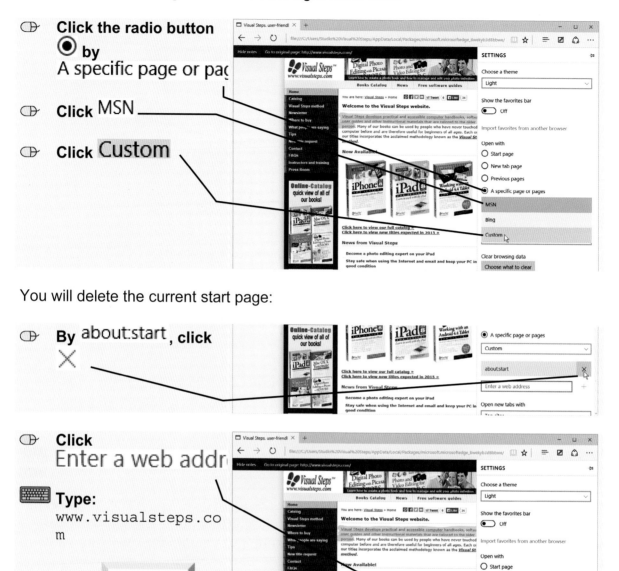

You will delete the current start page:

☞ **By** about:start **, click**
✕

☞ **Click**
Enter a web addr

⌨ **Type:**
www.visualsteps.co
m

⌨ **Press**
Enter ⏎

Now the home page has been added to *Edge*. The next time you open *Edge*, this page will be displayed.

☞ **Close *Edge*** ⍟¹

4.14 Browser History

Edge remembers the websites you have visited. To see how, open *Edge* again:

☞ **Open *Edge* ℰℰ³**

You will see the home page you have added in the previous section. This is how you open the list of websites you have previously visited (the browser history):

⊕ **Click ≡**

⊕ **Click ⟲**

You will see the history:

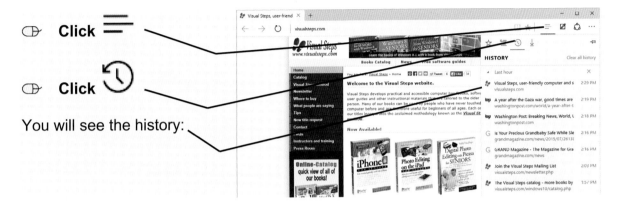

If you have not saved a certain website as a favorite, you might be able to find the site again in this list. Just click the hyperlink in order to visit the web page.

4.15 Deleting the Browser History

While you are surfing the Internet, *Edge* stores information on the websites you visit. This is also called the *browser history*. The browser history consists of various parts, such as temporary Internet files, the history, passwords, small files stored on your computer by websites in order to save information about you and your preferences (cookies), and information you have filled in on forms on websites or in the address bar (such as your name, address, and email address).

This is how you delete this data in *Edge*:

If you want to delete the history for an individual web page:

⊕ **By the desired web page, click ✕**

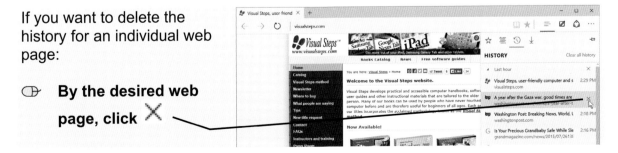

This is how you delete the entire browser history all at once:

⊕ **Click**
   Clear all history

You will see the components you can delete. In the dictionary at the back of this chapter you can read what each component is about.

⊕ **Check the box** ✅ **by the desired data**

⊕ **Click**

        Clear

The browser history will be deleted:

⊕ **Click** ≪

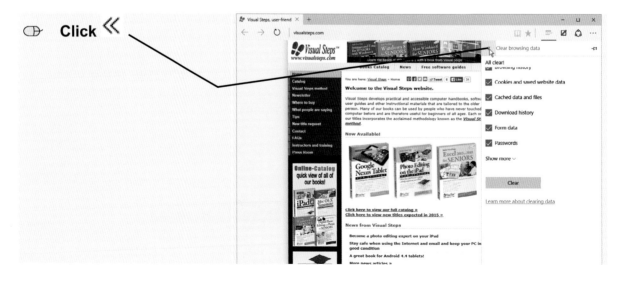

4.16 Security and Privacy Settings in Edge

In *Edge* you can select a security level for Internet access. In this way you can indicate how *Edge* should behave on different websites.
Take a look at the security settings:

☞ **Drag the scroll box downwards**

☞ **Click**

View advanced settings

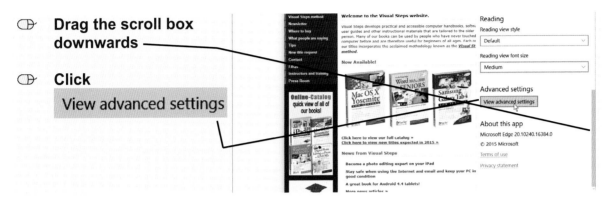

You will see the window with advanced settings:

☞ **Drag the scroll box down**

You will see that the setting for protection against malicious websites has been enabled:

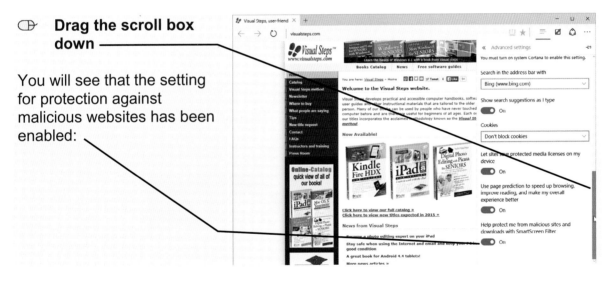

You may have heard of cookies. At if you live in one of the countries of the European Union you may have heard about the new cookie law that has been instituted in the countries of the European Union in 2012. *Cookies* are small text files that are placed on your computer while you are surfing the Internet. These small files contain information on the things you have filled in on a web page in a form or in other ways.

For example, if you book a trip with an online travel agency, the website will create a cookie that contains the dates and cities you have filled in. Because of this, you can navigate forwards and backwards through the web pages, without having to fill in the data again on every page.

Note that these text files cannot 'run' on your computer (they are not programs), and their maximum size is very small.

Please note:

Cookies are not dangerous. A website can only access the information you have provided yourself. Once a cookie has been saved to your computer, it can only be accessed by the website that has created the cookie.

One of the main provisions in the cookie law is that consumers are entitled to know whether a website uses cookies. The new law does not apply to all types of cookies. Cookies that are essential to the proper functioning of a website, such as filling a shopping cart, can be placed without your permission.

Asking for the visitor's permission is done in various ways. For example, a bar may be displayed above or below the window, as is seen in this example from the CNN website.

An example of a message you can choose to ignore. The rest of the page is visible:

There are also messages that requires you to accept the information in the window, in order to make use of the website.

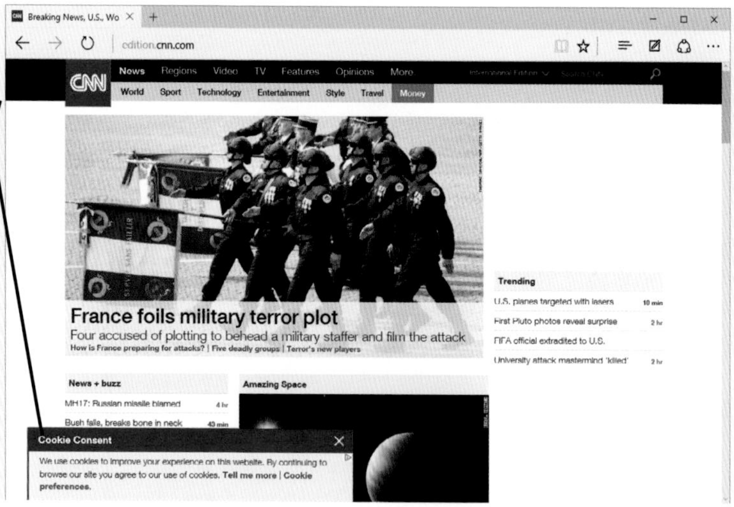

Please note:

The cookie law only applies to websites in the European Union. If you visit a foreign website outside the EU, you may not see any notifications regarding the use of cookies, but most likely they will surely be used.

In *Edge* you can block cookies entirely, if you wish. But keep in mind that this may restrict the functionality of a website.

⬚ **By** Cookies, **click** Don't block cookie

You will see three options:

Block all cookies: no cookie whatsoever will be accepted.

Block only third party cool *Third-party cookies* originating from the ads on the websites you visit (such as *pop-ups* and *banners*).

Don't block cookies: cookies will be allowed automatically.

🖑 **Please note:**
You may want to block all the cookies. But if you do this, there is always a chance of some websites not working properly. Of course you can experiment with different settings. If you do not like a setting, you can always select another one.

In this example we have not blocked any cookies:

⬚ **Click** Don't block cookie

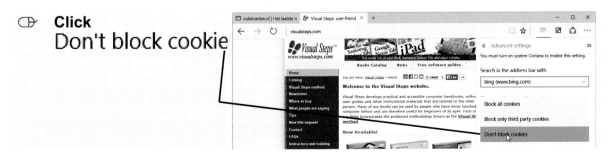

You can change even more settings in this window.

You will see several privacy options. Some of which are discussed:

Block pop-up windows:

Offer to save passwords:

Save form entries:

    👆 **Drag the scroll box downwards**

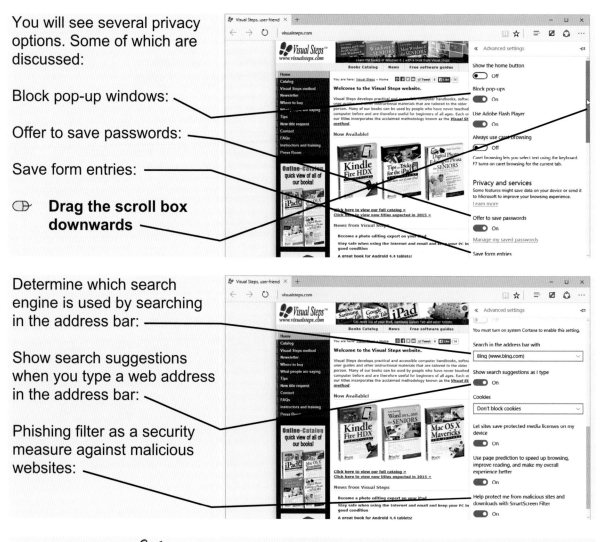

Determine which search engine is used by searching in the address bar:

Show search suggestions when you type a web address in the address bar:

Phishing filter as a security measure against malicious websites:

👉 **Close** *Edge* ✂️¹

By now you have learned a number of methods for effectively navigating the Internet, and finding your way to various websites. You have also viewed the security options in *Edge*. You can read more about the security measures for your *Windows 10* computer in *Chapter 7 Useful Settings and Security*.

4.17 Exercises

🦶

The following exercises will help you master what you have just learned. Have you forgotten how to do something? Use the number beside the footsteps 🦶[1] to look it up in the appendix *How Do I Do That Again?* at the end of this book.

Exercise 1: The SeniorNet Favorite

In this exercise, you will open the SeniorNet website and add it to your favorites.

☞ Open *Edge*. 🦶[3]

☞ Open the www.seniornet.org website. 🦶[27]

☞ Browse through a few pages of the SeniorNet website. Click some of the hyperlinks on the pages for practice.

☞ Go back to the homepage of SeniorNet by clicking the logo .

☞ Make the address for SeniorNet a favorite. 🦶[28]

☞ Close *Edge*. 🦶[1]

Exercise 2: Tabs

In this exercise you will be surfing the Internet and working with tabs.

☞ Open *Edge*. 🦶[3]

☞ Open a favorite website you have saved: www.seniornet.org. 🦶[29]

☞ Open the www.cnn.com website. 🦶[27]

☞ Open a link on a new tab. 🦶[30]

☞ Switch to the new tab. 🦶[31]

☞ Close *Edge*. ℰℓ^1

Exercise 3: Use the Reading View

In this exercise you will view a web page with the *reading view*.

☞ Open *Edge*. ℰℓ^3

☞ Open the www.cnn.com web page. ℰℓ^{27}

☞ Click an article.

☞ View the article in the reading view. ℰℓ^{32}

☞ Go back to the regular view. ℰℓ^{32}

☞ Close *Edge*. ℰℓ^1

Exercise 4: Take Notes

In this exercise you will work again with *Web Notes*.

☞ Open *Edge*. ℰℓ^3

☞ Open the saved favorite website www.seniornet.org. ℰℓ^{29}

☞ Highlight a piece of text. ℰℓ^{34}

☞ Add a note in a text box. ℰℓ^{35}

☞ Close the toolbar. ℰℓ^{36}

☞ Close *Edge*. ℰℓ^1

4.18 Background Information

Dictionary

Bing	Search engine powered by Microsoft. Currently, this is the second biggest search engine on the Internet. *Google* is the largest.
Browser history	The traces you leave on your computer while surfing the Internet. The history displays the websites you have recently visited.
Browser, Web browser	A program used to display web pages and to navigate the Internet. *Edge* is an example of a web browser.
Cached data and files	Web pages that are displayed in your web browser for the first time, are stored in the folder with temporary Internet files. This enables the browser to display frequently or previously visited pages much faster, since *Edge* will be able to open these from your computer's cached memory.
Cookies	Small text files that are placed on your computer by websites, in order to store information about you and your preferences.
Download History	List with files you have downloaded.
Edge	A program in *Windows 10* for viewing websites. This is meant to be the substitute for *Internet Explorer*.
Favorites	A list of the website addresses you have saved. You can use a favorite to quickly open a saved website.
Form data	Information you have filled in on web forms.
Home page	The web page that is displayed each time you open *Edge*.
Https://	If you see this prefix in the web address, the Internet connection is secured (encrypted data transfer).
InPrivate navigation	A function that prevents others from seeing your surfing behavior.

- Continue on the next page -

Internet	A network of computer networks which operates worldwide, using a common set of communications protocols. The part of the Internet that most people are familiar with is the World Wide Web (WWW). Also called simply the web.
Internet Explorer	A type of browser program with which you can view web pages on the Internet. In *Windows 10* the *Edge* browser is also available.
Internet provider	An Internet provider is a company that provides access to the Internet, usually for a fee.
Link (hyperlink)	A navigational tool on a web page that automatically takes the user to the information that is displayed, if the link is clicked. A link may consist of text or images, such as buttons, icons, or pictures. You can recognize a hyperlink by the pointer changing into a hand.
Reading list	You can add pages to the reading list and read them offline later on (when you are not connected to the Internet).
Reading view	A function in *Edge* that enables you to hide various elements on a web page, such as advertisements and animated images, so you will only see the text and any relevant images. Using the reading view can make it easier to read a page.
Malware	Stands for *malicious software*. A computer program intended to damage your computer. Viruses, worms, and Trojan horses are a few examples of these harmful programs.
Phishing	A type of Internet fraud, where criminals try to get their hands on personal information through an email or website.
Pop-up	A pop-up is a small window that is displayed above or on top of the window with the website you are visiting. Pop-ups are usually opened as soon as you visit a website, and mainly contain advertisements.
Privacy settings	A level of protection of your personal data by blocking access of certain programs, for example.
SmartScreen filter	The *SmartScreen* filter in *Edge* helps to protect you against phishing websites. If the website is on the list with reported phishing websites, you will see a warning message.

- Continue on the next page -

Spyware	A computer program that can display commercials and advertisements (such as pop-up ads). Spyware will often collect information about your surfing behavior so that it can be passed along to the spyware manufacturer or other third parties.
Tab	A part of *Edge* where another website or web page can be opened.
Virus	A virus is a program that replicates itself and tries to spread from one computer to another. It can cause damage (by deleting or damaging data) or annoy the user (by displaying messages or altering the information on the screen).
Web address	The web address of a website identifies a unique location on the Internet. A web address is also called a URL (Uniform Resource Locator). An example of a web address is: **http://www.visualsteps.com**.
Web notes	A function in *Edge* with which you can add notes to a web page. In this way you can add a reminder, or place additional information about the web page, for example. You can also highlight text.
Web page	A web page is a resource of information that is suitable for the World Wide Web and can be accessed through a browser.
Website	A website is a collection of interconnected web pages, typically common to a particular domain name on the World Wide Web on the Internet.
Zoom	Enlarge or reduce a web page. Zooming will enlarge or reduce every item on a page, including text and images.

Source: Windows Help, Wikipedia

Viruses, spyware, and malware
If you use the Internet regularly for surfing websites or sending and receiving email, your computer is at risk of being infected with viruses, spyware, or malware. *Windows 10* provides various security measures to prevent this, but you also need to be on the alert yourself when using the Internet.
In *Chapter 7 Useful Settings and Security* you will read how to scan your computer for viruses.

Speech recognition with Cortana
Microsoft has a speech recognition assistant called *Cortana*. Cortana plays an important role in *Windows 10*. It is so important, that *Cortana* is also located on the taskbar, as part of the search function. By means of a microphone, you can pose questions to this assistant on a variety of topics. The answers are found by utilizing the *Bing* search engine, among others. *Cortana* can also help you find and open files, programs and apps on the computer.
You need to take into account that voice recognition software, such as *Cortana*, is still undergoing development; this means some commands or questions will be misunderstood.
Cortana also stores a lot of information regarding your actions on your computer and saves it online in the cloud (a storage location on the Internet). This is intended to help you, but it also brings up privacy issues.
We will not discuss *Cortana* in this book any further, since your desktop computer may not have a microphone installed, and you would need to buy a separate microphone in order to use this function. But a tablet or a smartphone with *Windows 10* does have a built-in microphone, so you can use *Cortana* better on such a device.

If desired you can switch on and set up *Cortana* via the settings. At the taskbar, click
 and .

Recognize a secure website
Whenever you purchase anything on the Internet, you should always check whether the website is secure, before entering your bank account data. The main difference between a secure website and an unprotected website, is that on a secure website, the information is transferred with encrypted technology. The user enters his data, such as a credit card number. This information is encoded (encrypted) by using special programs that are transferred to the seller's computer, where the info is decrypted again. This can only be done by authorized parties. In this way you can prevent hackers from stealing information that is sent across the Internet.
The easiest and quickest way of identifying a secure website, is by checking the web address in the *Edge* address bar. If the address begins with https:// instead of http://, you can be sure that the website is secure. The extra 's' stands for 'secure'. Here is an example: https://www.bankofamerica.com/.

- Continue on the next page -

Another indication is the small 🔒 icon that is displayed in the address bar
🔒 Bank of America Corporation [US]　**bankofamerica.com**, when you
open the website. If this icon is missing, there is a big chance the website is not
secure. Only enter your personal data and credit card information if you are sure that
you are visiting a secure website that guarantees a safe method off communication.

Please note: many websites have both a secure and an unprotected section. For
example, if you order a book at www.amazon.com, the pages are not secure. But as
soon as you order the book, you will end up in the secure section.

Phishing

The Internet is used by ever more people, to manage online bank accounts, shop,
book trips, sell secondhand stuff, study, etc. Unfortunately, criminals have also found
their way to the Internet. One of the methods used more and more frequently is
called *phishing*. But what exactly is phishing?

Phishing is a method of persuading unsuspecting computer users to disclose their
personal data or financial information by posing as a legitimate person or
organization. In fact, phishing is a way of 'fishing' for information.

A familiar tactic in phishing is to send a fake email message that looks like a real
message sent by a familiar, trusted source. This might be your bank, credit card
company, a web store, or another website you have previously visited. These fake
messages are sent to thousands of email addresses.
In the email, the recipients are asked to check their bank data, for instance. The
message contains a hyperlink for this purpose. If the link is clicked it may lead you to
a website that may look like a bank's website. There you will be asked to enter
personal information, such as name and address, bank account numbers, and PIN
codes, supposedly to check if everything is OK.

If you fall for this trick and enter your data, the information will be sent immediately to
the criminals who have set the trap. Next, they may use your data to purchase items,
open new credit card accounts in your name, or abuse your identity in other ways.
These phishing mails and websites have a deceptively genuine look. They often use
the bank's logo in the email, and the website may look exactly like the legitimate
website.

- Continue on the next page -

An example of a phishing mail:

This mail asks the clients from this bank to enter their personal information on a certain website. Criminals can then gain access to these accounts and empty them out.

Bank of America 💠   Online Banking

Online Banking Alert

Remember: Always look for your SiteKey before you enter your passcode during Sign In »

This email was sent to: REDACTED

Message from Customer Service

A message from Customer Service is waiting in your Online Banking mailbox. If you haven't already read it:

 – Sign in to Online Banking at https://www.bankofamerica.com/

 – Select Mail at the top of the page.

This alert relates to your Online Banking profile, rather than a particular account.

Want to confirm this email is from Bank of America? Sign in to Online Banking and select Alerts History to verify this alert.

Want to get more alerts? Sign in to your online banking account at Bank of America and within the Accounts Overview page select the "Alerts" tab.

Because email is not a secure form of communication, this email box is not equipped to handle replies.
If you have any questions about your account or need assistance, please call the

Windows 10 protects you from online phishing in *Edge*. You can read more about this on the next page.

Criminals do not stop at online phishing anymore. There are ever more cases in which the victim is phoned at his home address, by so-called employees from their own bank, by someone from a non-existing '*Windows Maintenance Team*', by Microsoft, or by some other organization that sounds official.

Such a person will ask (often in poor English) to check certain items on the computer. They often use the pretext that the security of your computer is faulty. Sometimes the victim is asked to adjust the settings himself, but sometimes also the so-called employee will do this, by gaining remote access to the computer while the victim watches. They will also often try to pry personal codes and Internet banking passwords from their victims.

Do not go along with this! *Windows* or Microsoft employees will never call you at home, regarding problems with your computer. Likewise, your bank will never ask you to change your computer settings, or ask you for your personal codes for Internet banking services.

The SmartScreen filter
The *SmartScreen filter* in *Edge* will help to detect phishing websites. *SmartScreen* will also protect you from downloading or installing malware (harmful software). The *SmartScreen* filter uses three methods to protect you:

- The address of the website you visit is compared to a dynamic list of reported phishing websites and websites with harmful software. If the website you are visiting is listed on this list of reported phishing websites, *Edge* will display a warning page and a warning on the address bar, telling you that this website is blocked in order to protect you.

- The websites you visit are analyzed, in order to find out whether they have any characteristics of a phishing website. If any suspect web pages are found, you will see a *SmartScreen* message that warns you about that. You can also give your feedback if desired.

- *SmartScreen* checks the files you want to download on the basis of a list of reported websites with harmful software and programs that are known to be unsafe. If any similarities are found, *SmartScreen* will display a warning message telling you that the download has been blocked for your own safety. *SmartScreen* also checks the files you download on the basis of a list of known files that are often downloaded by *Edge* users. If the file you are downloading, is not on this list, *SmartScreen* will display a warning message.

Apart from this, you can let Microsoft check whether a specific web address is on the most recent list of phishing websites. And you can also report any suspicious websites.

In *section 4.16 Security and Privacy Settings in Edge* you have seen that these security settings are enabled by default in *Edge*.

Safe surfing

In this chapter you have looked at the various security settings in *Edge*. Remember that your own actions also play a big part when it comes to securing your computer. The first four bullets in this list are discussed in *Chapter 7 Useful Settings and Security*.

A list of points to consider:

- Make sure that *Windows Defender* or any other good antivirus and anti-spyware program is up-to-date and enabled.

- Make sure that *Windows Firewall* or any other good firewall is installed and activated.

- Make sure that *Windows* and any installed programs and apps are up-to-date.

- Let *Windows Defender* or the other antivirus and anti-spyware program scan your computer on a regular basis.

- If something strange happens while you are surfing the Internet, then break the connection right away.

- If you do not need to be connected to the Internet, break the connection. This diminishes the risk of others breaking into your computer.

- Protect your computer against pop-ups, unwanted emails, and phishing attempts, by using the settings that are recommended in this chapter and the final chapter of this book.

- Only download files and programs from trustworthy websites. Only download apps from the *Windows Store*.

- Enter as little personal information as possible on websites.

- Do not click hyperlinks in emails and chat messages from unknown persons, or links that seem suspect. Visit websites by typing the address known to you in the *Edge* address bar.

- Check the web address and the security settings on the websites you use for online banking operations, or when you buy something. The address (URL) needs to be the exact, correct, name, and begin with https://. Never offer information (credit card, bank info, pin codes or passwords), unless you are absolutely sure that it is a trustworthy website.

- Be careful with entering your email address on websites. Some websites try to collect email addresses in order to send spam to these addresses later on. Use an email account of a free service provider, such as *Hotmail* or *Gmail*, if you need to enter an email address on the Internet. If you receive a lot of spam at these addresses, just get a new address.

4.19 Tips

Tip

Internet Explorer

Although *Edge* is the new official Internet browser for *Windows*, *Internet Explorer* is still present as well, and can still be used.

Actually, *Internet Explorer* is a more extensive version of *Edge*. You can adjust more settings, but *Internet Explorer* can be a bit slower while surfing. It is also possible that *Internet Explorer* will no longer be supported in the long run. From that point on, it is wiser to use Edge in terms of online security.

This is how you open *Internet Explorer*:

Click

Type: internet explorer

Click

Internet Explorer
Desktop app

You will see the *Internet Explorer* window:

This window still looks the same in *Windows 10*.

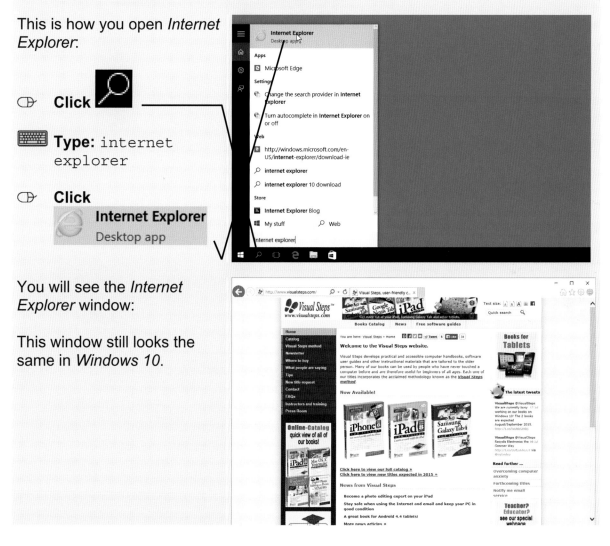

🔅 Tip

InPrivate navigation
With InPrivate navigation you can surf the Internet in *Edge* without leaving any
traces. You do this in a separate window. The history of visited websites, passwords,
cookies, and temporary files will automatically be removed as soon as you close the
window. This is how you surf InPrivate:

☞ **Click • • •**

☞ **Click**
New InPrivate win

You will see a new window
with information about
InPrivate:

At the top you see
InPrivate:

⌨ **Type the web address**

⌨ **Press Enter**

You will see the website in
the InPrivate view:

To close the InPrivate
window:

☞ **Click ✖**

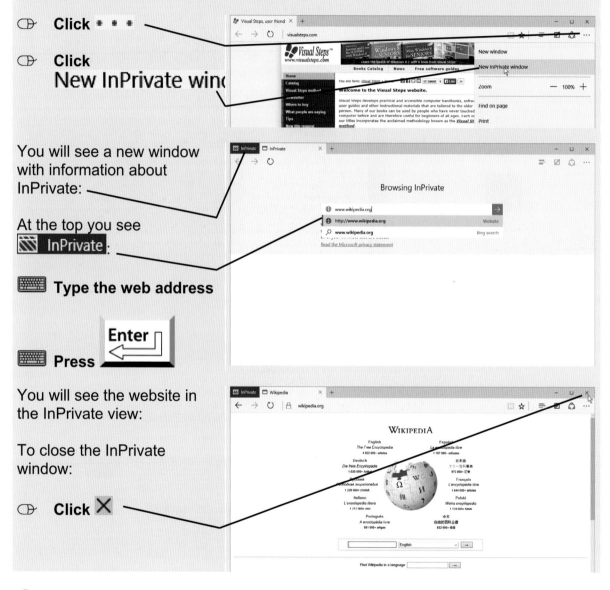

🔅 Tip

Searching the Internet using the search function
At the end of *Chapter 7 Useful Settings and Security* you can read how to search the
Internet using the search function on the taskbar.

💡 Tip

Search the Internet using the address bar

If you are looking for a specific subject, you can search the Internet. You can do this directly in the address bar of *Edge*:

In the address bar:

⌨ **Type a keyword, for example:** weather in canada

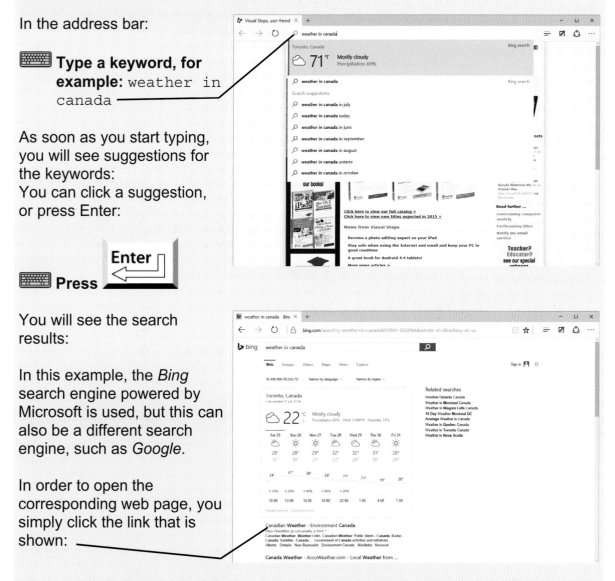

As soon as you start typing, you will see suggestions for the keywords:

You can click a suggestion, or press Enter:

⌨ **Press** Enter

You will see the search results:

In this example, the *Bing* search engine powered by Microsoft is used, but this can also be a different search engine, such as *Google*.

In order to open the corresponding web page, you simply click the link that is shown:

If you enter more than one word, you will get a list of web pages that contain at least one of those words. But if you place these words between quotation marks, the list will only display those pages that contain that exact combination of keywords.

💡 Tip

Setting up the default search engine

Bing is the default search engine in *Edge*. That is understandable, since *Bing* is manufactured by Microsoft. But you can change the default search engine in the settings. You can use the popular *Google* search engine, if you prefer:

☞ **Open the www.google.com website** ⬚²⁷

⊕ **Click** • • •

⊕ **Click** Settings

You will see the *Settings* window:

⊕ **Drag the scroll box downwards**

⊕ **Click**
   View advanced settings

Change the search engine:

⊕ **Drag the scroll box downwards**

By Search in the address bar with:

⊕ **Click**
   Bing (www.bing.com)

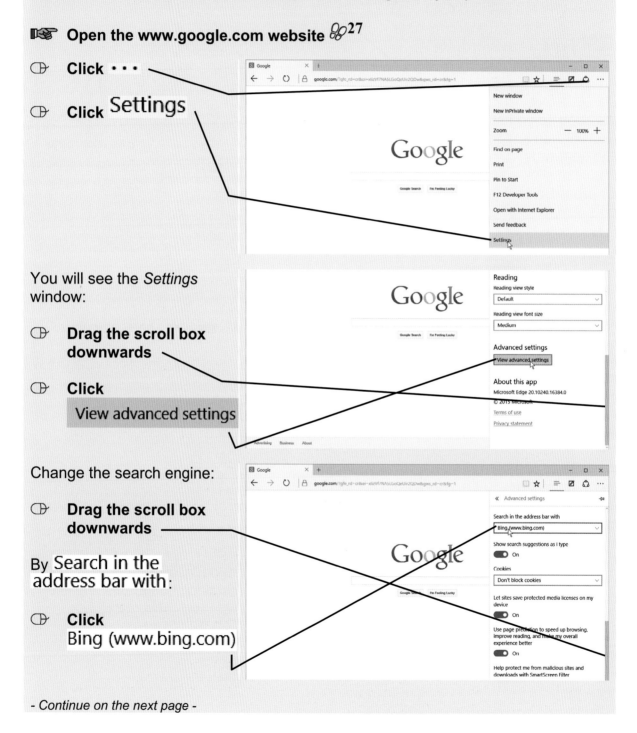

- Continue on the next page -

Click **\<Add new\>**

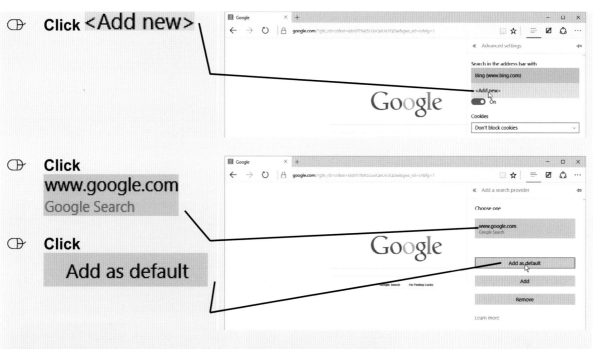

Click
www.google.com
Google Search

Click
Add as default

Now *Google* has been set as your default search engine.

💡 Tip

Add a website to the Start menu
You can also add your favorite website to the Start menu, as a tile. This way, you can very quickly open your favorite website.

👉 **Open the www.visualsteps.com web page** ⸕⸕²⁷

Click • • •

Click **Pin to Start**

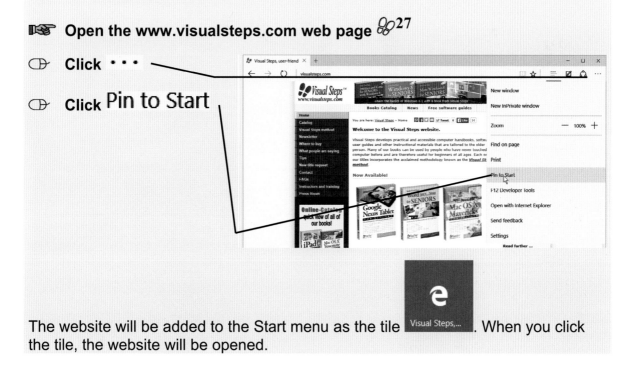

The website will be added to the Start menu as the tile ![Visual Steps tile]. When you click the tile, the website will be opened.

💡 Tip

Viewing news with the News app
If you would like to stay up-to-date with the news, the News app is a nice app. The app displays the news from different sources.

👉 **Open *News*** 🐾³

News from different sources will be displayed. You can see by **Chicago Tribune** en **The Guardian**:

Open a news item:

👆 **Click the item** ◀

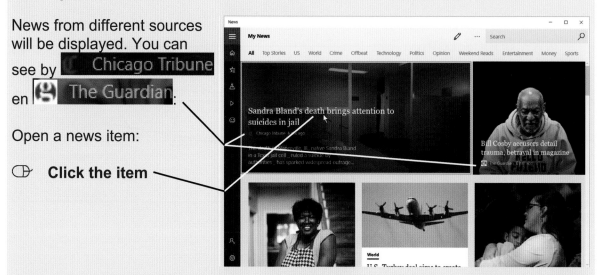

If your window looks different, you can drag the window borders. Then you will probably see a window similar to the one above.

You will see the item:

To return to the news overview:

👆 **Click** ←

You can determine for yourself which news you would like to see, for example the sports news or entertainment news. You can set this using the ✏ at the top-right of the start page of *News*.

5. Working with Mail

Mail is an app that lets you send and receive electronic mail, quickly and easily. In this chapter you will learn how to use this app. You will discover how easy it is to use *Mail*.

In this chapter you will learn how to:

- set up an email account;
- create an email message;
- send, receive, open, and reply to an email;
- delete email messages;
- send, open, and save attachments;
- change the signature.

5.1 Setting up an Account in Mail

You can use the *Mail* program to send and receive email messages. You will need to have an email address available in order to use this program.

This is how you open *Mail*:

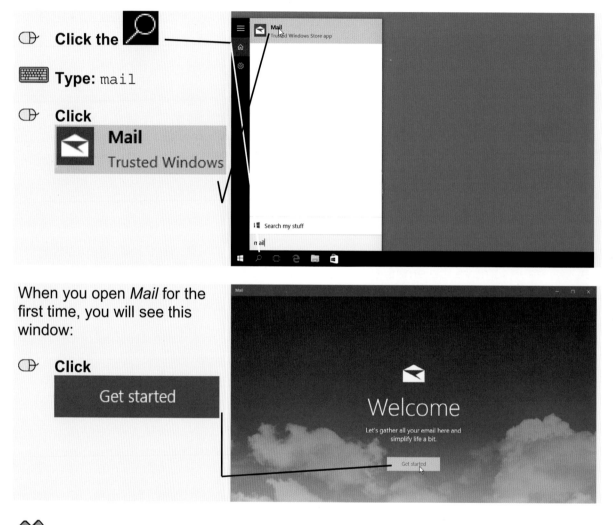

Click the 🔍

⌨ **Type:** mail

Click

Mail
Trusted Windows

When you open *Mail* for the first time, you will see this window:

Click

Get started

HELP! I do not see this window.
If you do not see this window, *Mail* has been previously opened. You can continue with the next step.

In order to use *Mail*, you will need to have an email account. This can be an account offered to you by your Internet provider, or you can use an account from an online email service such as *Hotmail*, *Outlook.com* and *Gmail*.

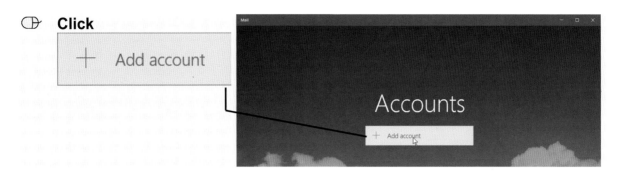

☞ **Click**

⊞ Add account

Accounts

+ Add account

✖ **HELP! I do not see this window.**

If you do not see this window, an email account has already been set up. You can continue with *section 5.3 Creating an Email Message*.

You will see a window with options for various types of accounts. In this example we will set up a POP/IMAP account. This is the type of account that is offered by Internet providers, such as AOL or Verizon. If you wish, you can also select another type of account such as a *Hotmail*, *Outlook.com* or *Gmail* account. In the next section you can read more about these accounts.

When you set up the email address you have received from your Internet provider, you will need to have the email address and the corresponding password available.

This is how you set up the account:

☞ **Click**

✉ Other account
POP, IMAP

If you want to use an email account provided by *Hotmail*, *Outlook.com* or *Gmail*, you can read how to do so in the next section.

✕

Choose an account

◻✓ Outlook.com
Outlook.com, Live.com, Hotmail, MSN

E Exchange
Exchange, Office 365

✉ Google

✉ Yahoo! Mail

✉ iCloud

✉ Other account
POP, IMAP

Close

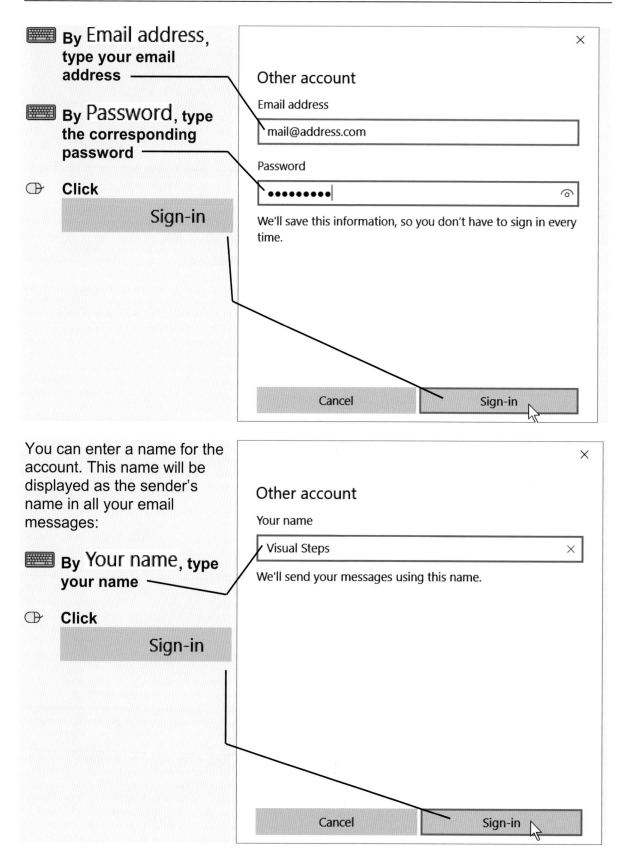

By Email address, type your email address ⎯

By Password, type the corresponding password ⎯

Click Sign-in

Other account

Email address

mail@address.com

Password

●●●●●●●●

We'll save this information, so you don't have to sign in every time.

Cancel   Sign-in

You can enter a name for the account. This name will be displayed as the sender's name in all your email messages:

By Your name, type your name ⎯

Click Sign-in

Other account

Your name

Visual Steps

We'll send your messages using this name.

Cancel   Sign-in

Now the account has been set up:

At the bottom of the window:

⬚ **Click**

<table><tr><td>Done</td></tr></table>

✕

All done!

Your account was set up successfully.

✉ mail@address.com

🩹 HELP! I see a message in the next window.

If you see a message in a window, after you have clicked

<table><tr><td>Done</td></tr></table>, there may have been some problem while you were setting up your email account. At the end of this chapter you will find the *Tip Setting up a POP/IMAP account if sending and receiving mail fails*, where you can read more about the advanced settings for email accounts.

👉 **Close *Mail*** 👣¹

👉 **Continue with *section 5.3 Creating an Email Message***

5.2 Setting Up a Hotmail, Outlook.com or Gmail Account

If you are using an email address that ends in hotmail.com, outlook.com, live.com, or gmail.com, you can set up an account like this:

👉 **Open *Mail*** 👣³

When you see the window below:

⬚ **Click**

Or if you see this window:

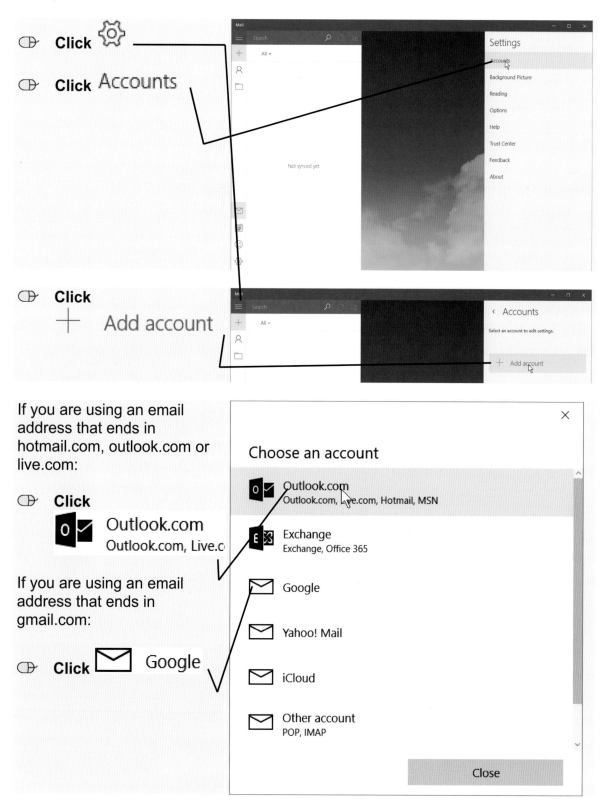

Click ⚙

Click Accounts

Click ➕ Add account

If you are using an email address that ends in hotmail.com, outlook.com or live.com:

Click 💠 Outlook.com
Outlook.com, Live.c

If you are using an email address that ends in gmail.com:

Click ✉ Google

Choose an account

💠 Outlook.com
Outlook.com, Live.com, Hotmail, MSN

📧 Exchange
Exchange, Office 365

✉ Google

✉ Yahoo! Mail

✉ iCloud

✉ Other account
POP, IMAP

Close

Log in with the account:

Use the login information for your account:

⌨ **Type your email address** ───

⌨ **Type the corresponding password**

☞ **Click**
Sign in

If you are using *Gmail*, click **Sign in**.

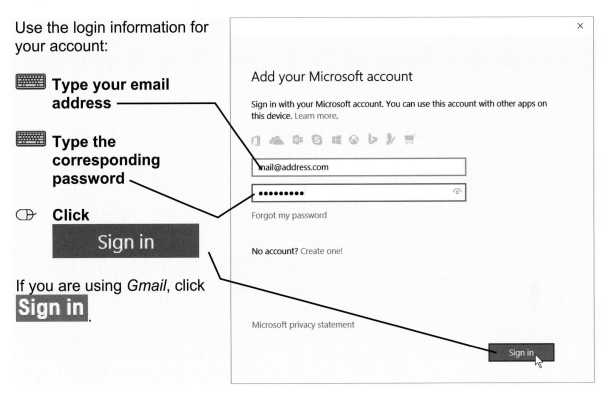

If you have selected *Outlook.com*, you will see this window:

You can set up your account for automatic synchronization of settings and files. In this example we will skip this step:

☞ **Click**
Sign in to just this app in

If you are using *Gmail*, you will need to give the *Mail* app permission:

☞ **Click**  **Accept**

The account has been added. You will see a message in the window:

At the bottom of the window:

☞ **Click**
    Done

> ×
>
> **All done!**
> Your account was set up successfully.
>
> 📧 mail@address.com

Close *Mail*:

☞ **Close Mail** ✌¹

5.3 Creating an Email Message

After you have set up an email account, you can send and receive mail with *Mail*:

☞ **Open Mail** ✌³

You may see this window:

You will see one or more
email accounts you have set
up:

☞ **If necessary, click the
    desired account** ————

☞ **If necessary, click**
    Ready to go

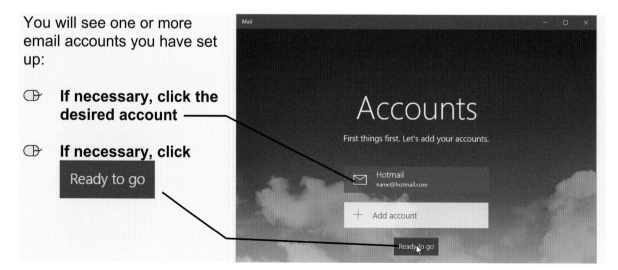

The *Mail* window appears:

In this example you do not see any incoming email messages. Your own window may contain a few email messages.

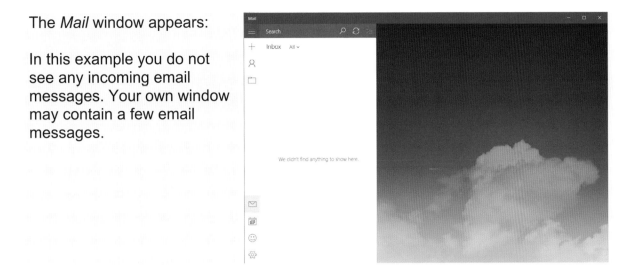

HELP! My window looks different.

If your window looks different, you can widen the window by dragging its border. Then you will probably see the same window as in the example above.

If you see different buttons in the *Mail* window, the *Mail* app on your computer may not be fully up to date. In this case, you may need to update the program first. You can read about this in *section 7.6 Updating Apps*.

You can practice sending an email by sending a message to yourself. In this way you will see how the sending and receiving part of email works. You will receive the message right away. You start by creating a new email message:

In the upper left corner of the window:

⊕ **Click** ✛

The right-hand side of the window is the formatting area where you can create a new email message:

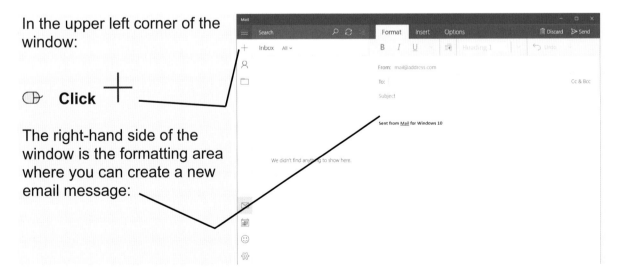

👆 **Click to the right of**
To:

⌨️ **Type the first letters of**
your own email
address

One you have typed a few
letters, your own email
address will appear in a small
popup window:

👆 **Click your email**
address

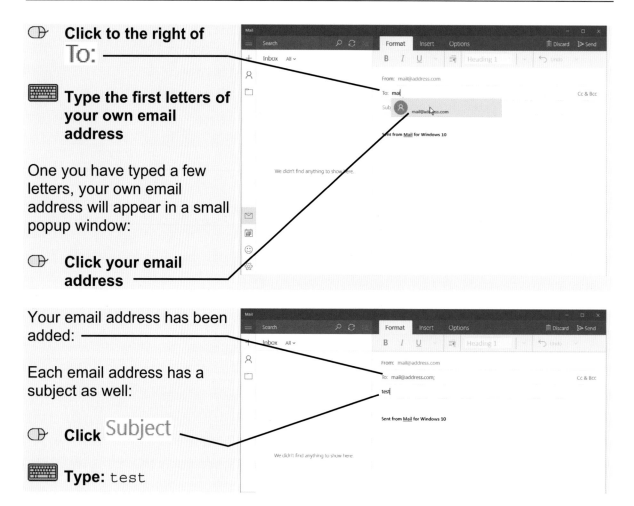

Your email address has been
added:

Each email address has a
subject as well:

👆 **Click Subject**

⌨️ **Type: test**

💡 Tip

Adding multiple email addresses
You can send an email to multiple addresses. If you want to send an email to more
than one person, you just type the next email address after the previous one. Just
make sure to type a blank space between the email addresses.

Type the message text:

👆 **Click the white area**
below the subject

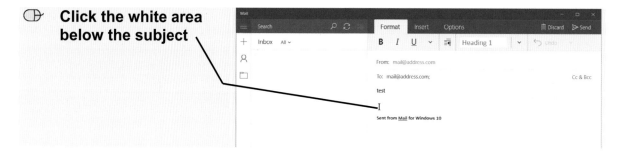

Here you can type the
message: ————————

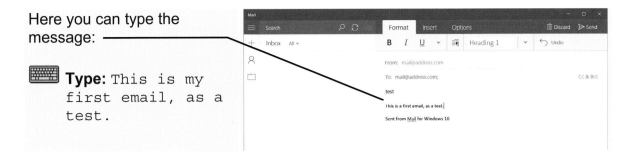

⌨ **Type:** This is my
first email, as a
test.

5.4 Sending and Receiving the Email Message

When you have finished typing the email message, you can send it:

In the upper right corner of
the window:

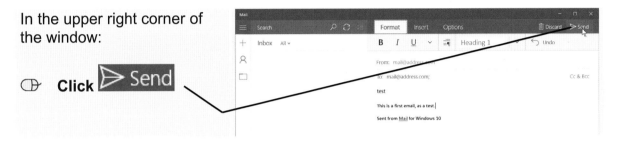

☞ **Click** ▷ Send

The message will be sent. The program will connect with your email provider. The
program will also check to see if any new email has been received. If that is the case,
Mail will retrieve the email message(s).

5.5 Reading an Email Message

All incoming email is saved in the folder named *Inbox*:

In the message list, you will
see the email you just sent:

The sender and the subject
are mentioned. The time of
receipt is stated as well.

HELP! No mail.

If you do not see any messages in the *Inbox*, it may mean the email has not arrived yet. With some email providers, it can take a little while to process a message. You can also try using the refresh button:

☞ **Click**

HELP! I have waited for a long time, but still no mail.

If you have waited quite a while and have not yet received anything, it may mean that your email account has not been properly set up. You may find the solution to this problem in the *Tip Setting up a POP/IMAP account if sending and receiving mail fails* at the end of this chapter.

Possibly, this message is part of a conversation. A conversation is a series of messages that belong together. You can recognize them by the arrow by the message:

☞ **By the conversation, click** ▶

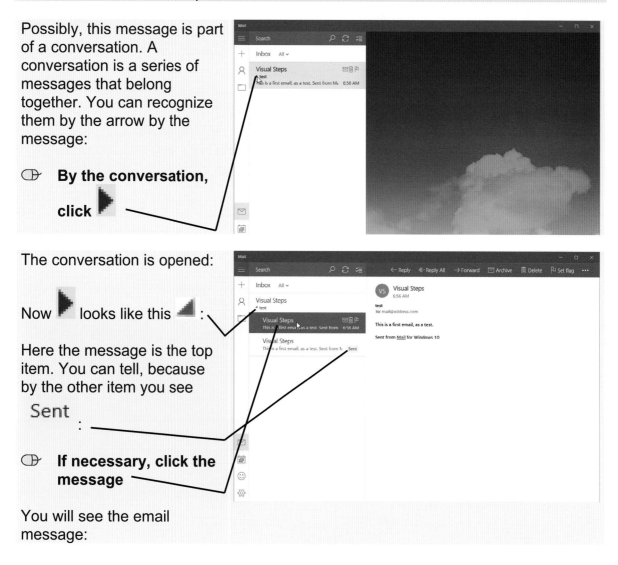

The conversation is opened:

Now ▶ looks like this ◢ :

Here the message is the top item. You can tell, because by the other item you see

Sent :

☞ **If necessary, click the message**

You will see the email message:

5.6 Replying To an Email

If you have received an email message and you want to reply back, you do not need to retype the sender's email address. *Mail* has several options for replying to an email. You can click any of the following buttons located at the top of the window:

← Reply

An answer message is created, where the correct email address is already filled in. The original email is also included.

← Reply All

You can send an email to multiple persons. Use this button if you want to create a new email message that will be sent to all the recipients in the original message. The original email will also be sent along with this message.

→ Forward

The original email will be turned into a new email message that can be sent to someone else.

In most cases you will want to reply to a message. Let's give it a try:

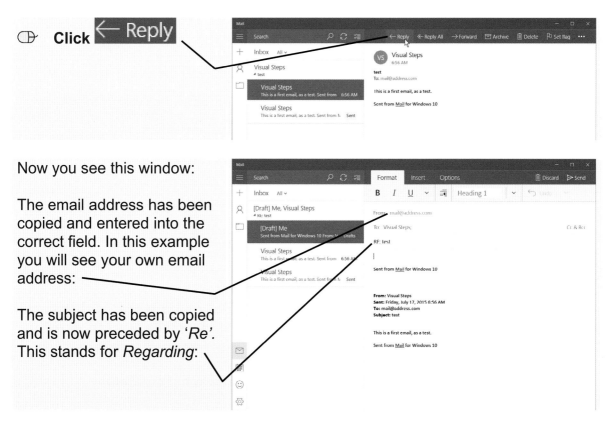

☞ **Click** ← Reply

Now you see this window:

The email address has been copied and entered into the correct field. In this example you will see your own email address:

The subject has been copied and is now preceded by '*Re*'. This stands for *Regarding*:

The text of the original message is automatically inserted into the reply. In itself this can be quite useful. The person who receives your reply will immediately see what the original message was all about. The downside is that this message will become longer and longer, as the correspondence continues.

You can type your reply at the top of the message:

Type: This is my reply.

Press

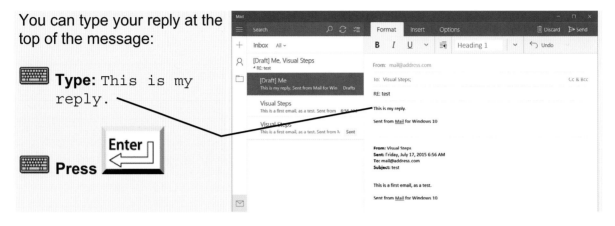

Now you can send the message, in the same manner as you learned earlier in the previous steps. You do not actually have to do that right now. You will delete the message:

Click Discard

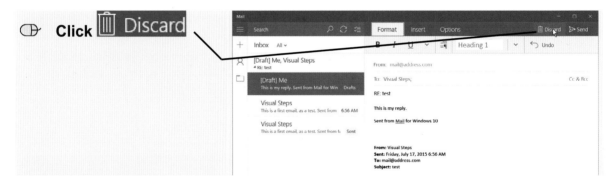

The message will be closed.

5.7 Including an Attachment

A very handy feature of an email program is the ability to send one or more files along with your email message. For example, you can add a photo or a document to your message. An item included with an email message is called *attachment*.

You can practice working with attachments by sending an email to yourself.

☞ **Create a new email message** &37

By To:, **type your own email address** ————

Click Subject

Type: Test with attachment

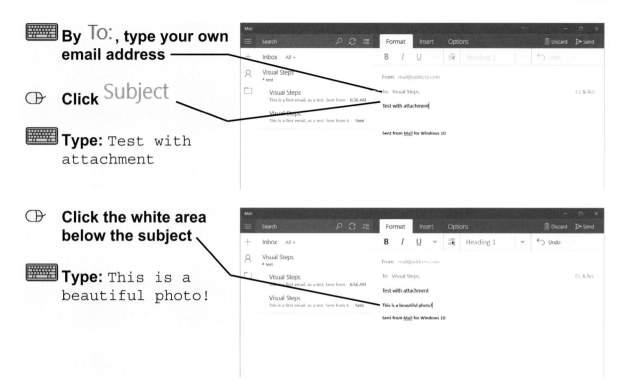

Click the white area below the subject

Type: This is a beautiful photo!

Add the attachment. In this example we have used an image. You can choose your own image:

At the top of the window:

Click Insert

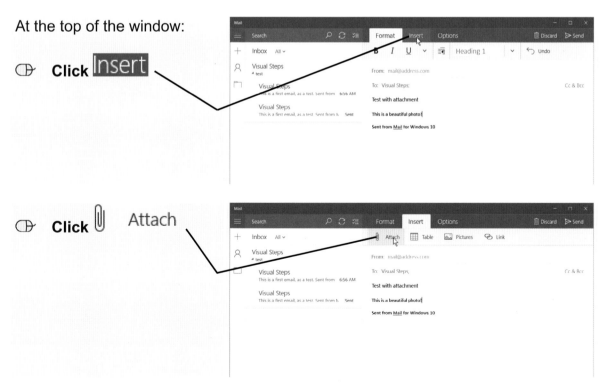

Click ⬚ Attach

You will see the *Open* window, and now you can select the image folder:

On the left-hand side of the
window:

Click 🖼 Pictures

Click the desired
photo

Click Open

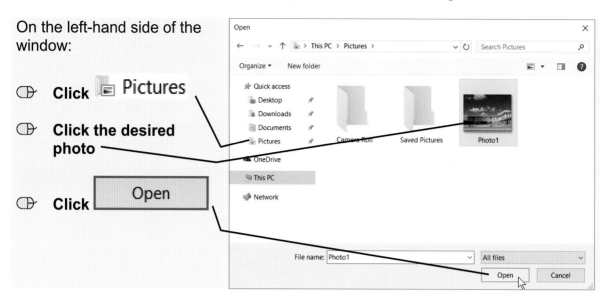

You will see the content of the *Pictures* folder. You may already have saved some photos in this folder. In this example, an image has already been saved in this folder. If you do not (yet) have any images on your computer, then just read *section 5.8 Opening an Attachment* and *section 5.9 Saving an Attachment*.
Or open the *Documents* folder and select a text file you have created in a previous chapter.

The attachment has been
added to your message:

Send the message:

Click ▷ Send

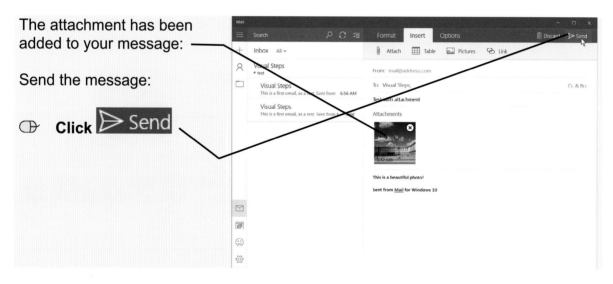

The email message with the image will be sent.

5.8 Opening an Attachment

An email you send to your own address will often be received right away, in the same session. But it can take a little while, especially if the attachment is a large file. When you see the message:

 **Click the message**

You will see the message on the right-hand side of the window:

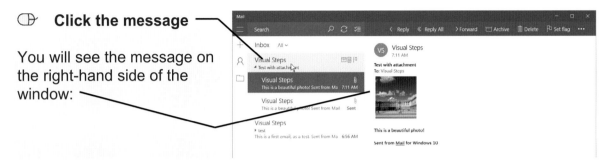

HELP! No mail.

If you do not see any messages in the *Inbox*, it may mean the email has not arrived yet. With some email providers, it can take a little while to process a message. You can also try using the refresh button:

 **Click**

In the case of a photo, you will see a thumbnail image of the photo:

The message on the left-hand side of the window includes a

paperclip ⛶, which means an attachment is included.

Usually you will immediately

see the paperclip ⛶ by the incoming email message.

In order to display the photo a bit larger:

 **Click the photo**

HELP! I do not see a photo.

If you see an icon instead of a photo, this is what you do:

☞ **Click**

In this example, the photo is displayed in the *Photos* app. This is the default setting in *Windows 10*. The app is one of the apps included in *Windows 10*. You can use the app to view, share, and print digital photos. In *Chapter 6 Introduction to Photos, Video and Music* you will learn more about this app.

After you have viewed the photo, you can close the window:

☞ **Click**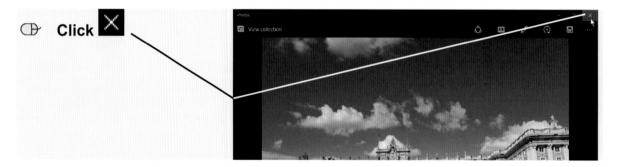

You will see the *Mail* window again.

5.9 Saving an Attachment

You can save an attachment that has been included in an email message and store it in a folder on your computer. Then you can use this attachment yourself, in a photo editing program, for example. This is what you need to do in the window of the open message:

☞ **Right-click the photo**

☞ **Click** Save

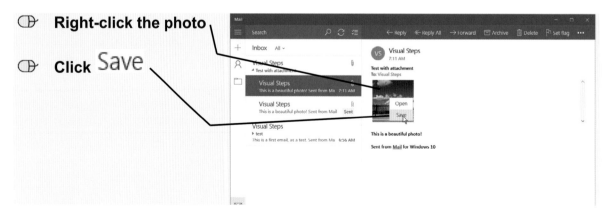

You will see the *Save As* window:

Here you see the name of the attachment: ———

On the left-hand side of the window you can click on the folder in which you want to save the photo: ———

By **File name:** you can change the name of the attachment: ———

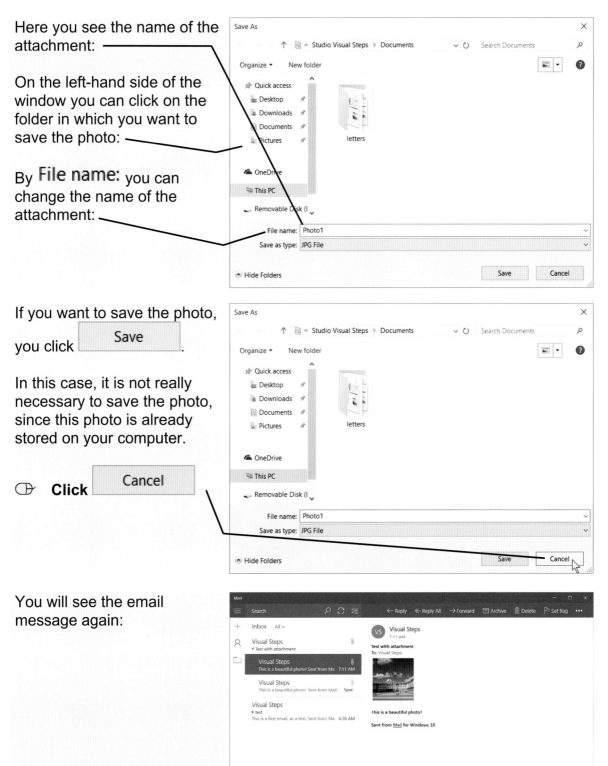

If you want to save the photo, you click **Save** .

In this case, it is not really necessary to save the photo, since this photo is already stored on your computer.

⊕ **Click** **Cancel**

You will see the email message again:

5.10 The Folders

Mail uses a system of folders for arranging your email messages: the folder list. Apart from the *Inbox*, there are some additional folders.

In the *Outbox*, the messages that still need to be sent are saved, for instance, if your Internet connection is temporarily unavailable.

Mail saves all the email messages you have sent in a separate folder, called *Sent items*.

Messages that appear to be unwanted, commercial email messages are moved to the *Junk* or *Spam* folder.

You can also delete sent and received messages from these folders. Deleted messages are saved in the *Deleted items* folder.

Finally, there is a folder for messages that have not been completed yet, these are saved in the *Drafts* folder.

➥ Please note:

Depending on your type of email account, you may see folder names that are a little bit different. You may also not be able to see some folders, such as the *Unwanted mail* or *Spam* folders.

The Sent Items folder contains copies of the emails you have sent. This folder also contains the messages you have just sent to yourself.

☞ **Click** ≡

You might not see all the folders in the account. Click ☐ to show all folders.

You will see a menu with a number of folders:

☞ **Click** Sent Items

And indeed, this *Sent items* folder contains the email messages:

To practice working with some of these other folders, you will be deleting an email message in the next section.

5.11 Deleting Email Messages

The *Inbox* and *Sent items* folders provide a very useful archive for lots of users. These folders contain all your email correspondence, and you can easily find email messages. You can save a large number or messages in these folders.

In practice, you will regularly delete all superfluous messages, in order to keep your folders neat and 'clean'. Before you can delete an email, you will need to select it first. In this example the sent message *Test with attachment* message will be deleted:

☞ **Click the message
Test with attachment**

The message is blue, which means it has been selected:

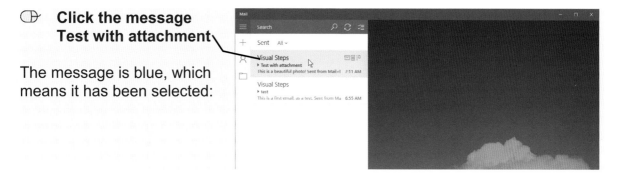

Let *Mail* delete this message:

☞ **Place the pointer on
the email message**

☞ **Click** 🗑

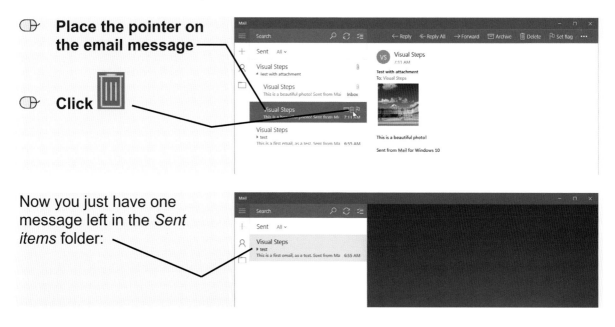

Now you just have one message left in the *Sent items* folder:

If you delete an email message in this way, it will not be permanently deleted. *Mail* saves all the deleted email messages in the *Deleted items* folder. This is an additional security measure. In case you have accidentally deleted a message, you can always retrieve it from this folder.

In next couple of steps you will learn how to permanently delete an email:

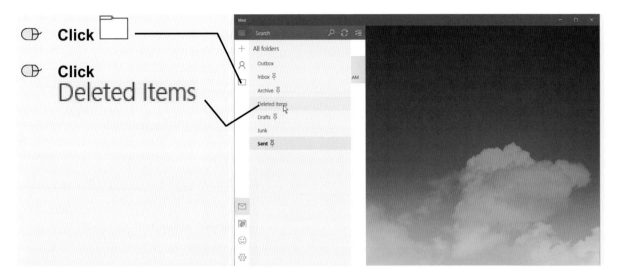

Click 📁

Click **Deleted Items**

You will see your email. You can delete a message in the *Deleted items* folder in the same way as you previously did:

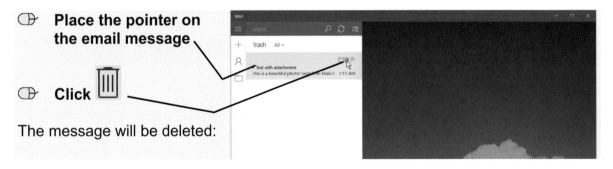

Place the pointer on the email message

Click 🗑

The message will be deleted:

Now the folder is empty. You can go back to the *Inbox*:

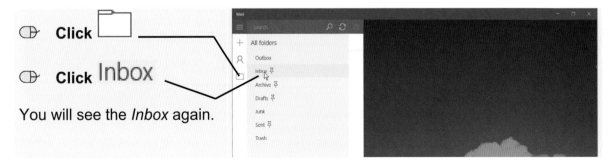

Click 📁

Click **Inbox**

You will see the *Inbox* again.

5.12 Your Signature

By default, each email you send is concluded with the text *Sent from Mail for Windows 10*. This text is called the default signature. You can replace this text with a standard salutation for all your messages, or by your name and address. This is how you change your email signature:

☞ **Click** ⚙, Options

By Use an email signature, you will see that the use of a signature is enabled, and in the text box you will see the current signature. You are going to change the signature. In this example we have used Kind regards, and the name:

☞ Delete the text in the box by
Use an email signature

⌨ **Type:** Kind regards, Your name

You can press the Enter key to move the text to a new line, if you wish.

☞ **Click an empty section of the window**

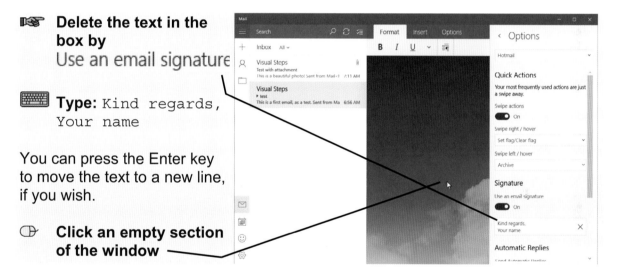

The signature will automatically be added to every email message you send.

☞ Close *Mail* 👣**1**

In the next couple of exercises you can repeat sending and receiving emails.

5.13 Exercises

☙

Have you forgotten how to do something? Use the number beside the footsteps to look it up in the appendix *How Do I Do That Again?*

Exercise 1: Creating an Email Message

In this exercise you are going to create a new email message.

☞ Open *Mail*. ☙^{3}

☞ Create a new email message. ☙^{37}

☞ Address it to yourself and add the subject *practice*. ☙^{38}

☞ Send the message. ☙^{39}

☞ Check whether you have received the message in the *Inbox*. ☙^{40}

☞ Read your email message. ☙^{41}

Exercise 2: Deleting an Email Message

☞ View the *Inbox*. ☙^{40}

☞ Delete the message you have received in the previous exercise. ☙^{42}

Exercise 3: Sending With Attachment

In this exercise you are going to create a new email message with an attachment.

☞ Create a new email message. ☙^{37}

☞ Address it to yourself and add the subject *practice with attachment*. ☙^{38}

☞ Add a picture as an attachment. ☙^{41}

☞ Send your message. ✂**39**

Exercise 4: Viewing the Attachment

☞ Check the *Inbox* and see if you have received the email with the attachment. ✂**40**

☞ Open the email message with the attachment. ✂**41**

☞ View the attachment. ✂**44**

☞ Close the window containing the picture. ✂**1**

☞ Close *Mail.* ✂**1**

5.14 Background Information

Dictionary

Attachment	A file that can be linked to an email message and sent along with it. This can be a document, picture, video or other type of file. Messages that contain attachments can be recognized by the paperclip icon in the message pane, next to the message title.
Conversation	A number of messages that belong together, such as emails with the same subject. These may be displayed together in *Mail*, in the *Inbox*.
Deleted items folder	Deleted emails are moved to the *Deleted items* folder. In order to permanently delete these items from your computer you will also need to delete the messages in this folder.
Drafts	Email message that are written and saved first, instead of being sent right away, are stored in the *Drafts* folder.
Email	Short for *electronic mail*. These are messages you send through the Internet.
Folder list	List op folders in the *Mail* app. Contains among others, the *Inbox* with received messages and *Deleted items* folder with the messages you have deleted.
Gmail	A free email service provided by *Google*.
Hotmail	A free email service provided by *Microsoft*.
IMAP	A method used by computers to send and receive email messages. This method will give you access to your email without having to download the messages to your computer.
Inbox	The *Inbox* is the folder in which all incoming email messages are collected.
Junk folder	*Mail* filters all messages that resemble unwanted, commercial email, and moves them to the *Junk* folder.
Message list	A list of messages stored in the folders of the *Mail* app.
Outlook.com	A free email service offered by *Microsoft*.

- Continue on the next page -

Password	With email a string of characters with which users can sign on and gain access to their email messages.
POP	Post Office Protocol. A standard method used by computers to send and receive email messages. POP messages are stored on an email server, until you download them to your computer. Then they are deleted from the server.
Sent items folder	In the *Sent items* folder, a copy of each sent message is stored, in case you may need it later on.
Signature	A signature can contain your name, email address, phone number and any other information that you want to include at the bottom of your email messages.
SMTP server	SMTP servers (Simple Mail Transfer Protocol) take care of sending your email messages to the Internet. The SMTP server processes outgoing email and is used alongside a POP or IMAP server for the incoming email.
Spam	Unsolicited, commercial email, also called *junk mail*.

Source: Windows Help, Wikipedia

Icons

Several icons are used in *Mail*. Here is an explanation of what they mean:

← a message to which you have replied;

→ a message you have forwarded;

the message contains an attachment;

a message flagged as 'important' by the sender.

The smaller the attachment, the faster it is sent and received

This is the rule on the Internet: the smaller the message is, the faster it will be sent from A to B. The same goes for attachments. In this case 'small' refers to the file size.

This is something you or the recipient of the message need to take into account, especially if you have a slow Internet connection. Nowadays most people in North America, Europe and Australia use a fast Internet connection, but there are some countries where this kind of connection is not available.

When you send an attachment, you will always be able to see the file name and the size, in kB or MB. This is a measure, just like meters and grams, feet and gallons.

One kilobyte equals (approximately) a thousand bytes.
20 kilobytes equal 20.000 bytes. Kilobyte is abbreviated to kB.
One megabyte equals (approximately) a thousand kilobytes.
This means that a megabyte equals (approximately) one million (a thousand times thousand) bytes. The abbreviation for megabyte is MB.

The speed with which something is sent or received depends on a number of factors, among others, the speed of your modem, the type of Internet connection, and the degree of traffic on the Internet. An email message that consists of only text, takes just a few seconds to send. A picture (unedited), taken with a modern digital photo camera (for example, 10 megapixels), is usually much larger. Sending such a photo will take up a lot more time. This can be especially hard on recipients who do not have a fast Internet connection, retrieving such a large file may cause them serious problems.

You can include many types of files with an email message, audio files and video files too. But be careful. Video files especially can be extremely large.
But if you have a fast broadband connection, such as DSL or cable, sending large files will not pose a problem.

There are other options for sharing files. You may want to create a web album or use *OneDrive* or *Dropbox*. You can add the desired files and then upload them to the Internet. You can then create a list of users that have access to your files and can download them if they want.

Please note: some Internet providers set a limit to the amount of data you can send along with an email. If the limit is exceeded, the message will not arrive. Usually you will receive a warning message when this happens.

5.15 Tips

Tip

Setting up a POP/IMAP account if sending and receiving mail fails

If you are using an email address given to you by your Internet provider, such as AOL or Verizon, you may not be able to receive any email right away. In this case, you can change a number of settings.

You will need to have your email address, the corresponding password, the name of your email provider's POP or IMAP server, and the name of your email provider's SMTP server. You will often have received this information from your provider. You can also find most of this information on the provider's website. Look for 'email settings' on the website, for example.

If you do not succeed in changing the settings, ask an experienced computer user for help.

This is how you change the settings:

☞ **Click** ⚙, Accounts

On the right-hand side of the window:

☞ **Click the account**

In this example, it is an AOL account.

- Continue on the next page -

You will see a window with account settings. Change the settings:

⌨ **Type your password**

Maybe your password has already been filled in, but you should just retype it

👆 **Click**
   Change mailbox sync
   Options for syncing email, co

If this option is grey in your window, then click
Save at the bottom, and open the window once more

AOL account settings

✉ mail@address.com

Password

••••••••

Account name

AOL

Change mailbox sync settings
Options for syncing email, contacts, and calendar.

Delete account
Remove this account from your device.

You will see this window. You can change the email settings:

👆 **Drag the scroll box downwards**

👆 **Click**
   Advanced mailbox s
   Incoming and outgoing ma

☑ Always download full message and Internet images

Download email from

the last 3 months   ⌄

Your name

Visual Steps

We'll send your messages using this name.

Sync options

Email

⬤ On

Advanced mailbox settings
Incoming and outgoing mail server info

Done	Cancel

- Continue on the next page -

Now you can choose between setting up your email account as a POP or an IMAP account:

- IMAP stands for *Internet Message Access Protocol*. This means you manage your email messages on the mail server. Messages that you have read will be saved on the mail server, until you delete them. IMAP is useful if you manage your email on multiple computers or devices. Your mailbox will look the same on all your devices.
  If you create any folders in which you arrange your email messages, these same folders will be present on every device. If you want to use IMAP, you will need to set up your email account as an IMAP account on all your devices.
- POP stands for *Post Office Protocol*. This is the traditional way of managing email. When you retrieve your messages, they will be deleted from the mail server right away. However, the default setting for POP accounts is for saving a copy on the mail server, even after the message has been retrieved. This means you can still retrieve the message on another device.

In this example we have chosen to use an IMAP account:

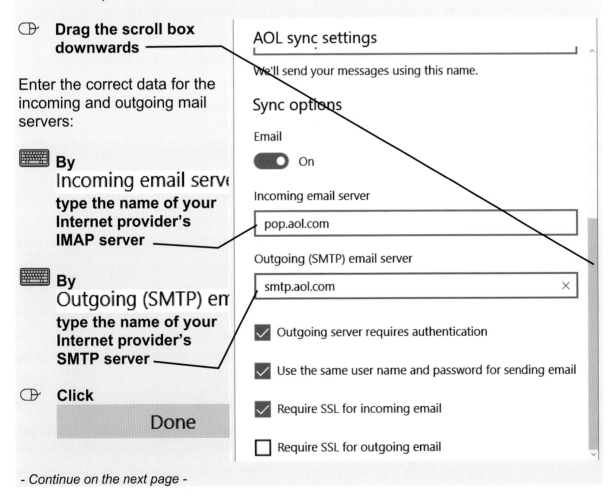

☞ **Drag the scroll box downwards**

Enter the correct data for the incoming and outgoing mail servers:

⌨ **By** Incoming email serve **type the name of your Internet provider's IMAP server**

⌨ **By** Outgoing (SMTP) em **type the name of your Internet provider's SMTP server**

☞ **Click** Done

- *Continue on the next page -*

The settings have been changed:

 Type your password

Maybe your password has already been filled in, but you should just retype it.

At the bottom of the window:

☞ **Click**

Save

The new settings are saved.

AOL account settings

✉ mail@address.com

Password

●●●●●●●●●

Account name

AOL

Change mailbox sync settings
Options for syncing email, contacts, and calendar.

☞ **Send an email to yourself, as explained in *section 5.3 Creating an Email Message* and *5.4 Sending and Receiving the Email Message***

If sending and receiving an email is still not working, contact your email provider's support desk, or ask an experienced computer user for help.

💡 **Tip**
Search for your emails
If you are looking for a specific email, but cannot find it, you can let the app find it for you:

☞ **In the top right-hand corner of the window, click** 🔍

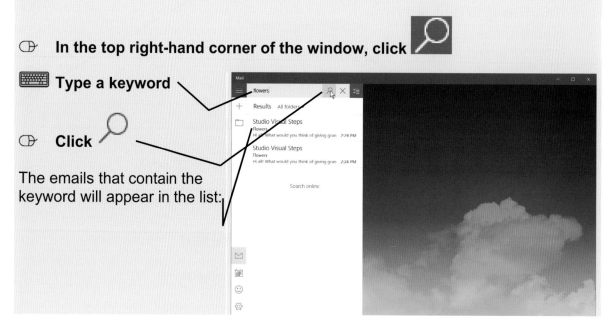 **Type a keyword**

☞ **Click** 🔍

The emails that contain the keyword will appear in the list:

🔆 Tip

CC and BCC
There are several ways of sending an email to multiple recipients:

☞ **Click** Cc & Bcc

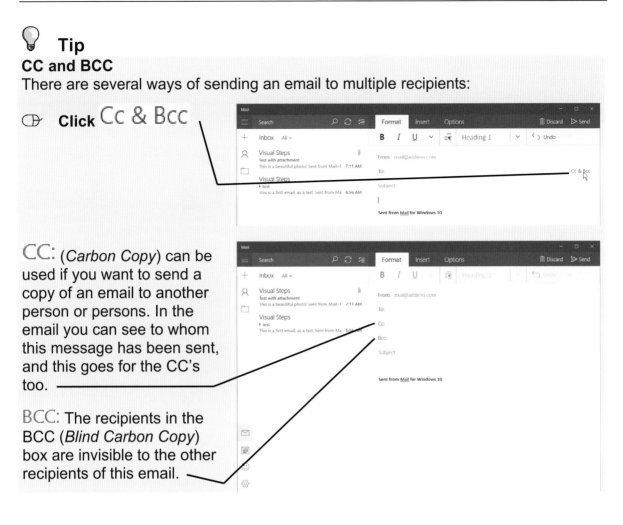

CC: (*Carbon Copy*) can be used if you want to send a copy of an email to another person or persons. In the email you can see to whom this message has been sent, and this goes for the CC's too.

BCC: The recipients in the BCC (*Blind Carbon Copy*) box are invisible to the other recipients of this email.

♡ Tip

Open an attachment
By double-clicking the attachment, you will automatically open a program or app with which you can view the attached file. The exact program or app to be opened depends on the settings on your computer.

If the attachment is a text document, in most cases *Microsoft Word* will be opened, or *WordPad* if *Word* is not installed on your computer.
If the attachment is a photo, the default setting in *Windows 10* is to open the *Photos* app. If you have installed a photo editing program on your computer, this default setting may have changed and the editing program will be opened instead.

If you receive an attachment that can only be opened with a program that is not installed on your computer, you will not be able to open the attachment. For some file types it is possible to download a so-called *viewer*. The viewer lets you view the file, but you cannot edit it. For example, on www.microsoft.com you can download free viewers for *PowerPoint* files (extension: PPS or PPT) and *Excel* files (XLS).

If the attachment is a computer program (for instance, an .EXE file), access to this file will usually be blocked by your antivirus program. You will see this on your screen and if you want you can unblock the files. But be cautious, especially with any files containing the extension .exe. These files could contain viruses. It is always best to download files or programs directly from the manufacturer's website or from the CD or DVD included in the program's packaging.

♡ Tip

Switching between email accounts
When you have set up multiple email accounts in Mail, you can swith between them:

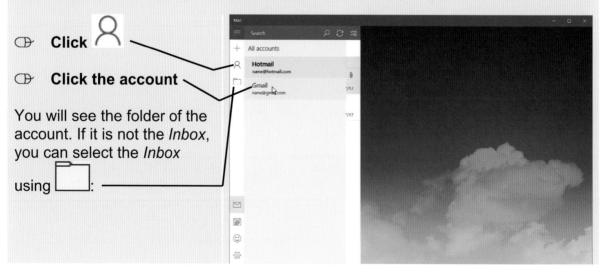

☞ **Click** ⊗

☞ **Click the account**

You will see the folder of the account. If it is not the *Inbox*, you can select the *Inbox*

using ▭:

💡 Tip

Formatting text in an email message

This is how you can change the font, the font size, and the style of the text in an email message:

☞ **Select the desired text** 👣**11**

Here you see the formatting options for rendering text bold or in italics, underlining it, or changing the text color.

To see more options:

☞ **Click** ⌄

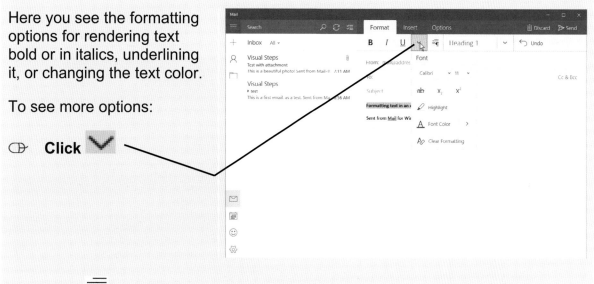

If you click ≡¶, you will see a window with options for lists and line spacing.

You can select a different text style with ⌄ by Heading 1.

💡 Tip

Link a Microsoft account to your computer

In various apps in *Windows 10* you will be asked whether you want to link your *Microsoft* account to your computer. Actually, a *Microsoft* account consists of an email address ending in hotmail.com, outlook.com, or live.com. You may have already set up this email account in *Mail*, and in the following tips you will also read about setting up this account for saving contact information and events in the calendar. If you set up this same email account in the apps on your tablet or smartphone as well, you will see the same data. This is called s*ynchronizing*.

Besides this, *Windows 10* also has an option for linking your *Microsoft* account to your user account. This is more extensive than the option described above. If you use this option and log on to another computer, tablet, or smartphone with *Windows* installed, you can synchronize your data right away, and also your files and settings. If an app offers you an option for linking your account, you can consider if this is useful to you, and follow the steps in the windows.

♀ **Tip**

Update your contacts in People
The computer is often used for communicating through email or social media. If you often correspond with the same persons, you can save the contact information of these persons in *People*, so you will not need to type these data over and over again.

☞ **Open *People*** ♧♧³

You will see the *People* window:

You may already see your contacts on the left-hand side of the window:——

Add a new contact:

⊕ **Click** ╋

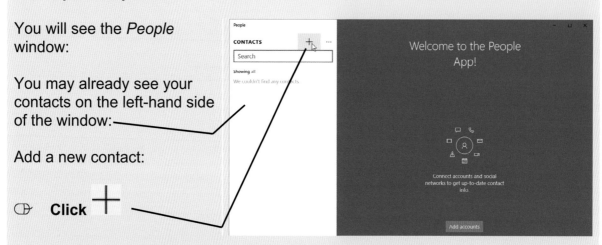

If your window looks different, you can drag the window borders. Then you will probably see a window similar to the one above.

If you had previously created any email accounts in *Mail*, you can select one of these accounts as a location for saving your contacts. You can always select a different account later on:

If this window appears:

⊕ **Click the desired account**

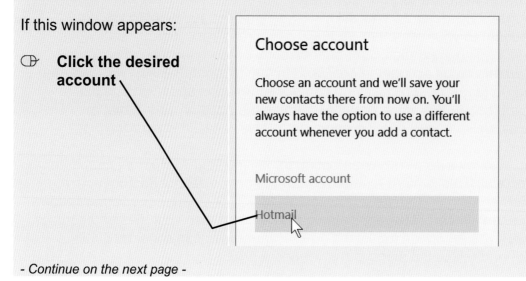

Choose account

Choose an account and we'll save your new contacts there from now on. You'll always have the option to use a different account whenever you add a contact.

Microsoft account

Hotmail

- Continue on the next page -

Add a contact:

☞ **Enter a name, phone number, and email address**

If you want to fill in more fields, you click the field:

Save the data:

⊕ **Click** 💾

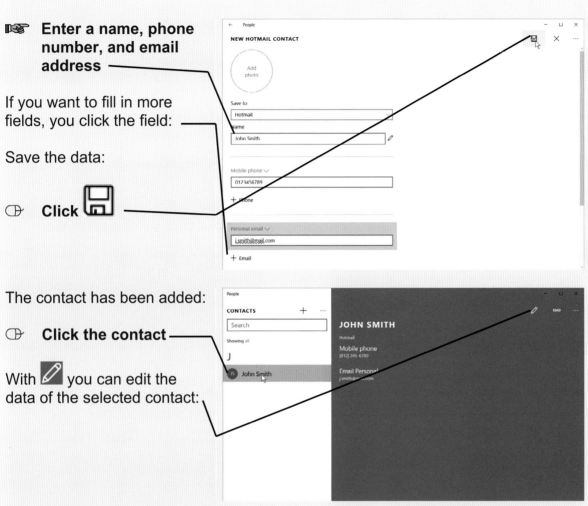

The contact has been added:

⊕ **Click the contact**

With ✏ you can edit the data of the selected contact:

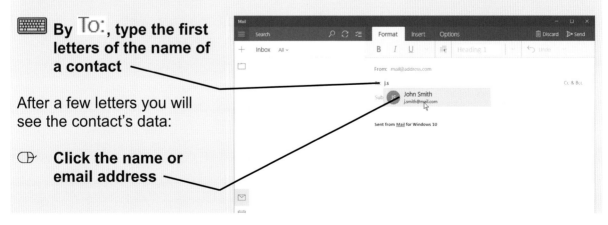

You can use a contact when you would like to send a new email message. In the window of a new message:

⌨ **By To:, type the first letters of the name of a contact**

After a few letters you will see the contact's data:

⊕ **Click the name or email address**

💡 Tip

Keep a calendar in Calendar

With *Calendar* you can keep track of appointments and other events in a calendar. For this you can often use the email account you have also set up in *Mail*.

☞ **Open** *Calendar* ³

When you open *Calendar* for the first time, you see a welcome window:

⊕ **Click** | Get started |

If this is the first time you use *Calendar*, you need to set the account you want to use:

For this you can often use the email account you have also set up in *Mail*.

⊕ **Click the account**

⊕ **Click** | Ready to go |

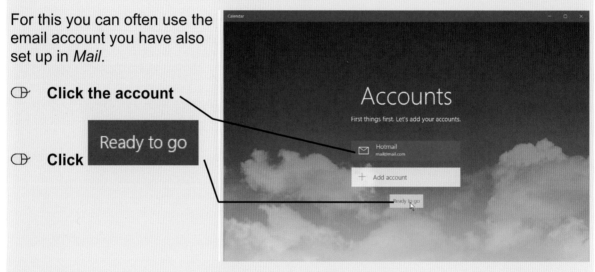

If you do not see an account, *Calendar* may have trouble in cooperating with the account set up in *Mail*. In that case, you can add an account. Usually, the calendar app goes together well with *Hotmail*, *Outlook.com*, and *Gmail* accounts.

You can create such accounts first, via signup.live.com or accounts.google.com, if you wish.

- Continue on the next page -

You will see the start window of *Calendar*. If your window looks different, you can drag the window borders. Then you will probably see a window similar to the one above.

Calendar views:

Monthly calendar:

Calendar:

If the selected account contains multiple calendars, you will see them here:

Change the view of the calendar, for example, select the week view:

☞ **Click** 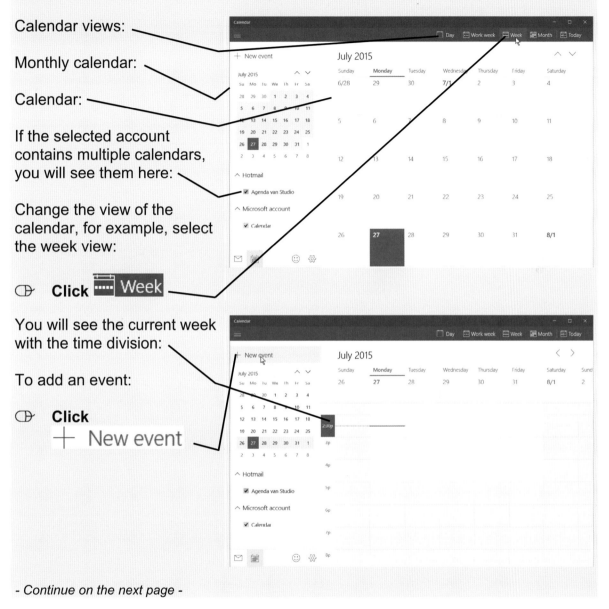 **Week**

You will see the current week with the time division:

To add an event:

☞ **Click**
   ✛ New event

- Continue on the next page -

Fill in the data for the event:

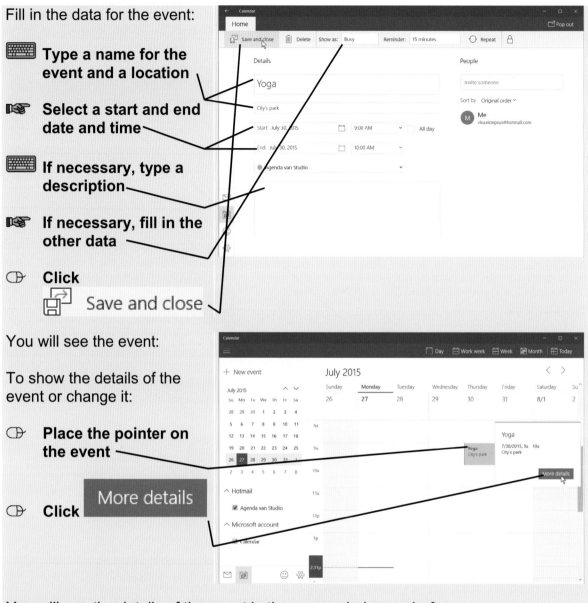

⌨ **Type a name for the event and a location**

☞ **Select a start and end date and time**

⌨ **If necessary, type a description**

☞ **If necessary, fill in the other data**

⊕ **Click**

     Save and close

You will see the event:

To show the details of the event or change it:

⊕ **Place the pointer on the event**

⊕ **Click** More details

You will see the details of the event in the same window as before.

6. Introduction to Photos, Video and Music

In this chapter you will be introduced to a few of the options offered by *Windows 10* for working with photos, video, and music.

Many people have large collections of digital photos stored on their computer. You can open these photos in the *Photos* app, and view them one by one, or in a more creative way as a slideshow. If a photo is upside down, you can rotate it in *Photos*. You will also see how to crop a photo, and read about the other photo editing options available in this app.

Windows 10 also offers various options for sharing your photos with others. We will show you how to use the *Photos* app to print your photos or send them as attachments in an email.

Do you have photos stored on your digital camera? In this chapter you will learn how to transfer these photos to your computer.

You will also become acquainted with the *Movies & TV* app and *Windows Media Player*. You can play your video files with *Movies & TV* and listen to music on a CD with your computer using *Windows Media Player*.

In this chapter you will learn how to:

- view photos in *Photos*;
- rotate a photo;
- crop a photo;
- use other photo editing options;
- view a slideshow;
- print and email photos;
- connect your digital camera to the computer;
- import photos from your digital camera;
- play a video file in the *Movies & TV* app;
- play a CD in *Windows Media Player*.

➤ Please note:

In order to be able to follow all the examples in this chapter, you will need to copy the practice files to your computer. In *Appendix B Downloading the Practice Files* at the end of this book you can read how to do this. You also need to have a music CD available.

6.1 Opening a Photo

With the *Photos* app you can view the photos that are stored on your computer. Open *Photos*:

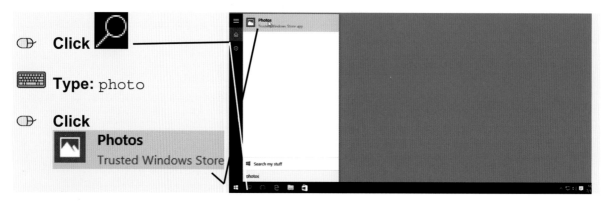

⬧ **Click** 🔍

⌨ **Type:** photo

⬧ **Click**

Photos
Trusted Windows Store

The *Photos* app will be opened. You will see a collection of photos. In this example, you see the practice photos. If you also have photos of your own saved on your computer, you may see different pictures in this window. This will not affect the following actions you need to perform.

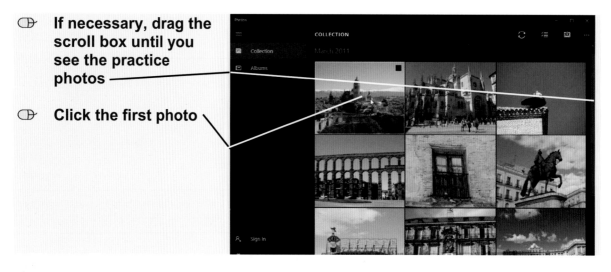

⬧ **If necessary, drag the scroll box until you see the practice photos**

⬧ **Click the first photo**

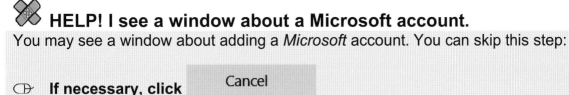 HELP! I see a window about a Microsoft account.

You may see a window about adding a *Microsoft* account. You can skip this step:

⟐ **If necessary, click**   Cancel

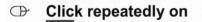 HELP! My window looks different.

If your window looks different, you can widen the window by dragging the window border. Then you will probably see a window similar.

You will see a large image of the first photo in the folder:

Use the button on the right-hand side of the window to view the next photo in the folder:

⟐ **Click**

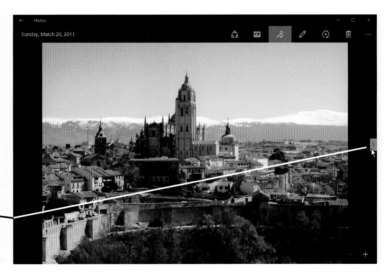

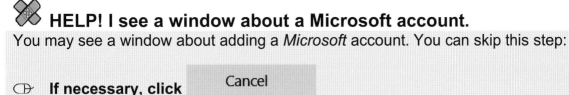 HELP! I do not see this button.

If the mouse has not moved for a while, the buttons will disappear. If you move the mouse a little bit, the buttons will re-appear again.

You will see the second photo:

You can view all the photos:

⟐ **Click repeatedly on**

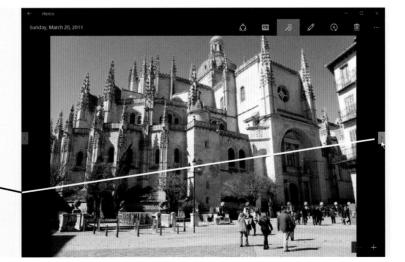

You will see all the practice photos. When you have reached the last photo, you will no longer see the button on the right-hand side. But you will see a button on the left-hand side . This button indicates that you can browse back to the previous photo.

Now you see this photo:

In the next section you will start working on this photo.

 HELP! I do not see this photo.
If you do not see the photo above, you need to go back to the first window of *Photos*:

☞ **Click**

☞ **If necessary, drag the scroll box upwards or downwards**

☞ **Click**

6.2 Rotating a Photo

Photos taken with your digital camera or photos that you have scanned may not be displayed in the correct orientation. You can easily solve this problem easily. To do this, you need to use the buttons that are displayed in the window. You can rotate the photo a quarter turn like this:

In the upper right corner of the window:

 Click

Now the photo is shown in the correct vertical orientation, also referred to as portrait mode:

☞ **Browse to the first photo**  $\mathcal{QQ}$45

6.3 Cropping a Photo

You will often see minor blemishes on a photo, things nobody really notices. In *Photos* you can easily crop a photo and remove some of these irksome blemishes. Here is how you do that:

☞ **If necessary, click the photo**

At the top of the window:

☞ **Click**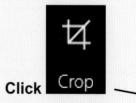

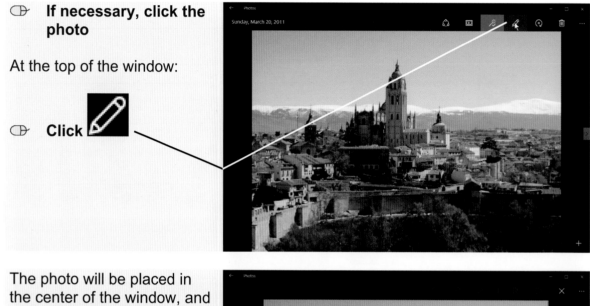

The photo will be placed in the center of the window, and to the left and right you will see photo editing buttons. You can practice working with the cropping option:

☞ **Click** Crop

A frame appears, all around the photo. If you intend to print the cropped photo afterwards, it is a good idea to crop the photo to the correct size. To do this you need to select a fixed height-width ratio:

☞ **Click** ▪▪▪

☞ **Click** [Aspect ratio]

A menu appears. Select the 4 x 6 ratio:

☞ **Click** 4 × 6

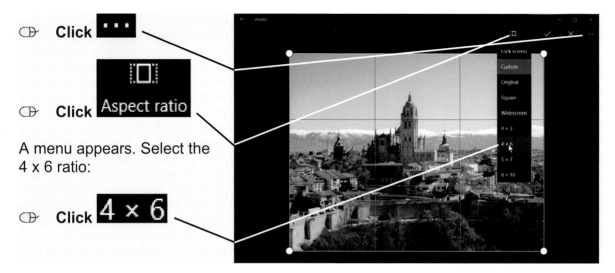

Now the frame will be adjusted to the 4 x 6 ratio. If you make the frame a bit smaller, the 4 x 6 ratio will remain unchanged:

☞ **Place the pointer on the corner handle in the lower right corner**

The pointer turns into ⬉:

☞ **Press the mouse button and hold it down**

☞ **Drag the handle to the left a bit**

☞ **Release the mouse button**

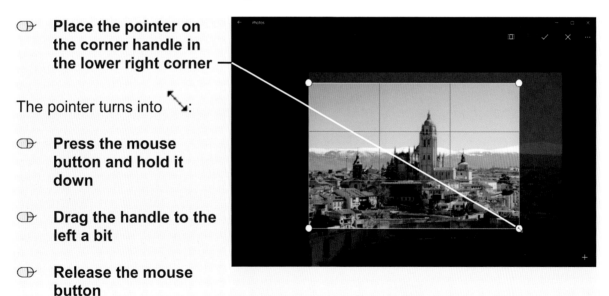

You can move the photo within the frame, so that you no longer see the city walls:

☞ **Place the pointer in the frame** ——————

The pointer turns into ⊕:

☞ **Press the mouse button and hold it down**

☞ **Drag the photo to the left and downwards**

☞ **Release the mouse button**

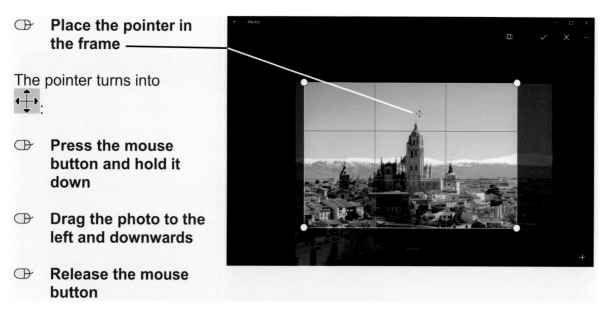

If you are satisfied with the size and position of the frame, you can crop the photo:

☞ **Click** ✔

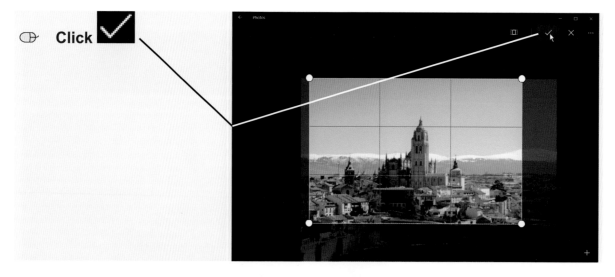

The photo will be cropped. If you are not satisfied with the cropped photo, you can restore the photo with the 🔄 button. Use the 💾 button to save the edits with the name of the original photo (the original photo will be overwritten). This means that the original photo will not be saved. This may not be what you want. Another option is to save the photo by copying it.

You can save a copy of the photo. Then the original will remain untouched:

☞ **Click**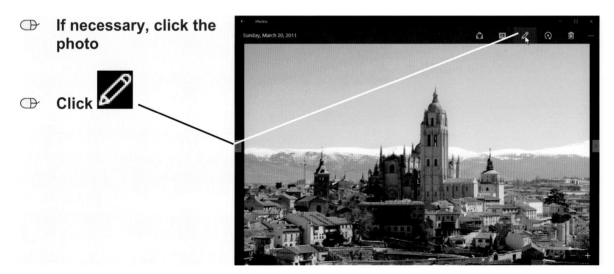

A copy of the photo has been saved in the same folder as the original photo. The file name now has the extension (2).

6.4 Photo Editing Options

Along with rotating and cropping, *Photos* has some other editing options. Take a look at these options:

☞ **If necessary, click the photo**

☞ **Click**

You will see the options on the left-hand side, for example, simple enhancements, filters, adjusting the exposure and colors, applying effects:

On the right-hand side you will see the functions of the selected option:

Click the desired edit. You will immediately see the effect of the edit in the window.

This is how you add a filter, for example:

⊕ **Click** Filters

On the right-hand side of the window:

⊕ **Click the desired filter**

You will see the result:

You can practice using these options later on, if you wish. For now you can cancel the edit of this photo:

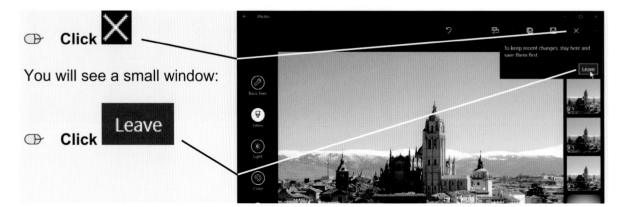

⊕ **Click** ✕

You will see a small window:

⊕ **Click** Leave

6.5 Viewing a Slideshow

A slideshow is a great way of viewing a series of consecutive photos. Your photos will be displayed on a full screen. Here is how you open a slideshow:

☞ **If necessary, click the photo**

☞ **Click**

The screen will turn dark for an instant, and then the slideshow will begin:

The photos will be displayed one after the other:

The series of photos will be repeated over and over again. You can stop the slideshow at any time by clicking a photo, like this:

☞ **Click the photo**

6.6 Printing Photos

In the *Photos* app you can also print a photo. You do that as follows:

☞ **If necessary, click the photo**

☞ **Click**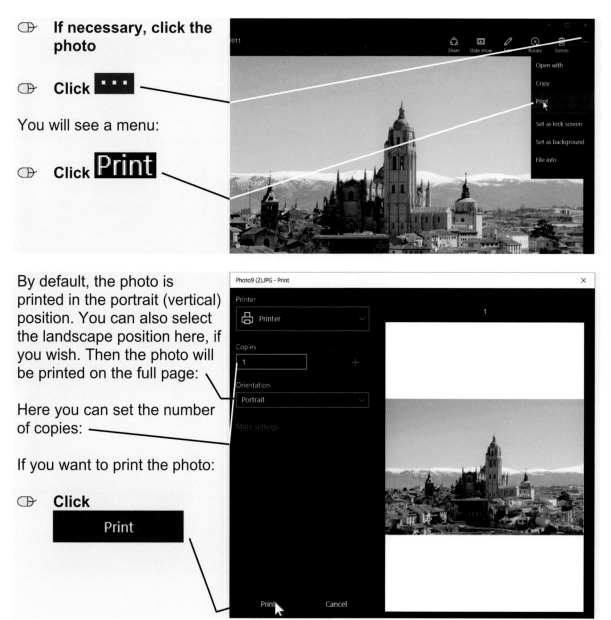

You will see a menu:

☞ **Click** Print

By default, the photo is printed in the portrait (vertical) position. You can also select the landscape position here, if you wish. Then the photo will be printed on the full page:

Here you can set the number of copies: ⸻

If you want to print the photo:

☞ **Click**
    Print

The photo is printed.

6.7 Sending Photos by Email

You can quickly share your photos with others by sending them by email. Just try it:

☞ **If necessary, click the photo**

☞ **Click**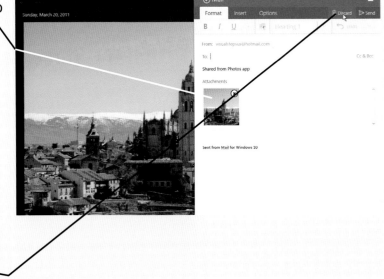

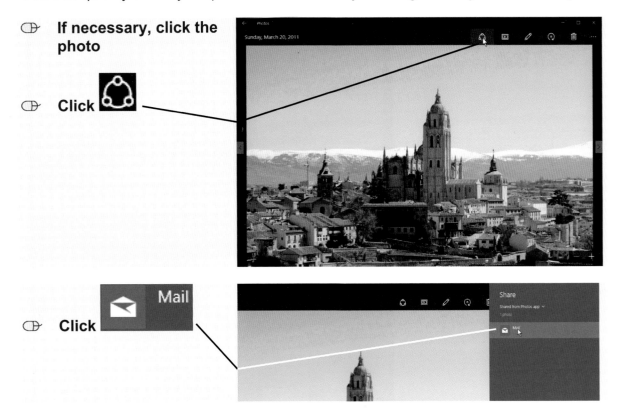

☞ **Click** Mail

A new email message is opened:

The photo has been added to the email as an attachment:

Now you can add a recipient, and a subject, and type a message if you wish. Then you can send the email message. For now this will not be necessary.

This is how you close the window with the email message:

☞ **Click**  Discard

You can go back to the photos overview:

⊕   **If necessary, click the photo**

⊕   **Click** ←

You will see the photos again:

6.8 Connecting Your Digital Camera To the Computer

If you want to view the photos that are stored on your digital camera in *Windows 10*, you need to *import* these photos to your computer. Importing means that the photos are transferred from the camera to your computer. There are two ways of doing this. By connecting the camera to the computer with a cable, or by directly copying the photos from the *memory card* on which they are stored. The memory card is a small card that can be taken out of the camera.

Most digital cameras come with a USB cable that can be connected to the computer's USB port. Some digital cameras can be connected with a firewire cable, to the computer's firewire port. The other end of the cable is plugged into a slot on the camera.

🔾 Please note:

In this section we will discuss importing photos from a digital photo camera. Devices such as a cell phone (smartphone), a digital video camera, or a tablet operate in a similar way. If you have stored your photos on one of these devices, you can transfer these as well. If necessary, ask an experienced computer user to help you, if you do not succeed in transferring the photos.

The most frequently used cable connection with a digital camera is the USB connection which you can put into a USB port:

Firewire is the alternative connection between a digital camera and a computer. The firewire plug is smaller:

☞ **Make sure the device is turned off**

☞ **Connect the cable to the camera**

☞ **Connect the USB or firewire cable to a corresponding port on the computer**

If you have a different cable, other than a USB or firewire plug, you need to connect it to the correct port on your computer (read your camera manual).

☞ **If necessary, turn on the device**

🔾 Please note:

Some cameras need to be switched to connect mode or play mode. In your camera's manual you will find the correct settings for your own camera.

Now *Windows* connects to your camera. If the camera has never been connected to the computer before, *Windows* will try to install a driver for the camera. This will happen automatically. You may see a message informing you of this procedure. The driver takes care of the correct communication between the camera, cell phone or external hard disk and the computer.

Once the device is correctly connected and has been recognized by *Windows*, you can import the photos to your computer. In the next section you can read how to do this.

 HELP! My camera is not recognized.

If *Windows* cannot connect to the camera, despite having installed the driver, you can try to do the following things to solve the problem:

1. Check whether the camera's battery is fully charged.
2. Check if the camera has actually been turned on and whether the camera has some sort of special connection mode that needs to be enabled first (read the camera manual).
3. Turn off the camera and restart the computer. Turn on the camera again.
4. Make sure the latest version of the driver program for your camera has been installed. It is recommended to download the driver from the Internet. If necessary, ask an experienced computer user to help you.
5. Check if something is wrong with the cable. Try to connect the cable to a different port on the computer, or use a different cable.
6. Try to connect the camera to another computer, to see if the connection works with the other computer. If this does not work, chances are that there is something wrong with your camera. Contact the manufacturer's service desk. Look up this information on the manufacturer's website.
7. Try to transfer the photos to the computer by using the camera's memory card.

You can also transfer photos directly from the memory card, also called an SD card. You will need to have a card reader to do this.

Nowadays many computers are equipped with a built-in memory card reader that can read several types of cards.

The card readers can also be bought separately, and connected to one of the computer's USB ports. If you intend to buy a card reader, you need to make sure that your type of memory card is supported by the reader.

If necessary, you can check the camera's manual to find out where the memory card is located.

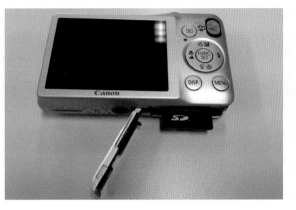

☞ **If necessary, connect the external card reader to your computer**

☞ **Insert the memory card into the card reader (in the card reader in your pc or the external card reader)**

In the next section you can read how you transfer photos from your camera to your computer.

6.9 Importing Photos From Your Digital Camera

You can start importing the photos:

⊕ **Click**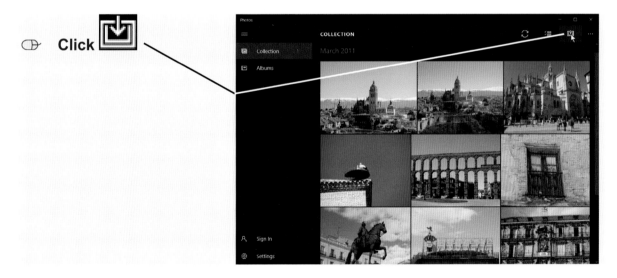

When multiple devices are connected to your computer, you will see this window:

☞ **Click the name of your camera**

☞ **Click** Choose a device to imp

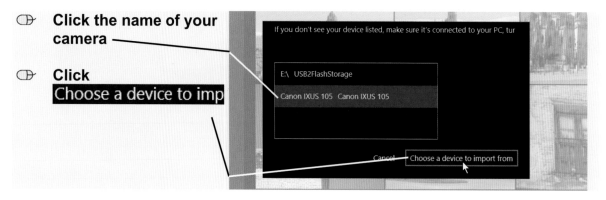

Windows will show how many new photos are found. In this example five pictures are found. For now, you will import all photos:

☞ **Click** Import

After the import process has finished, you will see the *Photos* window again:

In order to view the new photos:

☞ **Drag the scroll box down**

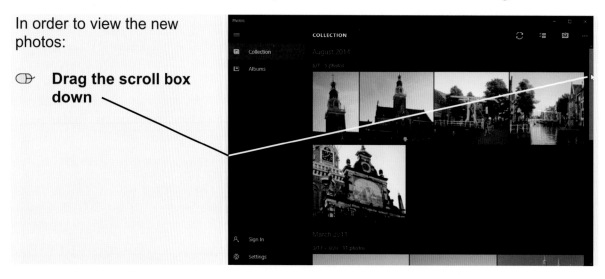

Now all the photos have been copied from the camera to the computer. The computer will remember which photos have been copied. The next time you connect your camera, the computer will not recognize these photos as new, and will not copy them. Only the new photos you have taken after you have imported the previous photos, will be imported.

💡 Tip
Transferring photos through File Explorer
When we were writing this book, it was not possible to import just a few selected photos through the *Photos* app. But you can do this in *File Explorer*. In the *Tips* at the back of this chapter you can read how to do this.

Now you can close *Photos*:

☞ **Close *Photos*** 🐾¹

☞ **Disconnect the camera from the computer**

💡 Tip
Change the name of the folder
If you want to change the name of the folder, you can do that in *File Explorer*. You will find your photos in the *Pictures* folder:

☞ **Open *File Explorer*** 🐾¹⁷

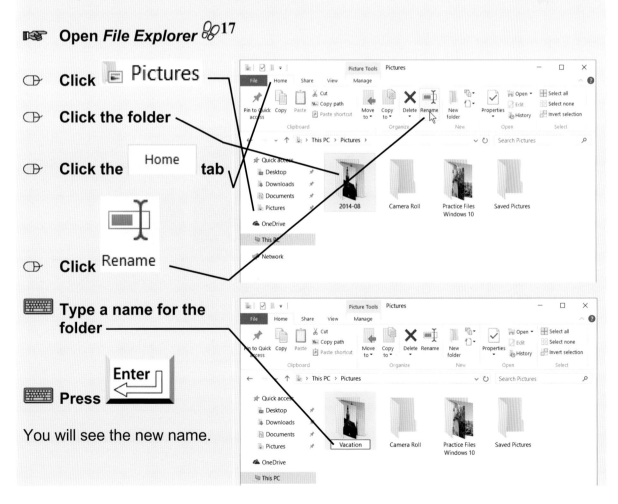

👆 **Click** 🖼 **Pictures**

👆 **Click the folder**

👆 **Click the** Home **tab**

👆 **Click** Rename

⌨ **Type a name for the folder**

⌨ **Press** Enter

You will see the new name.

Tip

More about working with digital photos
Besides the options for working with digital photos in the *Photos* app, there are several other programs available for photo editing. If you are interested in editing and/or managing photos on your computer, you can take a look at the Visual Steps titles regarding digital photo editing. On the
www.visualsteps.com/show_serie.php web page you will find an overview of all available books. All of these books have been written using the same step-by-step method as in this book. You will be presented with lots of examples and screen shots, and learn how to work with the program that is discussed.

6.10 Playing a Video File

You can use the *Movies & TV* app to play video files that are stored on your computer. The practice files also include a video. You can use this file to practice with in this section.

☞ Open *Movies & TV* &&³

Movies & TV will open. Apart from playing videos on your hard disk, this app can also play movies and TV shows that can be purchased or rented.

Click 🎥 Videos

You will see the practice files. You may see more video files on your own computer.

Play a practice file:

Click *Video1*

✂ HELP! My window looks different.

If your window looks different, you can widen the window by dragging the window border. Then you will probably see a window similar to the one above.

The short video will be played:

If you do not move the mouse, the buttons and the progress bar

─────○──────── at the bottom of the window will disappear: ──────

They will reappear as soon as you move the mouse once more.

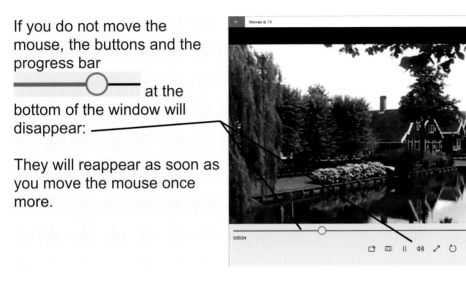

💡 Tip

Pause play

If you pause with the **||** button, the button will turn into ▷.

When the video has finished playing, you can replay it by

clicking the ▷ button: ──────

For now this will not be necessary.
Close the window:

☞ **Click** ✕ ──────

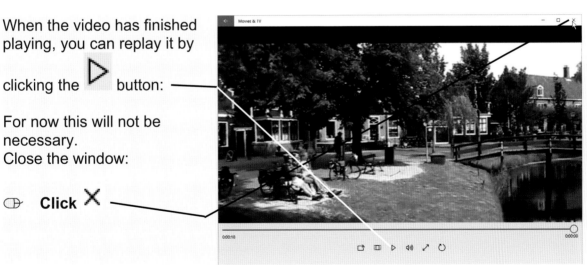

➥ Please note:

Unfortunately, you cannot play a DVD with the app. In *Windows 10* you will need to have a separate program in order to play a DVD. You can also download an app in the *Store*. On the website that is accompanied with this book, you can find a bonus chapter about downloading apps. See *Appendix C Opening the Bonus Online Chapters*.

6.11 Opening Windows Media Player

Windows Media Player is a program that you can use to play music, among other things. You open it like this:

☞ Open *Windows Media Player* 𝒪𝒪³

If this is the first time you have opened *Windows Media Player*, you can adjust a number of settings that determine how the program works. For now, you can use the default settings.

➥ Please note:

If you have previously opened *Windows Media Player* you will not see the next window. If that is the case, you can continue with the next step.

⊕ **Click a radio button ⦿ by Recommended setting**

⊕ **Click** ⟦ Finish ⟧

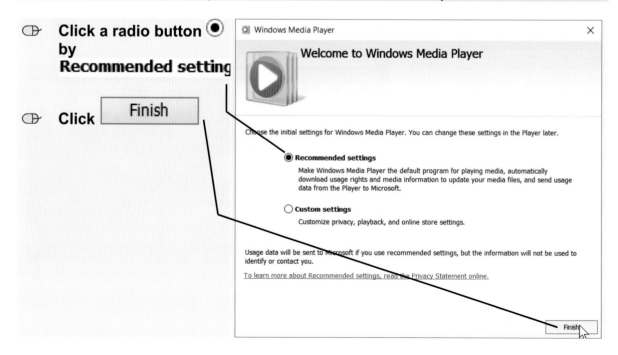

Once the settings have been adjusted, *Windows Media Player* will search your computer for music files.

In this example no music files are found:

But your own computer may contain some music files.

6.12 Playing a Music CD

On most computers, *Windows Media Player* is set as the default music player for most common audio files. When you insert a music CD into the CD/DVD player, *Windows* will immediately start to play it with *Media Player*.

➥ Please note:

In order to follow the examples in this section and the next few sections, you will need to have a music CD. Here is an example:

See what happens when you insert a music CD into the computer:

☞ **Insert a music CD from your own collection into your computer's CD/DVD drive**

☞ **Carefully close the tray**

✖ HELP! I do not have a CD/DVD drive.

Some computers do not have a CD/DVD drive. If this is the case, you can just read through this section.

HELP! Nothing happens after I have inserted a CD.

If nothing happens after you have inserted the original CD, this CD might be protected against playback on computers. Try a different music CD instead.

⊕ **Click**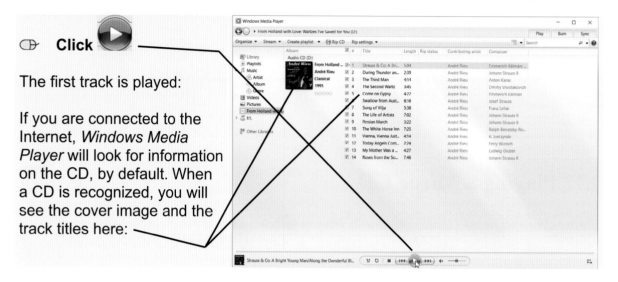

The first track is played:

If you are connected to the Internet, *Windows Media Player* will look for information on the CD, by default. When a CD is recognized, you will see the cover image and the track titles here:

HELP! I see a much smaller window.

This means *Windows Media Player* is displayed in the *Play now* view. You can return to the larger window:

⊕ **Click**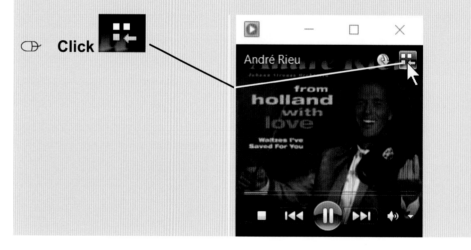

HELP! The volume is too loud or too soft.

If you want to turn the volume up or down, you can use the *Volume* slider ———.

To turn the volume down:

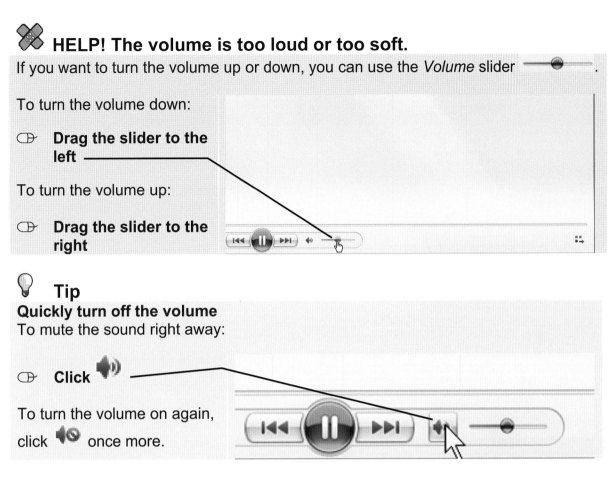

- ☞ **Drag the slider to the left** ————

To turn the volume up:

- ☞ **Drag the slider to the right**

💡 Tip

Quickly turn off the volume
To mute the sound right away:

- ☞ **Click** 🔊

To turn the volume on again, click 🔇 once more.

Just like with your regular CD/DVD player you can skip to the next track by clicking just once. At the bottom of the window:

- ☞ **Click** ▶▶❙

André Rieu   01:52

💡 Tip

Quickly skip to your favorite song
If you know exactly which track you want to hear on this CD, you can play it right away:

- ☞ **Double-click the track or the track's title, for example** Track 6

The track will be played right away.

This is how you return to the previous track:

Track number 2 is played:

☞ **Click**

With the shuffle button, the tracks will be played in a random order.

The repeat button allows you to repeat a track.

If you click these buttons again you will stop the shuffle or repeat actions.

You can also pause the music:

☞ **Click**

turns into   :

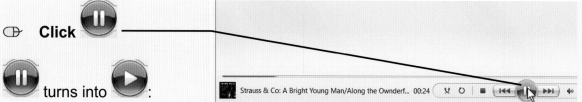

If you want to completely stop the music from playing:

☞ **Click**

Now you can close *Windows Media Player*:

☞ **Close *Windows Media Player* ⁰⁰1**

☞ **Remove the CD from the CD/DVD player**

In this chapter you have learned what you can do with photos, music CDs, and video files in *Windows 10.* By doing the exercises in the next section you can repeat what you have learned.

6.13 Exercises

The following exercises will help you master what you have just learned. Have you forgotten how to do something? Use the number beside the footsteps to look it up in the appendix *How Do I Do That Again?*

Exercise 1: View a Photo and a Slideshow

In this exercise you can take a look at a photo and view a slideshow.

☞ Open *Photos*. 3

☞ Click a photo from one of the practice files.

☞ Browse to the photo of the man on horseback. 45

☞ Browse to the photo of the stork's nest. 45

☞ View the slideshow of all the photos in the folder. 46

☞ Stop the slideshow. 47

☞ Go back to the start window of the *Photos* app. 48

☞ Close *Photos*. 1

Exercise 2: Play a Video

In this exercise you can practice playing a video.

☞ Open *Movies & TV*. 3

☞ Play the video file called *Video2*. 49

☞ Pause play. 50

☞ Resume play. 51

☞ View the rest of the video.

☞ Close *Movies & TV*. $\mathscr{CO}^1$

Exercise 3: Play a Music CD

In this exercise you can practice playing a music CD in *Windows Media Player*. You can also give the shuffle option a try.

☞ Open *Windows Media Player*. $\mathscr{CO}^3$

☞ Insert a music CD into your CD/DVD player.

☞ Skip to the next track. $\mathscr{CO}^{52}$

☞ Pause play. $\mathscr{CO}^{50}$

☞ Resume play. $\mathscr{CO}^{51}$

☞ Play the tracks in random order. $\mathscr{CO}^{53}$

☞ Skip to the next track. $\mathscr{CO}^{52}$

☞ Repeat one of the tracks. $\mathscr{CO}^{54}$

☞ Disable the shuffle (random play) function. $\mathscr{CO}^{55}$

☞ Disable the repeat function. $\mathscr{CO}^{56}$

☞ Stop the CD from playing. $\mathscr{CO}^{57}$

☞ Remove the music CD from your CD/DVD player.

☞ Close *Windows Media Player*. $\mathscr{CO}^1$

6.14 Background Information

Dictionary

Driver	Software that ensures that a device (such as a digital camera or a printer) can communicate with *Windows*. Every device needs a driver in order to function.
Firewire	A fast cable connection between the computer and an external device, such as a photo camera.
Import	Transferring digital photos from your digital camera to your computer.
Memory card	Memory in the shape of a card on which you can permanently store data. There are several types of memory cards. Their capacity ranges from 4 GB to 512 GB or more. Also called SD card.
Movies & TV	An app with which you can view video files on your computer. You can also rent or purchase movies through the Internet.
Mute	(Temporarily) turn off the sound.
Photos	An app with which you can view, share, rotate, and crop photos, among others.
Shuffle	Playing tracks in random order.
Slideshow	An automatic display of all your images on a full screen.
Track	A song or another individual audio fragment.
USB port	A rectangular communication port in the computer universally suited for many devices such as photo cameras.
Windows Media Player	A program for playing and managing music and videos.

Source: Windows Help, Wikipedia

Other apps

Besides the apps we have already discussed, there are a number of other standard apps available in *Windows 10*:

Alarms & Clock   An app with which you can set an alarm, use a world clock, a timer, and a stopwatch.

Camera   With this app you can take pictures and record videos with your computer and the devices connected to it.

Get Office   A promotional app from Microsoft, regarding the Microsoft Office suite and corresponding services.

Get started   Help function for working with *Windows 10*.

Phone companion An app with which you can synchronize your cell phone with your computer.

Money   An app with news regarding financial subjects.

OneDrive   Through *OneDrive* you can save your files in the cloud, a storage space on the Internet. In this way you can easily access your files on other computers, as well as on your tablet or smartphone.

OneNote   A notes app with which you can easily take notes in various ways. For example, by using text, images, and tables. This data can easily be shared with others via the Internet.

Get Skype   An app for downloading *Skype*. *Skype* is an app for making free phone calls via the Internet. This app requires the use of a microphone.

Sports   An app that displays sports news. Comparable to the *News* app.

Store   Through the *Store* you can download apps, free of charge or at a cost.

Voice recorder   An app that can record voices. This app requires the use of a microphone.

Xbox   An app that lets you connect with the Xbox game computer community on your own computer, and keeps you up to date with the latest games.

3D Builder   A program for creating, printing, and scanning 3D objects.

6.15 Tips

⚪ Tip
Import individual photos through File Explorer
With *Photos* you can only import all the (new) photos on your camera to your computer at once. If you want to select individual photos and transfer them to your computer, you need to use *File Explorer*. This is how you do it:

☞ **Connect your digital camera to the computer**

☞ **Open** *File Explorer* ✂️ **17**

Open the window with the photos:

⊕ **Click** 🖥️ **This PC**

⊕ **Double-click your camera**

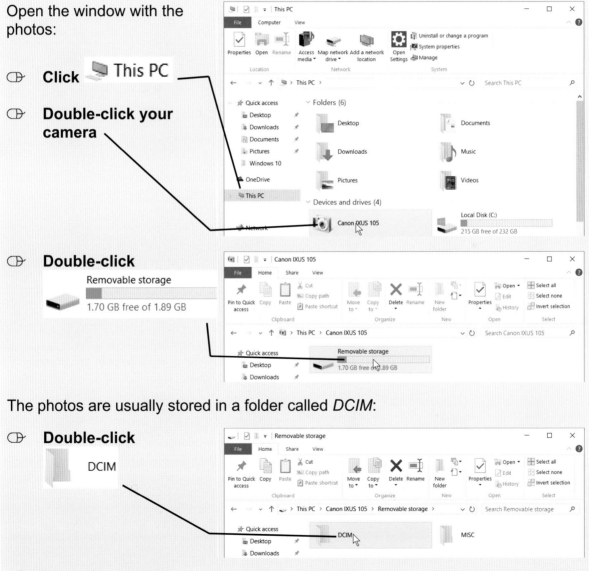

⊕ **Double-click**
Removable storage
1.70 GB free of 1.89 GB

The photos are usually stored in a folder called *DCIM*:

⊕ **Double-click**
DCIM

- Continue on the next page -

🖰 **Double-click the folder with the photos**

Please note: sometimes you may need to search for a while to find the folder containing the photos.

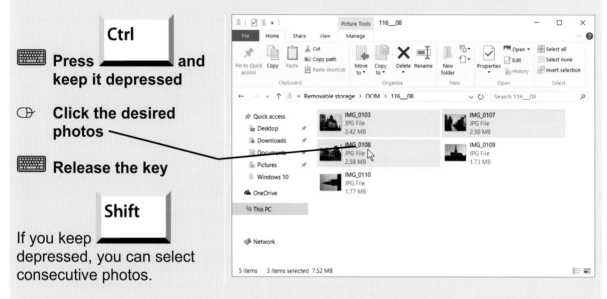

You will see the thumbnail images of the photos stored on your camera. This is how you copy these photos to the *Pictures* folder on your computer, for example:

⌨ **Press** **Ctrl** **and keep it depressed**

🖰 **Click the desired photos**

⌨ **Release the key**

Shift

If you keep depressed, you can select consecutive photos.

In this example we will transfer the photos to the *Pictures* folder:

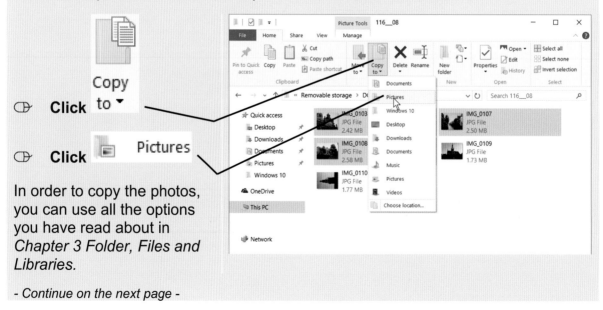

🖰 **Click** Copy to ▾

🖰 **Click** 🖼 Pictures

In order to copy the photos, you can use all the options you have read about in *Chapter 3 Folder, Files and Libraries.*

- Continue on the next page -

The photos will be copied. After they have been copied, you can disconnect the camera.

Disconnect the camera from the computer

Tip

Listen to music with Groove Music

You can also play and manage the music files on your computer with *Groove Music*. Besides this, you can use this app for downloading music from the *Store*.

Open *Groove Music* 3

You will see the start window of *Groove Music*:

Search for music on your computer:

Create a playlist:

Buy music online in the *Store*:

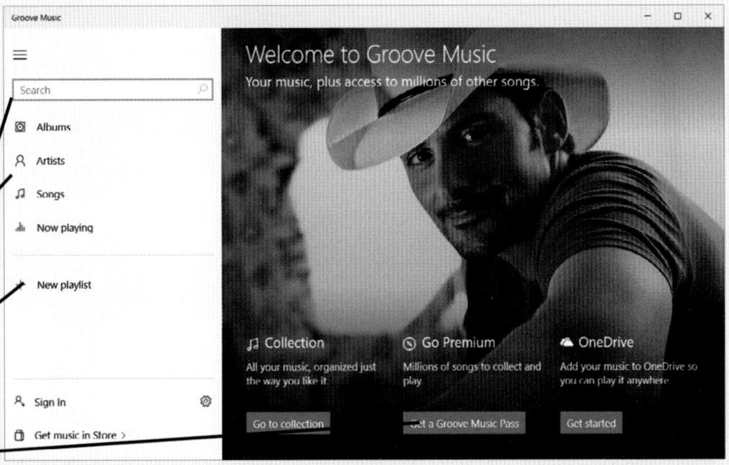

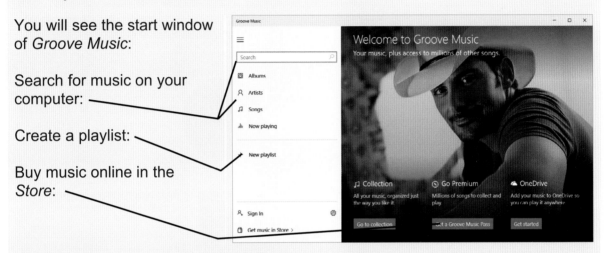

This is how you play music on your computer. You can search for an artist, for example:

Connect your speakers or headphone to your computer

Click Artists

You will see all the artists of which you have songs saved on your computer:

Click an artist

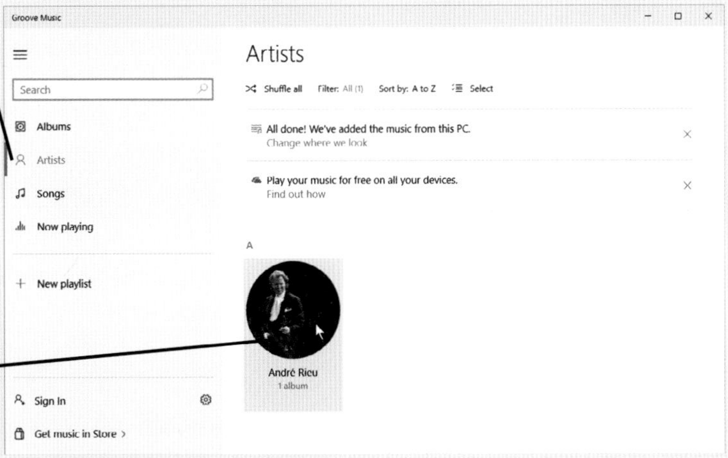

- Continue on the next page -

An album by this artist
appears:

☞ **Click a track**

You will see several options:

☞ **Click** ▶

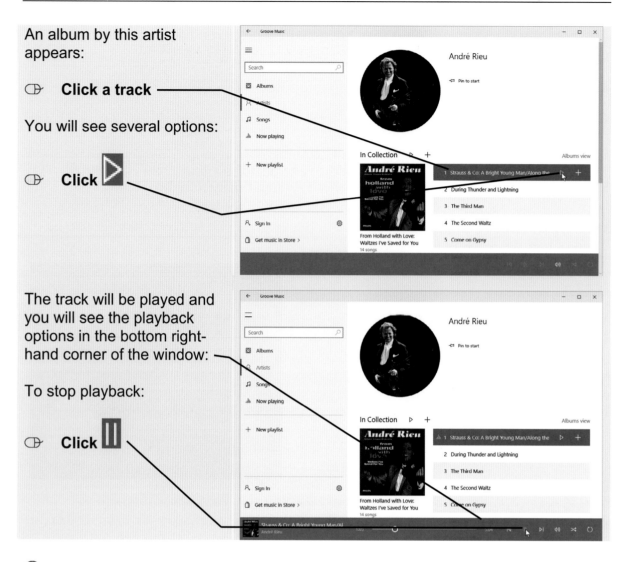

The track will be played and
you will see the playback
options in the bottom right-
hand corner of the window:

To stop playback:

☞ **Click** ❚❚

💡 **Tip**

Learn more about music in Windows Media Player or Groove Music
You can do even more with *Windows Media Player* or *Groove Music*. For example,
you can create playlists, and copy music from a CD to your computer. You can learn
more on this subject in the sequel titles concerning *Windows 10*. You will find an
overview of all the books on *Windows 10* at
www.visualsteps.com/show_serie.php

7. Useful Settings and Security

In *Windows 10* you can also adjust many components of your computer and set them up according to your own needs or preferences, just like in previous *Windows* versions. In this chapter you can read how to adapt the lock screen and desktop to your own personal taste. Just go ahead and experiment a bit, and see if the new settings suit you. All the settings you change can easily be restored to their original state, so do not be afraid to try things.

Good security measures are essential to computers that are connected to the Internet. As a computer user, you are responsible for the security of your own computer. A good security system reduces the risk of introducing viruses or other harmful software on your computer. *Windows 10* helps you to get the job done with *Windows Defender*. This is a program that offers complete protection against computer viruses and other types of unsolicited software. In this chapter you will read how the real-time protection functions of *Windows Defender* protect your computer, and how you can scan your computer for viruses or other harmful software.

The *Security and Maintenance* window is another security tool in *Windows 10*. In the *Security and Maintenance* window you can check the security settings for *Windows 10* on your computer and change them, if necessary.

You have the possibility of creating multiple desktops in *Windows 10*; this is a feature that was originally designed for mobile devices. With this option you can easily group programs and apps on a desktop, and keep *Windows* well-ordered.

In this chapter you will learn:

- how to add program and app tiles to the Start menu;
- how to change the size of the Start menu;
- how to move tiles and create groups in the Start menu;
- about *Settings*;
- about *Windows Update*;
- how to update apps;
- how to create multiple desktops;
- how to change the image of the lock screen and desktop background;
- how to change the size of letters and icons;
- how to set up the screensaver;
- how to adjust the power options;

- more about the *Notification* window and *Notification* center;
- how to view the *Security and Maintenance* window;
- about *Windows Firewall*;
- how to scan your pc for malware with *Windows Defender*.

➥ Please note:

Some of these adjustments require you to have certain user rights on the computer. For example, if you currently have *Guest* access to the computer you currently use, your rights for changing the settings will be limited.

If some settings require certain user rights, *Windows* will ask you for a password. If you do not know this password, you will only be able to read through the relevant sections. Or you can ask the administrator of the computer to give you permission.

7.1 Adding Program or App Tiles to the Start Menu

You can use the tiles in the Start menu to open a program or app. It is very easy; you just need to click the desired tile. You can also change the order of the tiles in the Start menu to suit your own needs. As you work with your computer for a while longer, you may find that you use some programs and apps more frequently than others. You may have also installed a new program or app on your computer. These programs and apps are sometimes placed in the Start menu right away, but sometimes they do not appear in the Start menu.

You can easily add tiles for programs and apps that are not displayed in the Start menu. One example of such a program is *WordPad*. You can practice adding a new tile to the Start menu for that program. Here is how you do it:

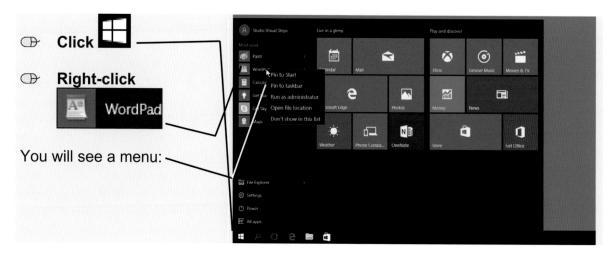

☞ **Click** ⊞

☞ **Right-click**

WordPad

You will see a menu:

HELP! I do not see .

If you do not see the *WordPad* button, this is what you do:

Click 🔍

Type: wordpad

Right-click
WordPad
Desktop app

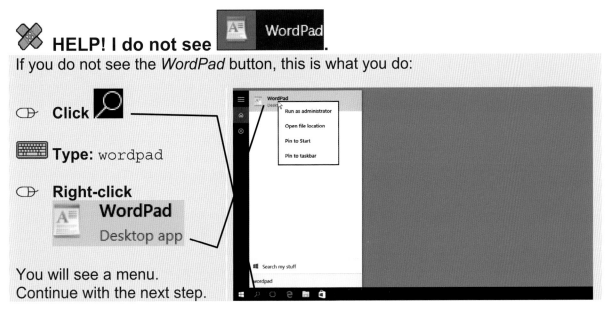

You will see a menu.
Continue with the next step.

Add *WordPad* to the Start menu:

Click Pin to Start

Notice that you can also attach the program or app to the taskbar.

This way, you can easily and quickly open frequently used programs and apps right from the taskbar.

WordPad has now been added to the Start menu as a new tile. From now on you can open this program right away, by clicking the tile:

7.2 Changing the Size of the Start Menu

If you have just started using *Windows 10*, the Start menu will not be very extensive. In due time, you will probably have more programs and apps. Some of these programs and apps will appear in the Start menu and the number of tiles will gradually increase. You can easily enlarge the Start menu to view more programs and apps at once. You do that like this:

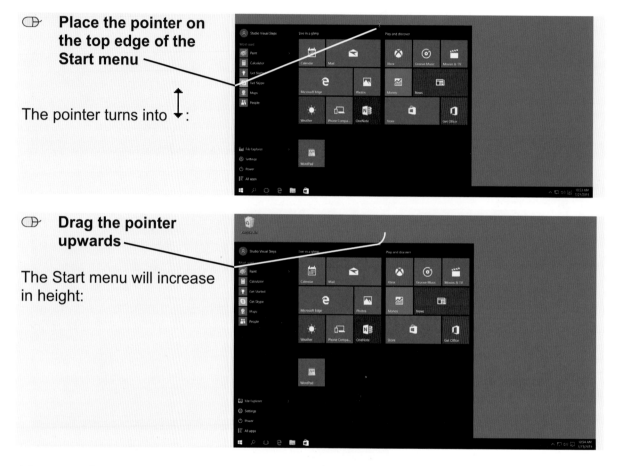

☞ **Place the pointer on the top edge of the Start menu**

The pointer turns into ↕ :

☞ **Drag the pointer upwards**

The Start menu will increase in height:

You can also make the Start menu wider or smaller, if you wish. To do that, place the pointer on the right edge of the Start menu and then drag the pointer to the right or left.

7.3 Moving Tiles and Creating Groups in the Start Menu

You can change the order of the tiles, if you wish, or arrange the tiles in various groups. In the following exercise you will be creating a new group for the *WordPad* and *Mail* tiles:

☞ **Drag the *Mail* tile**

to the right-hand side of the *WordPad* tile

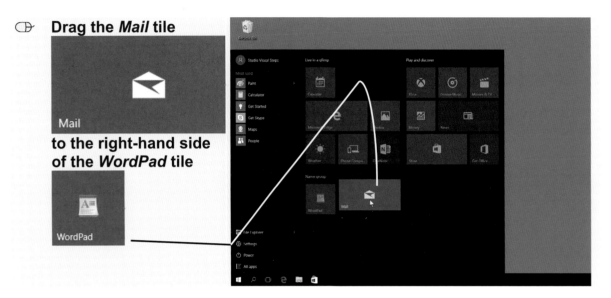

Now these two tiles are joined in a group. You can name this group. In this example, we will call it *Exercise*. You can also choose another name for the group, if you wish. And you do not need to use the same tiles as in this example; you can also add other tiles to the group.

☞ **Click above the two tiles**

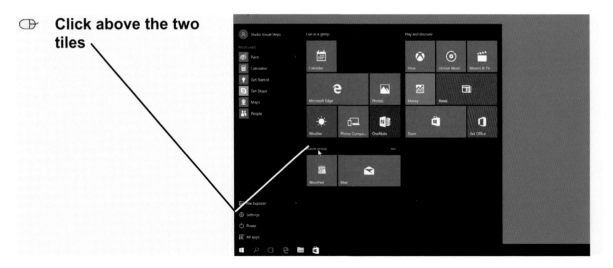

Name the new group, call it *Exercise*:

Type: Exercise ⎯⎯⎯⎯⎯⎯⎯⎯⎯⎯

Press Enter

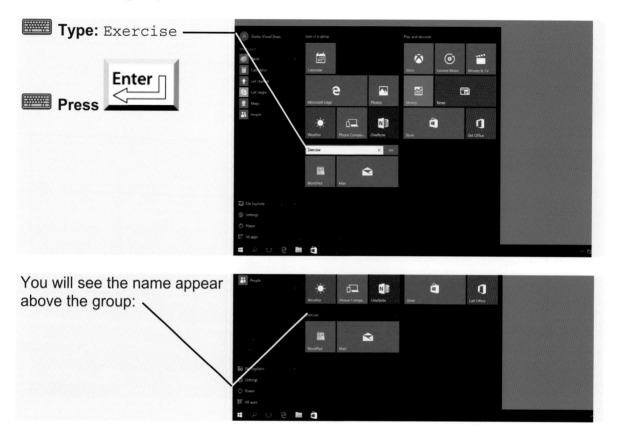

You will see the name appear above the group:

If you want to remove the tiles from the group, you can just drag them out of the group. When all the tiles have been removed from the group, the group name will automatically disappear.

7.4 Settings

If you would like to change any of the desktop or system settings in *Windows 10*, you need to use *Settings* app. You can open the *Settings* app from the Start menu:

☞ **If necessary, click** ⊞

☞ **Click**

The *Settings* window will be opened:

The window is filled with all sorts of subjects, arranged by category:

Each category is indicated by an icon:

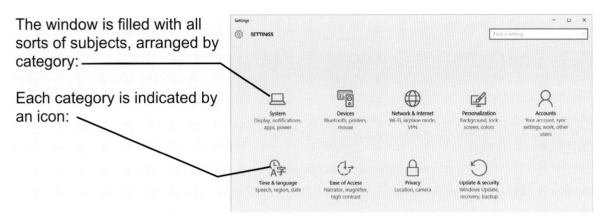

You can open the window for a particular category by clicking its icon. In the next section you will be taking a look at *Windows Update*.

7.5 Windows Update

Windows Update is an important component in *Windows*. The main function is to check if you are using the most recent version of *Windows 10*. *Windows 10* is constantly being updated, extended and enhanced. It is of particular importance that you have the latest updates and revisions to the security measures. These additions and improvements are distributed by Microsoft in the form of software updates.

➥ Please note:

Microsoft never sends software updates through email. If you receive an email with an attachment that claims to be Microsoft software, or a *Windows Update*, you should never open the attachment. Delete the email at once, and do not forget to delete this email from the *Deleted items* folder as well. This type of email is sent by criminals who try to install harmful software on your computer.

If you want to be sure that you are using the most recent version of *Windows 10*, you need to check to see if *Automatic updates* is enabled. You do that as follows:

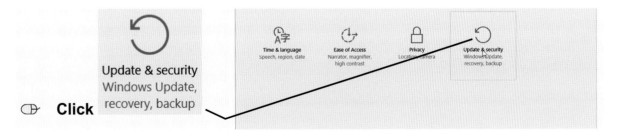

The *Update and Security* window will be opened on the *Windows Update* tab:

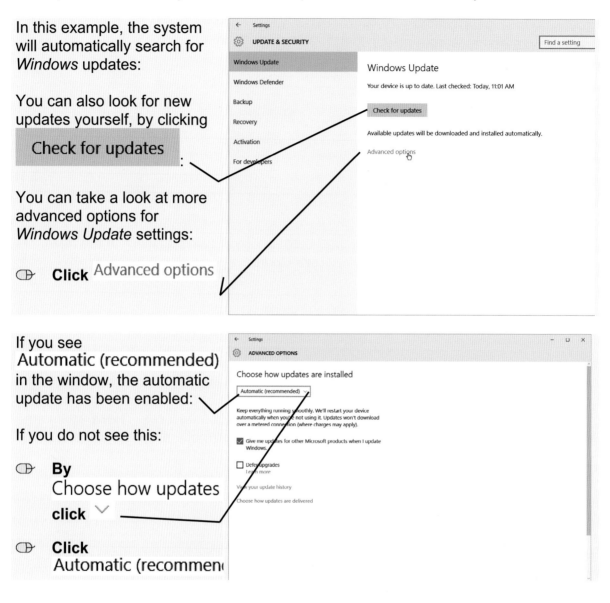

In this example, the system will automatically search for *Windows* updates:

You can also look for new updates yourself, by clicking

Check for updates
:

You can take a look at more advanced options for *Windows Update* settings:

⊕ **Click** Advanced options

If you see Automatic (recommended) in the window, the automatic update has been enabled:

If you do not see this:

⊕ **By** Choose how updates **click** ⌄

⊕ **Click** Automatic (recommen

You can also enable the installation of updates for other Microsoft programs, if desired:

If you do not see a
checkmark ✅ by
Give me updates for other Micr
Windows.

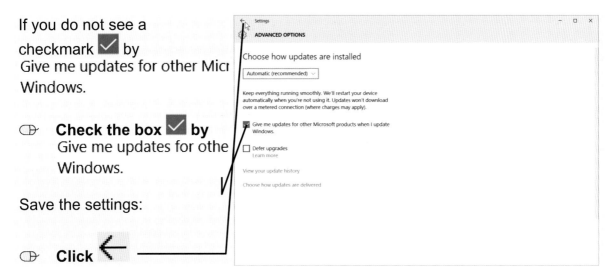

☞ **Check the box ✅ by**
    Give me updates for othe
    Windows.

Save the settings:

☞ **Click ←**

In the *Update and Security* window:

☞ **Click ←**

Now the *Windows Update* settings have been saved.

☞ **Close *Settings* 🐾¹**

7.6 Updating Apps

The default setting in *Windows 10* for updates made to apps is for them to be downloaded automatically. However, the updates are not always downloaded immediately. Your computer may also have a different setting for these updates. You can manually search to see if updates for apps are available. You do that like this:

☞ **Open the *Store* 🐾³**

Tip
Open the Store from the taskbar
You can also open the *Store* from the taskbar:

☞ **Click** ⊞ **on the taskbar**

Store will be opened. Here you can update apps, like this:

☞ **Click** 👤

☞ **Click** Settings

Update apps automatically is ⬤ On.

If this is not the case on your computer, you need to drag the slider ⬤:

Open the page where you can check for updates manually:

☞ **Click** 👤

☞ **Click** Downloads

Check for updates:

☞ **Click**
Check for updates

If any updates are found, you will see ⬇ to download the updates. Just click it and follow the instructions in the window, if necessary.

Close the window:

☞ **Close the *Store* window** ᵍᵍ**1**

🢂 **Please note:**
Windows programs will usually receive automatic updates. Programs manufactured by other companies, such as *Picasa* by *Google*, will often have an option in the Help, Extra, or Options menu with which you can check for updates. Some programs will tell you if there are any updates as soon as you open them.

7.7 Creating Multiple Desktops

A new feature in *Windows 10* is the option of creating multiple desktops. In this way you can arrange *Windows* in an orderly manner, for example, by creating separate desktops for private matters and work-related tasks. Also, you can use a program or app on one of the desktops, while it is not opened on the other desktop. This way, you can execute separate tasks. Just take a look at this:

☞ **Open *WordPad*** ᵍᵍ**3**

The *WordPad* window is opened on the desktop. You create a new desktop:

In the bottom left-hand corner of the taskbar:

☞ **Click**

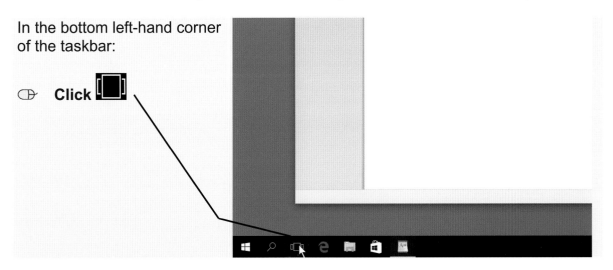

You will see the Task View and are going to create a new desktop:

In the bottom right corner of
the screen:

⊕ **Click** New desktop

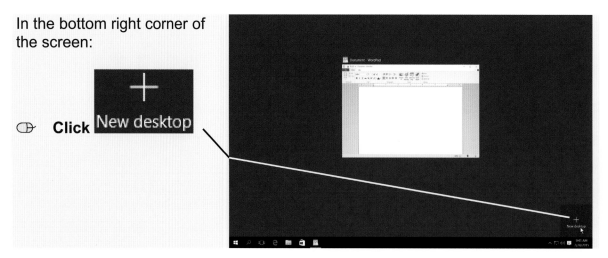

Now there are two desktops:

⊕ **Click**
Desktop 2

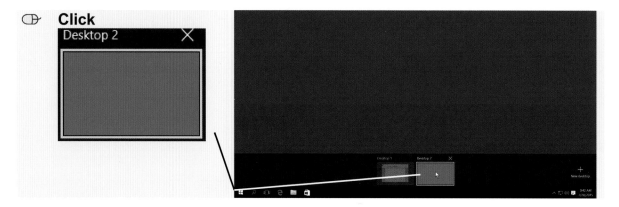

The *WordPad* program is not opened on the second desktop. Here you can open a
second version of *WordPad*, for example, and work on another document.

For now you are going to close the second desktop:

⊕ **Click**

You will see the Task View
and close the second
desktop:

⊕ **Click**

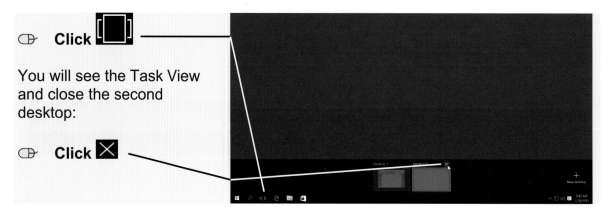

You will see the Task View:

☞ **Click the *WordPad* window**

☞ **Close *WordPad* 🐾¹**

7.8 Changing the Image of the Lock Screen

You can change the image of the lock screen as well:

☞ **Open *Settings* 🐾⁵⁸**

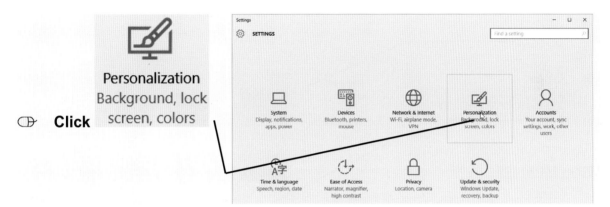

Personalization
Background, lock
☞ **Click** screen, colors

You will see the *Personal Settings* window. Here you can change the image on the lock screen:

On the left-hand side of the
window:

☞ **Click** Lock screen

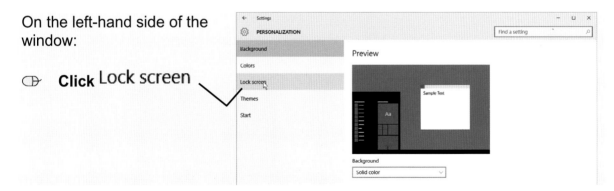

You can select one of the standard images provided by *Windows*. Click the desired image: ─────

Another option is to use one of your own images that you have saved on your computer:

⊕ **Click** [**Browse**]

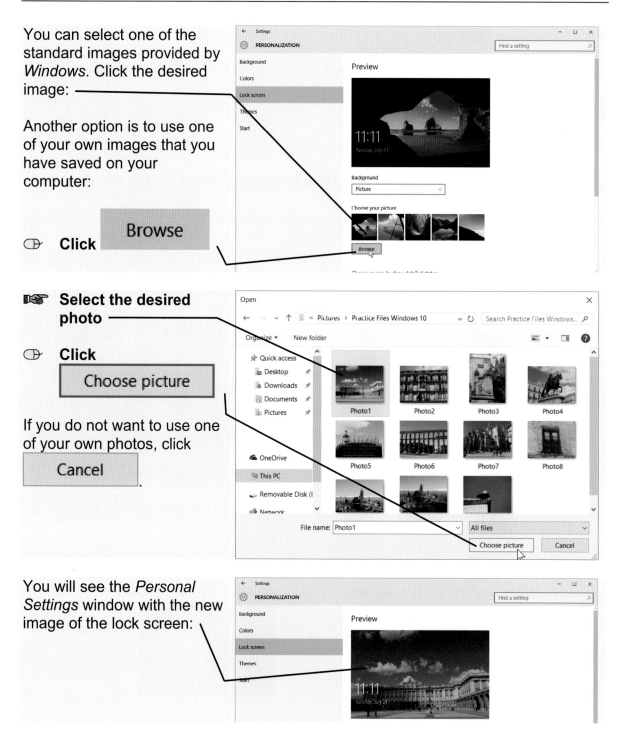

☞ **Select the desired photo** ─────────

⊕ **Click** [**Choose picture**]

If you do not want to use one of your own photos, click [**Cancel**].

You will see the *Personal Settings* window with the new image of the lock screen: ↖

In the next section you will learn how to change the desktop background.

7.9 Changing the Desktop Background

Many people like to use a calm background (also called wallpaper) when they are working on their computer. But if you think your own background is rather dull and want to see something livelier, or you just want something else for a change, you can set a new background. Selecting a different background is very easy. You can change the desktop background by selecting an image or color yourself:

If you want to use an image that comes with the *Windows* system:

In the upper left corner of the window:

☞ **Click** Background

If necessary:

☞ **By** Background **,**
   click ⌄

☞ **Click** Picture

Note that you can also display a slideshow with multiple photos.

☞ **Click the desired image**

If you want to use an image that is already stored on your computer, click

Browse . Then select the desired image, as explained in *section 7.8 Changing the Image of the Lock Screen.*

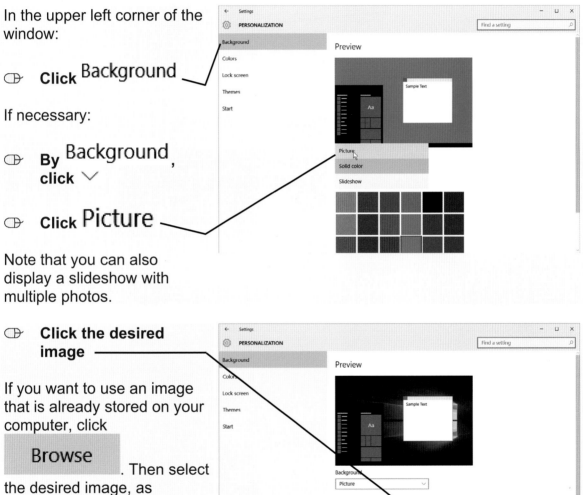

If you prefer not to use an image, but a specific color instead:

☞ **By** Background **,**
   click ⌄ ───────

☞ **Click** Solid color

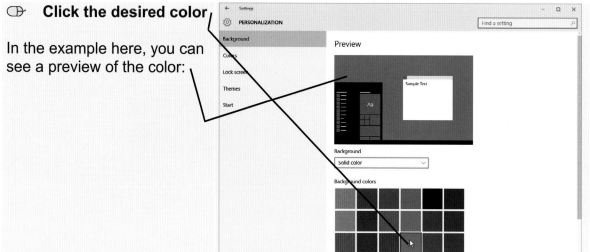

☞ **Click the desired color**

In the example here, you can
see a preview of the color:

In order to save the desktop background and go back to the *Settings* home screen:

In the upper left corner of the
window:

☞ **Click** ⟵ ───────

You will see the new desktop background you have chosen. If on second thought you
are not satisfied with the background, you can repeat the actions in this section.

7.10 Changing the Size of Letters and Icons

If you find it difficult to read letters and icons, you can display them in a larger size. The *Settings* window is still open:

☞ **Click**

System
Display, notifications, apps, power

You will see your display settings:

If you want to display text and other items larger:

☞ **Drag the slider to the right**

To apply the change:

☞ **Click** **Apply**

If you want to permanently change the font size, you need to sign off:

☞ **Click** **Sign out now**

You will be logged off.

☞ **Sign on** &2

Notice that the size of the text and other items on the desktop have been adjusted.

7.11 Setting up a Screen Saver

If you have not used your computer for a while, you may see an animated image on your screen. This is known as a *screen saver*. You can set your own screen saver in *Windows*.

☞ **If necessary, open *Settings* &⁹⁸58**

If certain topics are not displayed in the *Settings* window, you can find them easily by using the search box in the *Settings* window. Search for a screen saver:

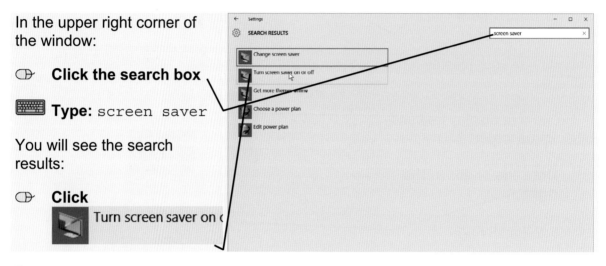

In the upper right corner of the window:

☞ **Click the search box**

⌨ **Type:** screen saver

You will see the search results:

☞ **Click**

 Turn screen saver on c

💡 **Tip**

The search box in Settings
If you want to know more about a specific setting, or want to change a setting, but cannot find it in *Settings*, you need to use the search box in the top right-hand corner of the window.

A new window is opened. In order to set up a screen saver:

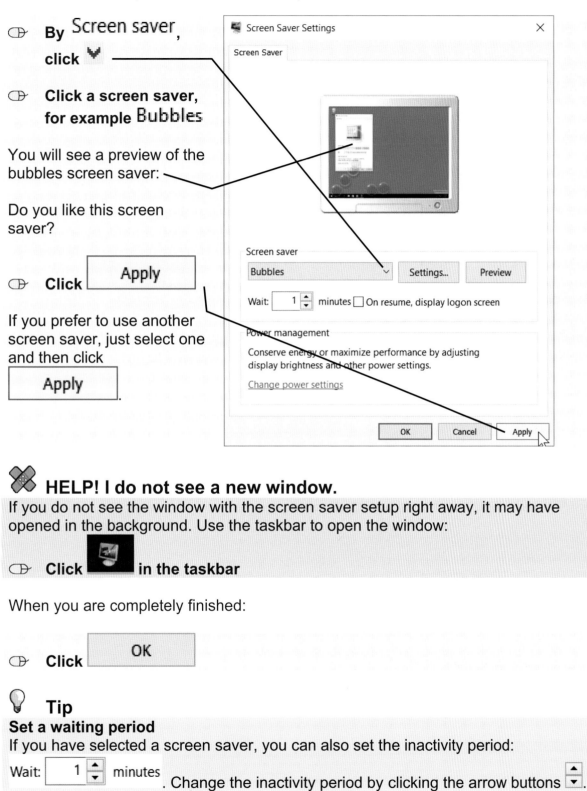

- **By** Screen saver,
  click ⌄

- **Click a screen saver,**
  for example Bubbles

You will see a preview of the
bubbles screen saver:

Do you like this screen
saver?

- **Click** Apply

If you prefer to use another
screen saver, just select one
and then click

Apply
.

HELP! I do not see a new window.

If you do not see the window with the screen saver setup right away, it may have
opened in the background. Use the taskbar to open the window:

- **Click** [icon] **in the taskbar**

When you are completely finished:

- **Click** OK

Tip

Set a waiting period

If you have selected a screen saver, you can also set the inactivity period:

Wait: 1 minutes . Change the inactivity period by clicking the arrow buttons ⏶⏷.

⬤ **Tip**
Screen saver with photos
If you have some nice pictures on your computer, you can use them as a screen saver. By Screen saver, select the Photos option. Next, you click
Settings... . Now you can choose the desired settings in the window that appears. In this case, you are actually using the screen saver as a slideshow. The slideshow will start after a period of time of inactivity.

7.12 Adjusting the Power Scheme

The *Windows* power scheme is a collection of settings that manage the energy usage of your computer. Sometimes it can be useful to take a closer look at the power scheme. For example, if you think your screen turns dark too soon or if you have a laptop that goes into sleep mode when left idle for just a few seconds.

Take a brief look at the power scheme of your computer.

System
Display, notifications,
☞ **Click**   apps, power

You will see the *System* window:

☞ **Click** Power & sleep

You can view more
extensive energy settings:

☞ **Click**
Additional power settings

Windows contains the following default power schemes that will help you manage the energy usage of your computer:

- **Balanced (recommended)** : This scheme ensures full performance when necessary, and saves energy when the computer is not used for a while.
- Power saver : This scheme saves more energy, compared to the option above. The computer and the monitor can be disabled or switched to sleep mode earlier.
- High performance : This scheme ensures optimum performance. Laptop users will notice that their battery depletes faster if they use this scheme.

Your own computer may have other schemes available that have been given by the computer manufacturer.

By **Balanced (recomme** click Change plan settings

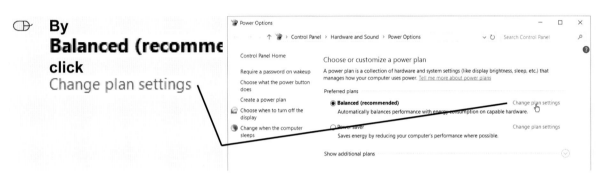

If the performance of your desktop computer or laptop is satisfactory, you do not need to change these settings. In that case, you can just read through this section. But if you are not satisfied, for instance, because your screen turns dark too soon, or your laptop goes into sleep mode too quickly, you can adjust the settings. Desktop computer users will see the following settings.
You can change the settings by selecting a different period of time by

Turn off the display: and Put the computer to sleep:.

When you have finished changing the settings:

Click Save changes

If you do not want to change anything, click Cancel .

Laptop users will also see settings for On battery and Plugged in . You can change these too, if you wish.

HELP! I cannot change the power scheme.
If your computer is part of a company or organizational network, such as a school or a business, the systems administrator may have disabled or even removed some components. In that case, you may not be able to adjust the power scheme.

☞ **Close the *Power Options* window** ℘1

☞ **Close *Settings*** ℘1

♡ Tip
How do I wake up my computer from sleep mode?
The sleep mode saves energy. Before the computer goes into sleep mode, all the open documents, programs and apps are saved. The computer can be taken out of sleep mode very quickly (usually within a few seconds) and you can resume working. Enabling the sleep mode can be compared to the pause play function on a DVD player. The computer immediately stops all operations and starts them up again so you can continue working where you left off.

Most computers can be woken up from sleep mode by pressing the power switch of the device. However, computers may differ in this respect. You might also need to press a key, click the mouse, or open the cover of a laptop or notebook, in order to disable the sleep mode.

☞ **Read the documentation or manual that came with your computer**

There you will find more information on this subject.

In this section you have learned how to customize the settings of your computer's *Power Plan*. Not satisfied about a particular setting? You can always go back to the original settings. Just follow this section and restore the default settings.

7.13 Notification Window

If you are using *Windows 10*, you will regularly see notifications displayed in the bottom right-hand corner of the screen. These are messages sent by *Windows* and other programs, for example, concerning updates or any problems.

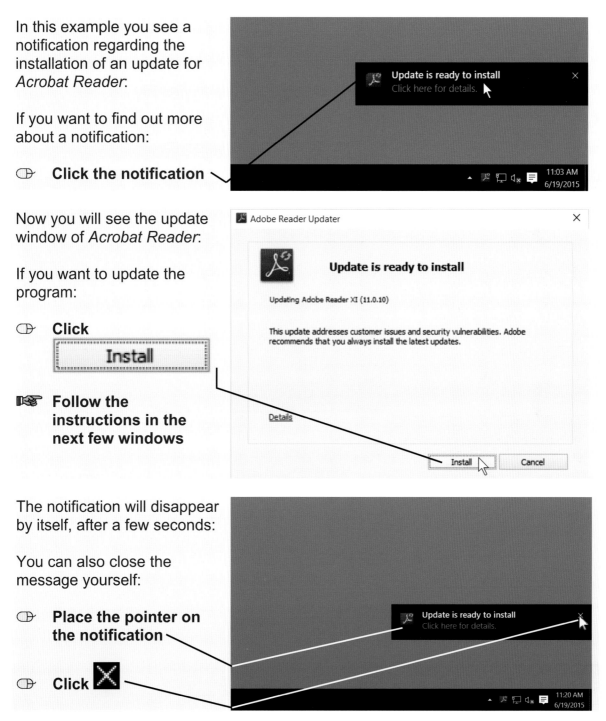

In this example you see a notification regarding the installation of an update for *Acrobat Reader*:

If you want to find out more about a notification:

☞ **Click the notification**

Now you will see the update window of *Acrobat Reader*:

If you want to update the program:

☞ **Click** Install

☞ **Follow the instructions in the next few windows**

The notification will disappear by itself, after a few seconds:

You can also close the message yourself:

☞ **Place the pointer on the notification**

☞ **Click** ✖

Besides separate notifications on the screen, you can also view a summary of all the notifications in the *Notification center*:

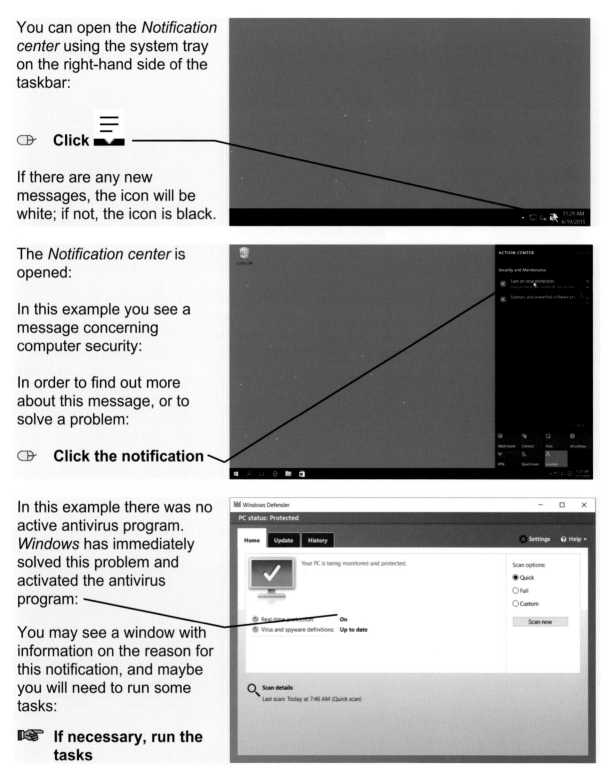

You can open the *Notification center* using the system tray on the right-hand side of the taskbar:

☞ **Click**

If there are any new messages, the icon will be white; if not, the icon is black.

The *Notification center* is opened:

In this example you see a message concerning computer security:

In order to find out more about this message, or to solve a problem:

☞ **Click the notification**

In this example there was no active antivirus program. *Windows* has immediately solved this problem and activated the antivirus program:

You may see a window with information on the reason for this notification, and maybe you will need to run some tasks:

☞ **If necessary, run the tasks**

☞ **Close the window** **1**

Once you have seen a notification, it will no longer be regarded as new, and the icon

in the *Notification* window will be black ▆. You will open the *Notification* window again:

⊕ **Click** ▆

The previous notification has been removed:

There are some more buttons at the bottom, and among them is a button that directly opens *Settings*. You will probably not use this button very soon.

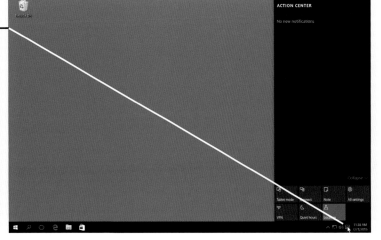

7.14 Security and Maintenance

In the *Security and Maintenance* window you check the security settings of your computer in *Windows 10*. You can also see your computer's maintenance status in this window, and solve any computer problems. This is how you open the window:

☞ **Open *Settings*** 🦶**58**

⊕ **Click the search box**

⌨ **Type:** security

⊕ **Click**
     Security and Mainter

You will see the *Security and Maintenance* window in the *Control Panel*:

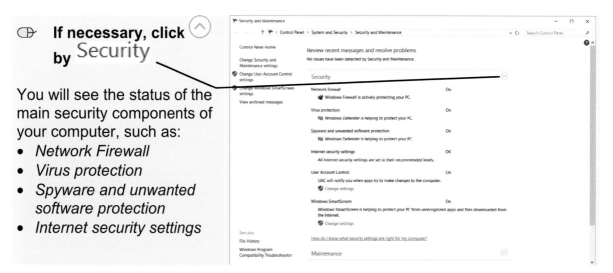

☞   **If necessary, click** ⌃
     by Security

You will see the status of the
main security components of
your computer, such as:
- *Network Firewall*
- *Virus protection*
- *Spyware and unwanted
  software protection*
- *Internet security settings*

You will see at a glance what the current problems are on your computer. In the
window displayed above, all the items are turned on. The window on your own
screen may look different. The settings on your computer may differ from the settings
in this example.

7.15 Windows Firewall

A *firewall* is software or hardware that regulates the incoming and outgoing data
traffic from your computer to and from the Internet and/or other networks. Depending
on your firewall settings, data traffic will be blocked or allowed.
The word firewall sounds a lot safer than it actually is. A firewall does not protect your
computer against viruses. If your email program is allowed to connect to the Internet
by the firewall, you may still receive an email with an attachment containing a virus.
The firewall does not check the content of the data that are transferred.

In the top left-hand corner of
the window:

☞   **Click**
     Control Panel Home

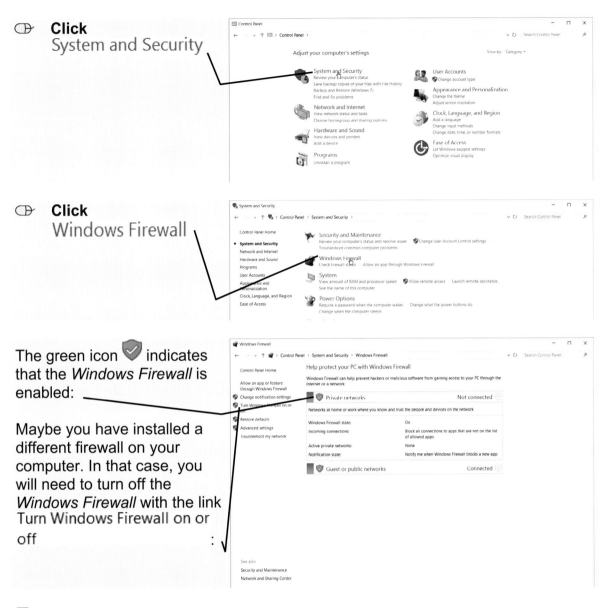

⊕ **Click**
   System and Security

⊕ **Click**
   Windows Firewall

The green icon ⬤ indicates that the *Windows Firewall* is enabled:

Maybe you have installed a different firewall on your computer. In that case, you will need to turn off the *Windows Firewall* with the link Turn Windows Firewall on or off :

➥ **Please note:**

The simultaneous use of two or more firewalls will cause conflicts. In many cases, using the Internet will become much slower, or even impossible.

☞ **Close the window** ✂¹

7.16 Virus Protection with Windows Defender

A virus is a well-known term, but in fact, viruses are just one type of the increasing threats to every computer that connects to the Internet. The general term for this is *malware*. Malware is short for *malicious software*. This is software that is specifically developed to damage your computer. Viruses, worms, spyware, and Trojan horses are all types of unwanted software.

The source of an infection may be an attachment to an email, or a program you have downloaded. Your computer can also be infected when you exchange data through USB sticks that are infected with malware, or CDs, DVDs, or other storage media. Some of the malware programs are designed to be executed at unexpected moments, and not just during installation.

Windows Defender is included in the *Windows 10* software package, and helps protect the computer against malware, in two ways:

- **Real-time protection**
  With *Windows Defender* you will be warned when malicious software tries to install itself, or is installed to your computer. You will also be warned in case any apps try to change major settings.
- **Scan**
  With *Windows Defender* you can scan your computer whenever you want. For example, in case your computer does not work properly, or if you have received a suspicious-looking email. Run a scan in order to check whether you have unintentionally downloaded any malware.

Open *Windows Defender*:

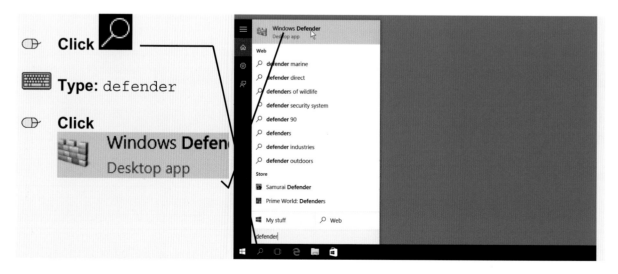

The home window of *Windows Defender* appears:

By default, *Windows Defender* is enabled:

Real-time protection: is **On**:

In this example, a quick scan has previously been executed:

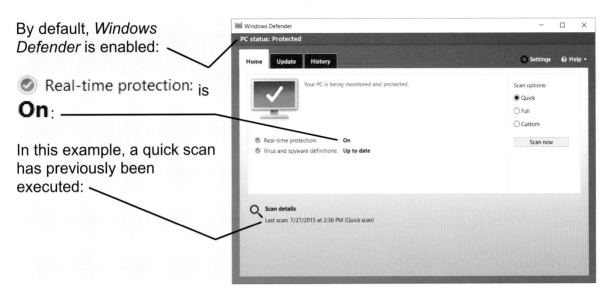

Windows Defender closely cooperates with *Windows Update*. As soon as new spyware and malware definitions are available, these will automatically be downloaded and installed. In this way, the program can always dispose of the most recent information. By default, there is an extra check before a scan is executed. You can also update *Windows Defender* yourself:

☞ **Click the**

Update tab

Here you see the most recent update of the definitions:

This is how you check for new definitions:

☞ **Click**

Update

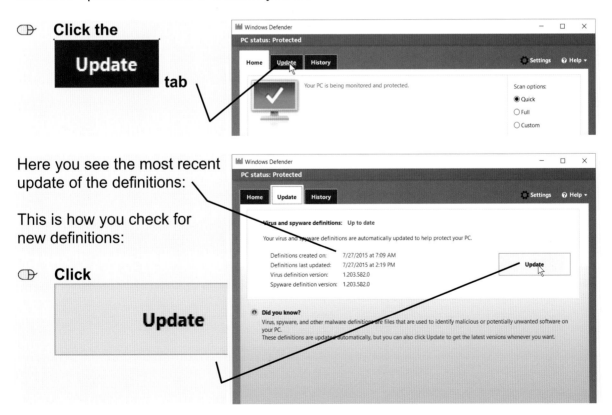

If any new definitions have been found, *Windows Defender* will be updated at once:

In this example you see the progress of the installation process of the new definitions:

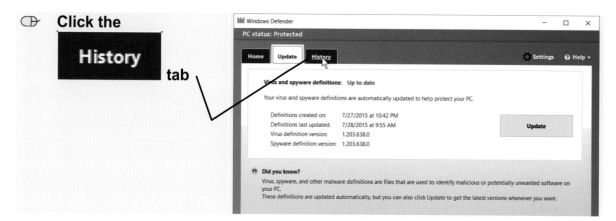

7.17 The Real-time Protection Function of Windows Defender

The real-time protection function of *Windows Defender* immediately warns you in case malware or spyware tries to install itself on your computer.

As soon as *Windows Defender* detects harmful software, you will see a message such as this one in the bottom right-hand corner of the screen:

Malware Detected
Windows Defender is taking action to clean detected malware.

The harmful software will immediately be placed in quarantine, to prevent it from being executed. You can take a look at it later on, and decide if you want to delete or restore the item in question. This is how you do it:

☞ **Click the**

History tab

In order to protect the privacy of the user, you will not immediately see which items have been placed in quarantine:

☞ **Click**

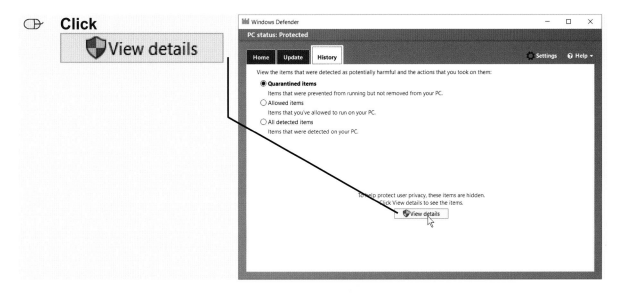

You will see an overview of the items that have automatically been placed in quarantine. You can read more about quarantine in the next section. The list on your computer may be empty.

You will see an overview of the items that have automatically been placed in quarantine. You can read more about quarantine in the next section. The list on your computer may be empty.
If you see an item you know to be harmful, you can check the box by this item and use the button to restore it:

Remove all:

☞ **Click**

All harmful software has been deleted.

7.18 Scanning Your Computer with Windows Defender

You can scan your computer with *Windows Defender* any time you want. For example, in case your computer does not work properly, or if you have received a suspicious-looking email. In order to be sure that your computer has not been infected by a virus or other unwanted software, you can run a scan on your computer.

You can choose between three types of scans:

- Quick: only scans the locations where unwanted software is regularly found.
- Full: scans all the files and folders on your computer.
- Custom: only scans the folders you have selected.

In order to get an idea of how a scan works, you are going to execute a quick scan.

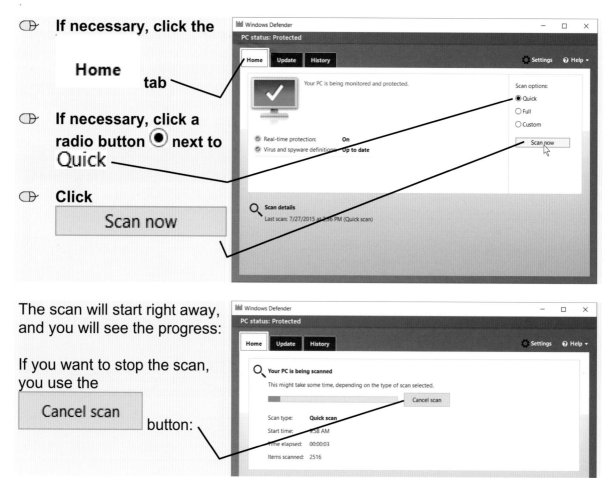

☐➤ **If necessary, click the**

   Home tab

☐➤ **If necessary, click a radio button ⦿ next to** Quick

☐➤ **Click** Scan now

The scan will start right away, and you will see the progress:

If you want to stop the scan, you use the Cancel scan button:

A full scan may take up to an hour or longer, depending on the speed of your computer and the number of files. The quick scan is much faster.

After the scan has finished, you will see a scan report:

In this example, no suspect files have been found:

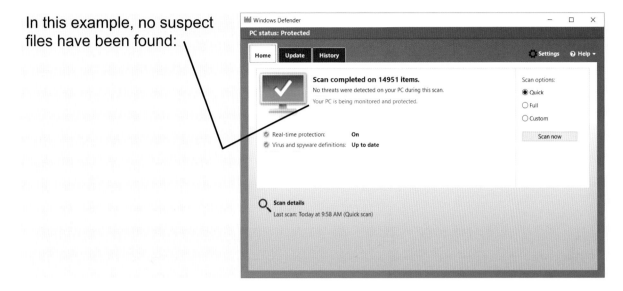

If you do not open unknown email attachments, or use suspect programs, there is only a small chance of unwanted programs entering your computer. Nevertheless, *Windows Defender* will surely find a suspect file, every now and then.

If anything has been found, you will see a message. You will see a description of the malicious software, the seriousness of the threat, and the action recommended by *Windows Defender*. Here there are various options:

- **Remove** : the infected file or virus will be removed from your computer. This means the content of the file will be lost if you have not made a backup copy. This is usually the course of action if there is no other solution for the problem.
- **Quarantine** : the item will be moved to a folder where it can do no harm. If you appear to be needing this item later on, you can restore it. Select this option if you are not sure about an item.
- **Allow** : the item will not be detected in future scans. Select this options if you know the item and are sure you want to keep it.

If no suspect files have been found on your computer, then just read through the next part of this section.

If a harmful program has been found, you will see this message:

You can view the details:

☞ **Click** Show details

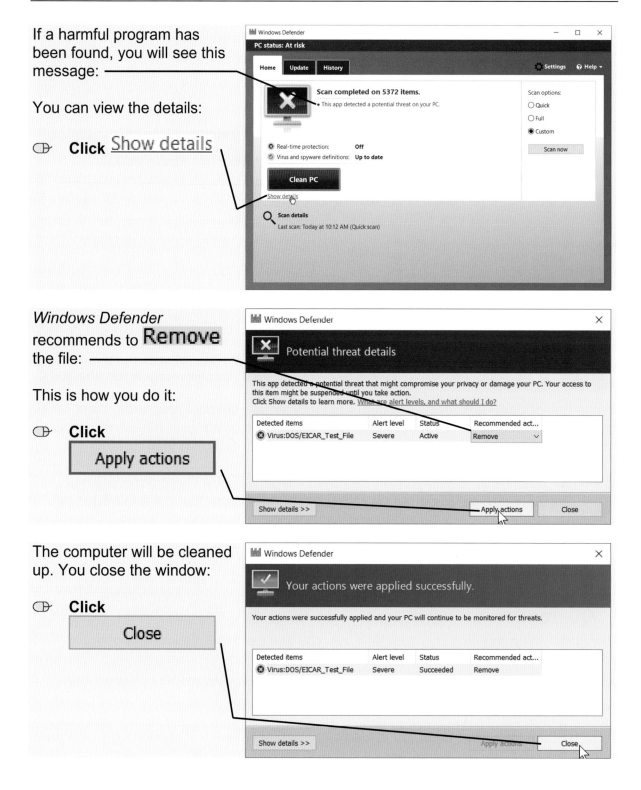

Windows Defender recommends to **Remove** the file:

This is how you do it:

☞ **Click**

Apply actions

The computer will be cleaned up. You close the window:

☞ **Click**

Close

You have learned a number of the options of this program. Close *Windows Defender.*

☞ **Close** *Windows Defender* ᐉᐉ**1**

💡 Tip
Create regular backups
Your computer is full of files that are important to you, such as precious photos, emails from relatives and friends, important documents, the addresses of your favorite websites, and the addresses of your contacts. Do not even think about what it would mean, if you were to lose all the files, or even part of them due to a virus or some other computer problem? That is why you need to create a backup on a regular basis!
In a follow-up book on *Windows 10* you will find more information on this subject.

You have almost reached the end of this chapter and you have seen that you can adjust various settings that will make using the computer easier for you. You have also learned how to keep your *Windows 10* computer up-to-date, check the security settings, and scan your computer for viruses and spyware.

This chapter does not contain any extra exercises. If you wish, you can experiment even further with the settings you have learned to adjust in this chapter. In the next section you will find information about Visual Steps and some follow-up titles.

💡 Tip
Bonus chapters
On the website accompanied to this book **www.visualsteps.com/windows10** you will find some bonus chapters. One of them is about downloading apps in the *Store*.

7.19 Visual Steps Website, Newsletter and Follow-Up Books

By now we hope you have noticed that the Visual Steps method is an excellent method for quickly and efficiently learning more about computers, tablets, other devices and software applications. All books published by Visual Steps use this same method.
In various series, we have published a large number of books on a wide variety of topics including *Windows*, *Mac OS X*, the iPad, iPhone, Samsung Galaxy Tab, Kindle, photo editing and many other topics.

On the **www.visualsteps.com** website you will find a full product summary by clicking the blue *Catalog* button. For each book there is an extensive description, the full table of contents and a sample chapter (PDF file). In this way, you can quickly determine if a specific title will meet your expectations. You can order a book directly online from this website or other online book retailers. All titles are also available in bookstores in the USA, Canada, United Kingdom, Australia and New Zealand.

Furthermore, the website offers many extras, among other things:
- free computer guides and booklets (PDF files) covering all sorts of subjects;
- frequently asked questions and their answers;
- information on the free Computer Certificate that you can acquire at the certificate's website **www.ccforseniors.com**;
- a free email notification service: let's you know when a new book is published.

There is always more to learn. Visual Steps offers many other books on computer-related subjects. Each Visual Steps book has been written using the same step-by-step method with short, concise instructions and screenshots illustrating every step.

Would you like to be informed when a new Visual Steps title becomes available? Subscribe to the free Visual Steps newsletter (no strings attached) and you will receive this information in your inbox.
The Newsletter is sent approximately each month and includes information about
- the latest titles;
- supplemental information concerning titles previously released;
- new free computer booklets and guides;
When you subscribe to our Newsletter you will have direct access to the free booklets on the **www.visualsteps.com/info_downloads.php** web page.

Photo Editing on the iPad for SENIORS
ISBN 978 90 5905 731 9

Topics covered in this title:

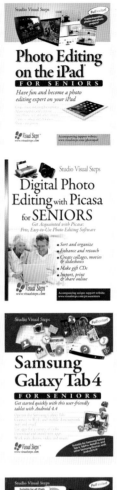

• crop, rotate and straighten photos • adjust exposure and contrast
• add effects, text and other objects • create a collage and
slideshow • share your photos

Digital Photo Editing with Picasa for Seniors
ISBN 978 90 5905 368 7

Topics covered in this title:

• sort and organize photos into albums • enhance and retouch
photos • create collages and make gift CDs • create movies and
slideshows • print and share photos online • import photos

Samsung Galaxy Tab 4 for Seniors
ISBN 978 90 5905 240 6

Topics covered in this title:

• operate the Samsung Galaxy Tab 4 • connect to Wi-Fi and
mobile data networks • surf and email • use apps for a variety of
tasks • download and install new apps • work with photos, video
and music

iPad with iOS 9 and higher for Seniors
ISBN 978 90 5905 681 7

Topics covered in this title:

• navigate the screens • connect to a Wi-Fi or 3/4G network • surf
the Internet and use email • use built-in applications • download
apps from the App Store • work with photos, video and music
• use Facebook, Twitter and Skype

For more information on these books and many others, click **www.visualsteps.com**

7.20 Background Information

Dictionary

Control Panel	In the *Control Panel*, you can change all sorts of computer settings. In *Windows 10* this function is mostly replaced by *Settings*.
Custom scan	An option in *Windows Defender* that only scans the folders you have selected.
Desktop background	The desktop background is the area you work in on your computer. You can select one of the backgrounds that come with *Windows*, use a digital photo from you own collection, or set a plain, single-color background.
Firewall	Software or hardware that contributes to the security of a computer. A firewall can block or allow data traffic to or from your computer.
Full scan	An option in *Windows Defender* that scans all the files and folders on your computer.
Malware	Short for *malicious software*. This is unwanted software that has been developed in order to damage a computer, such as viruses and spyware.
Power scheme	A power scheme or plan is a group of hardware and system settings that are used to manage the power usage of your computer. Power plans can help you save energy, enhance system performance or maintain a balance between these two functions.
Quick scan	An option in *Windows Defender*. By executing this scan, the system will only scan the locations that often contain unwanted software.
Real-time protection	This function makes sure that *Windows Defender* constantly watches all the activities while you are surfing the Internet. Attempts to install malware on your computer, will be blocked.

- Continue on the next page -

Screen saver	An animated image or pattern that is displayed on the screen when the mouse or keyboard have not been used for a certain period of time. *Windows 10* offers a number of different screen savers.
Security and maintenance window	A window that shows the checked computer security settings and the *Windows updates*.
Settings	In *Settings* you can change all sorts of settings for your computer.
Sleep mode	The sleep mode is intended to save energy. Before the sleep mode is enabled, all open documents, programs and apps are saved in the computer's memory. The computer can restore itself quickly (waking out of sleep mode usually within a few seconds) so you can resume working.
Spyware	Software that can display adverts (such as pop-up adverts), collect information on you as a user, or change settings on your computer, without asking you for permission.
Virus	A program that tries to spread itself from one computer to another, and causes damage (by deleting or damaging data), or annoys users (by displaying messages or altering information that is displayed on the screen).
Windows Defender	A complete solution for your Internet security, included in *Windows 10*. The program will protect your computer against all sorts of malware, such as viruses and spyware.
Windows Update	A system that checks whether you are using the most recent version of *Windows 10*.
Worm	A program that copies itself, just like a virus. A malicious user can use a worm to take over your computer, for example.

Source: Windows Help, Wikipedia

7.21 Tips

⚟ Tip

Search for settings using the search function on the taskbar
You can very easily find settings by using the search function on the taskbar. You do that like this:

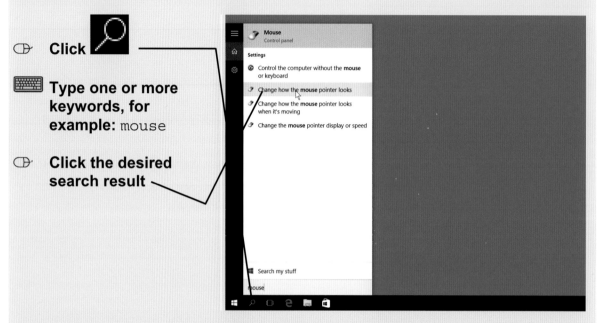

☞ **Click**

⌨ **Type one or more keywords, for example:** `mouse`

☞ **Click the desired search result**

The corresponding window will be opened.

⚟ Tip

Other antivirus programs
Windows Defender is integrated within *Windows 10* and offers real-time protection against viruses, spyware, and other malicious software. Of course, there are lots of other good antivirus programs on the market.
The best-known programs are *Norton* and *McAfee.* But less well-known programs such as *Norman*, *Avira*, or *AVG* also do a good job. The manufacturers of these programs often offer free demo versions for a limited period of time, such as fifteen, thirty, or sixty days. Visit these websites for more information:

- *McAfee*: www.mcafee.com
- *Norton*: www.symantec.com
- *Norman*: www.norman.com
- *Avira*: www.avira.com
- *AVG*: www.avg.com

💡 Tip

Setting up the mouse

You can change various settings for the mouse and the pointer. You do this through the *Settings* app:

☞ **Open *Settings*** 👣⁵⁸

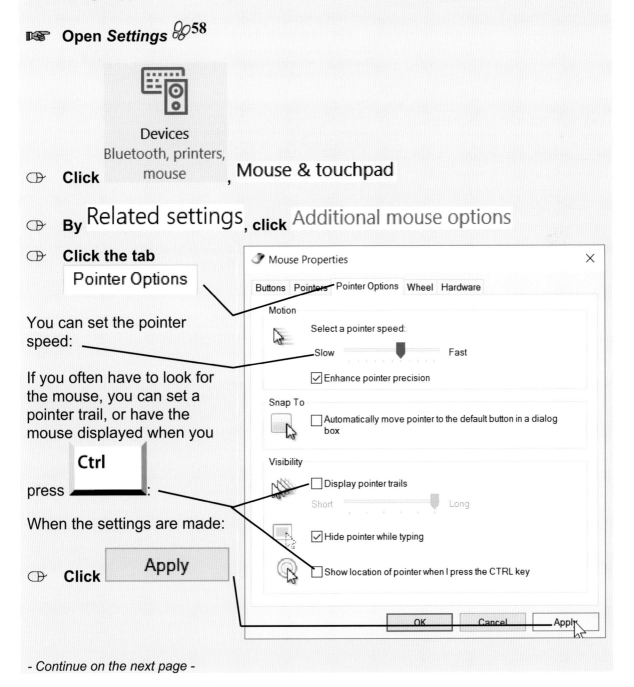

Devices
Bluetooth, printers,
⊕ **Click**   mouse   , Mouse & touchpad

⊕ **By** Related settings, **click** Additional mouse options

⊕ **Click the tab**
   Pointer Options

You can set the pointer
speed:

If you often have to look for
the mouse, you can set a
pointer trail, or have the
mouse displayed when you

Ctrl

press   :

When the settings are made:

⊕ **Click**   Apply

- Continue on the next page -

You can also set the double-click speed:

⊕ **Click the** Buttons **tab**

Mouse Properties ✕

Buttons | Pointers | Pointer Options | Wheel | Hardware

Button configuration

☐ Switch primary and secondary buttons

Select this check box to make the button on the right
the one you use for primary functions such as
selecting and dragging.

By moving the slider you can
set the double-click speed:

Are you left-handed? Then
swap the functions of the left
and right mouse buttons:

Double-click speed

Double-click the folder to test your setting. If the folder
does not open or close, try using a slower setting.

Speed: Slow ━━━━━━━▼━━━━━ Fast

Please note: from now on
you need to use the *left
mouse button* when you see
the instruction *Right-click*.

ClickLock

☐ Turn on ClickLock   Settings...

Enables you to highlight or drag without holding down the mouse button.
To set, briefly press the mouse button. To release, click the mouse button
again.

When the settings are made:

⊕ **Click** Apply

OK   Cancel   Apply

On the Pointers tab you can also set the size and shape of the pointer. If you

want to use a bigger pointer ↖ , you select
Windows Standard (extra large) (system scheme). You can also select a black

pointer ▲, if you wish.

After you have finished adjusting all the mouse settings:

⊕ **Click** OK

💡 Tip

Set up the search function

The search function may be set up as a button, or as a search box on your computer. This is how you change it:

☞ **Right-click the taskbar**

☞ **Place the pointer on Search**

☞ **Click the desired option**

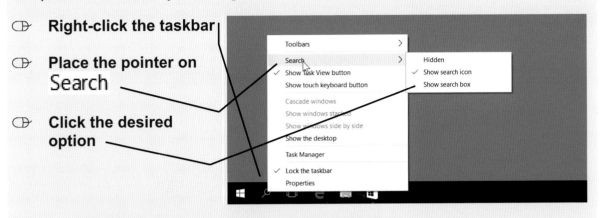

It is also possible to search the Internet through the search function. If this option has not yet been enabled, you can enable it like this:

☞ **Click** 🔍

☞ **Click** ⚙

☞ **By Search online and i**
click ⬛

You will see more options, such as the Bing safety setting, among others. Bing is the name of the search engine that is used.

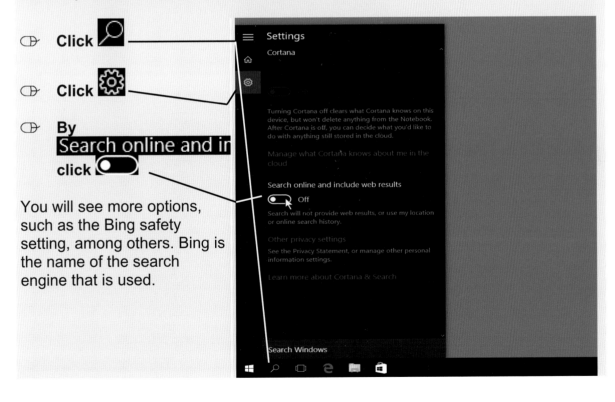

⚬ Tip

Turn live tiles on or off
In the Start menu you will see some tiles with an image that keeps changing all the time. These are Live tiles that display current information, for example, the weather, or news items. You can turn the information on these Live tiles on and off.
This is how you turn on a Live tile:

☞   **Right-click a tile**

☞   **Click**
     Turn live tile on

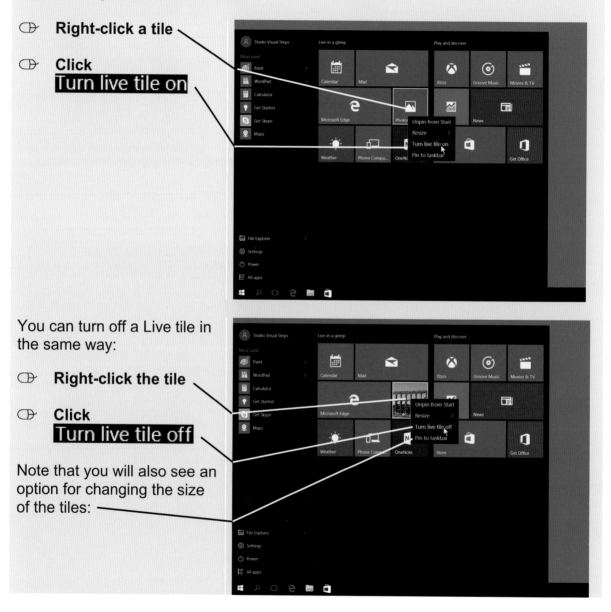

You can turn off a Live tile in the same way:

☞   **Right-click the tile**

☞   **Click**
     Turn live tile off

Note that you will also see an option for changing the size of the tiles: ─

Appendix A. How Do I Do That Again?

The actions and exercises in this book are marked with footsteps: 🐾1
In this appendix you can look up the numbers of the footsteps and read how to execute certain operations.

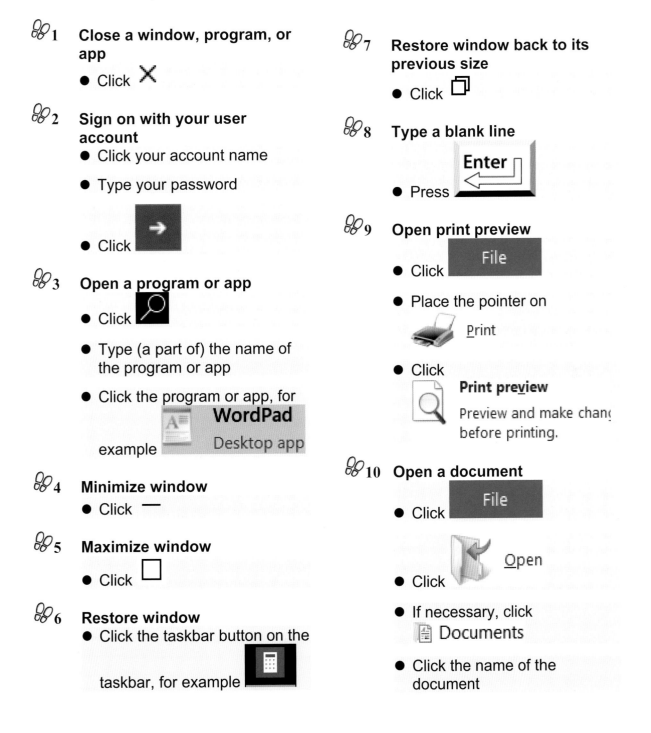

🐾1 **Close a window, program, or app**
- Click ✕

🐾2 **Sign on with your user account**
- Click your account name
- Type your password
- Click →

🐾3 **Open a program or app**
- Click 🔍
- Type (a part of) the name of the program or app
- Click the program or app, for example **WordPad** Desktop app

🐾4 **Minimize window**
- Click —

🐾5 **Maximize window**
- Click ☐

🐾6 **Restore window**
- Click the taskbar button on the taskbar, for example 🖩

🐾7 **Restore window back to its previous size**
- Click ❐

🐾8 **Type a blank line**
- Press Enter ↵

🐾9 **Open print preview**
- Click File
- Place the pointer on 🖨 Print
- Click 🔍 **Print preview** Preview and make chan(before printing.

🐾10 **Open a document**
- Click File
- Click 📂 Open
- If necessary, click 📄 Documents
- Click the name of the document

- Click [**Open**]

11 Select text
Select a word:
- Double-click the word

Select multiple words:
- Click in front of the first word

- Drag the mouse over the words

Or:
- Click in front of the first word

- Move the cursor with the arrow key (right arrow)

12 Close *WordPad*
- Click ✕

Save a document:
- Click [**Save**]

If the document has not been previously saved:
- If necessary, select the desired folder

- By **File name:**, type the desired file name

- Click [**Save**]

Do not save the document:
- Click [Don't Save]

13 Save a document
- Click [File]

- Click 💾 Save

- Type the name of the document next to **File name:**,

- Click [**Save**]

14 Open a folder
In an open folder window:
- Double-click the folder

15 Open a folder on a higher level
- Click ↑

16 Open the *letters* folder
- Click the first > in the address bar

- Click your name

- Double-click Documents

- Click letters

17 Open *File Explorer*
On the taskbar:
- Click 🗀

18 Open *Personal folder*
- Click the first > in the address bar

- Click your name

19 Go back to a previous folder or go to the next folder
- Click ← or →

20 Create a new folder
- Click the | Home | tab

- Click folder

New
- Type a name for the folder

- Press **Enter**

21 Copy a file to another folder
- Click the file

- Click Copy

- Double-click the folder

- Click Paste

22 Change the name of a file or folder
- Click the file or folder

- Click Rename

- Type the desired name

- Press **Enter**

23 Open the *Libraries* window
Via the File Explorer address bar:
- Click ›

- Click Libraries

24 Create a new library
- Click ▾

- Click Library

- Type the desired name

- Press **Enter**

25 Include a folder in a library
- Double-click the library

- Click | Include a folder |

- Click the desired folder

- Click | Include folder |

In order to include another folder:
- Click the | Manage | tab

Manage
- Click library

- Click | Add... |

- Click the desired folder

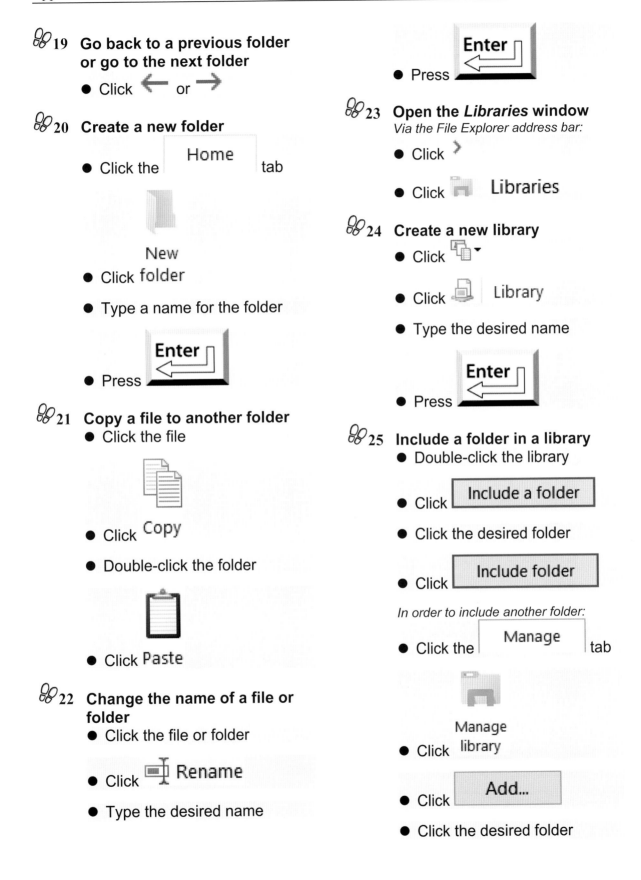

- Click [Include folder]

- Click [OK]

🦶26 Delete a library
- Click the library

- Click the [Home] tab

- Click ✖ Delete

🦶27 Open a web page
- Click the address bar

- Type the web address

- Press [Enter ↵]

🦶28 Add a website to the favorites
- Click ☆

- If necessary, click Favorites ☆

- Click [Add]

🦶29 Open a favorite
- Click ☰

- If necessary, click the ☆ tab

- Click the favorite

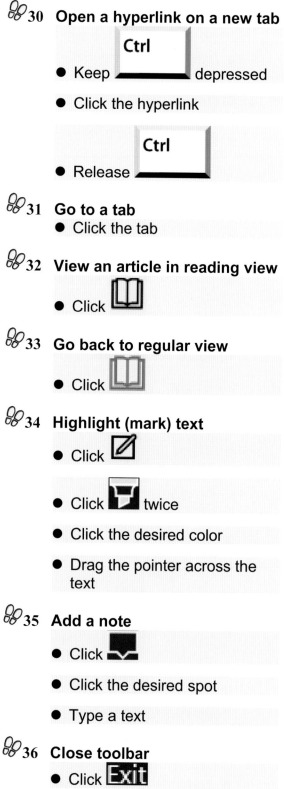

🦶30 Open a hyperlink on a new tab
- Keep [Ctrl] depressed

- Click the hyperlink

- Release [Ctrl]

🦶31 Go to a tab
- Click the tab

🦶32 View an article in reading view
- Click 📖

🦶33 Go back to regular view
- Click 📖

🦶34 Highlight (mark) text
- Click ▱

- Click ⬜ twice

- Click the desired color

- Drag the pointer across the text

🦶35 Add a note
- Click ⬇

- Click the desired spot

- Type a text

🦶36 Close toolbar
- Click Exit

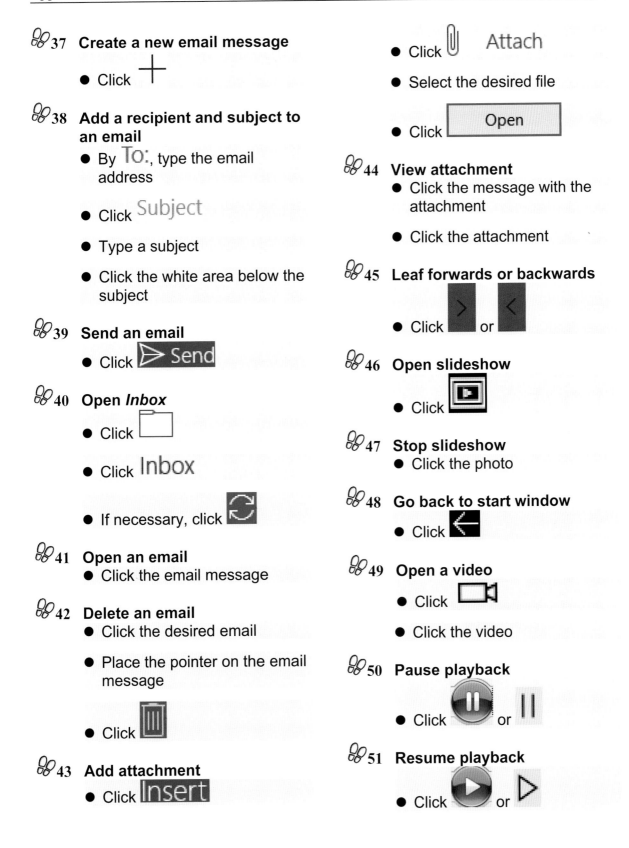

37 Create a new email message

- Click ┼

38 Add a recipient and subject to an email
- By To:, type the email address

- Click Subject

- Type a subject

- Click the white area below the subject

39 Send an email
- Click ▷ Send

40 Open *Inbox*

- Click 📁

- Click Inbox

- If necessary, click 🔄

41 Open an email
- Click the email message

42 Delete an email
- Click the desired email

- Place the pointer on the email message

- Click 🗑

43 Add attachment
- Click Insert

- Click 📎 Attach

- Select the desired file

- Click Open

44 View attachment
- Click the message with the attachment

- Click the attachment

45 Leaf forwards or backwards

- Click > or <

46 Open slideshow

- Click ▶

47 Stop slideshow
- Click the photo

48 Go back to start window

- Click ←

49 Open a video

- Click 🎥

- Click the video

50 Pause playback

- Click ⏸ or ‖

51 Resume playback

- Click ▶ or ▷

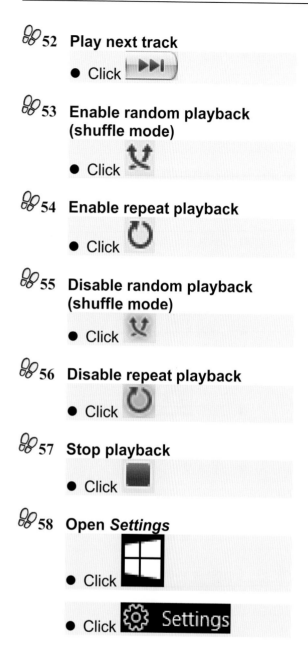

%52 Play next track

- Click ▶▶▎

%53 Enable random playback (shuffle mode)

- Click ⤬

%54 Enable repeat playback

- Click ↻

%55 Disable random playback (shuffle mode)

- Click ⤬

%56 Disable repeat playback

- Click ↻

%57 Stop playback

- Click ◼

%58 Open *Settings*

- Click ⊞

- Click ⚙ Settings

Appendix B. Downloading the Practice Files

In some chapters you will need to use several practice files. You can download these from the website accompanying this book.

☞ **Open *Edge*** 🐾³

☞ **Open the web page www.visualsteps.com/windows10** 🐾²⁷

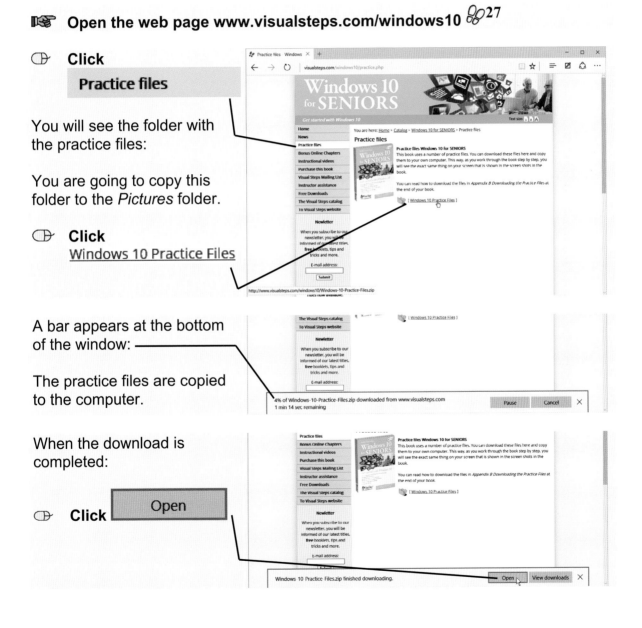

🖘 **Click**

    Practice files

You will see the folder with the practice files:

You are going to copy this folder to the *Pictures* folder.

🖘 **Click**

    Windows 10 Practice Files

A bar appears at the bottom of the window:

The practice files are copied to the computer.

When the download is completed:

🖘 **Click** **Open**

The *Practice files* folder is stored in the *Downloads* folder on the computer and this folder is now opened. This folder is a compressed folder. This means that the files in the folder are compressed so that the file size is smaller. If you want to use the files in a compressed folder, you need to unzip (or extract) the folder first:

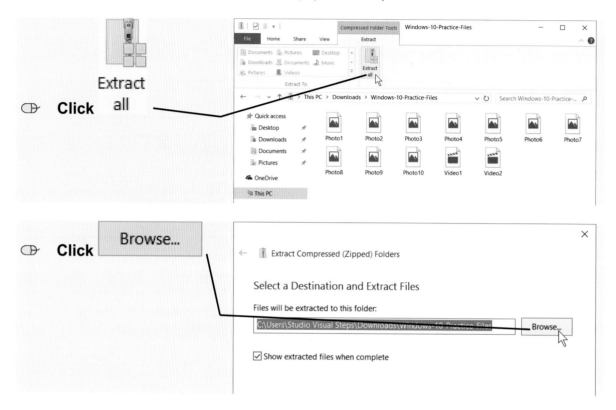

You are going to create a new folder with the name *Practice files Windows 10*:

☞ **Click**

| Select Folder |

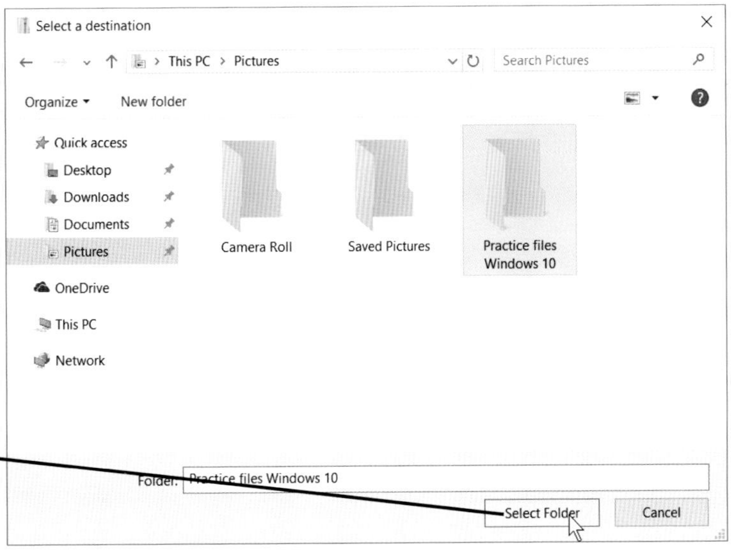

Now you are going to extract the files in this new folder:

☞ **Click** | Extract |

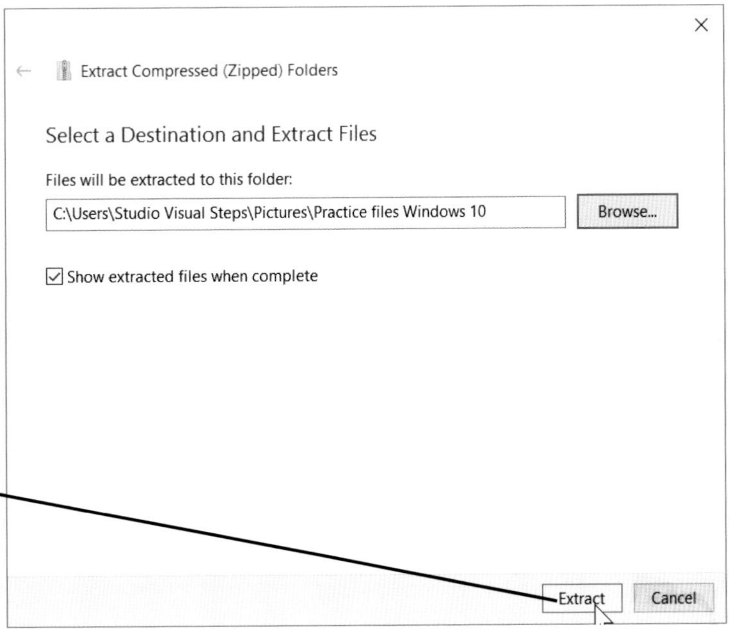

While the files are being
extracted, you see this
window:

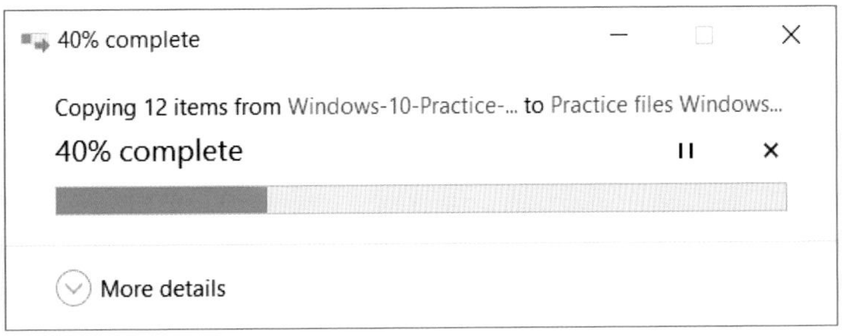

You will see the practice files that go with this book. There are a couple of photos and two videos. You are going to move the videos to the *Videos* folder:

☞ **If necessary, by**
🖥 This PC , click ❯

Click   Video1
and keep the mouse
button pressed

☞ **Drag the file to**
🎞 Videos

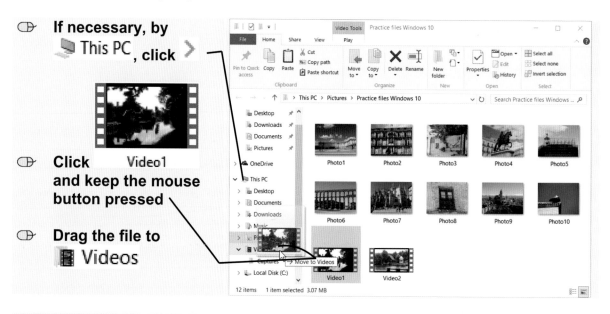

☞ **Do the same thing with the file called Video2**

☞ **Close the window** 👣¹

The compressed folder *Windows-10-Practice-Files* has been saved in the *Downloads* folder. This window is still opened. You can delete the compressed folder:

☞ **Click 📥 Downloads**

☞ **If necesary, click the**
folder

☞ **Click the   Home   tab**

☞ **Click ✖**

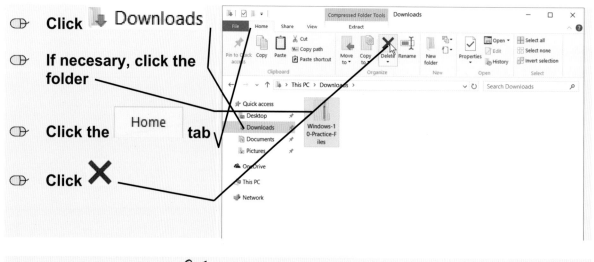

☞ **Close all windows** 👣¹

Now you can continue with the chapter.

Appendix C. Opening the Bonus Online Chapters

This is how you open the bonus online chapters on this book's website:

☞ **Open *Edge* ⌇³**

☞ **Open the web page www.visualsteps.com/windows10 ⌇²⁷**

You will see the website that goes with this book:

⊕ **Click**
   Bonus Online Chapters

Now you will see this web page:

To open the bonus chapter:

⊕ **Click**
   Start downloading »»

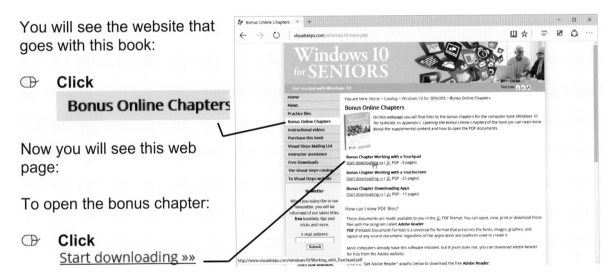

You will see a new tab in *Edge*. The PDF files are secured by a password. You need to enter the password to open the PDF file:

⌨ **Type: 56985**

⊕ **Click**
   OK

Now you will see the Bonus Chapter:

You can see the rest of the chapter by dragging the scroll box:

The blue progress bar at the top indicates the progress of the download. When this bar is gone, the whole document is opened:

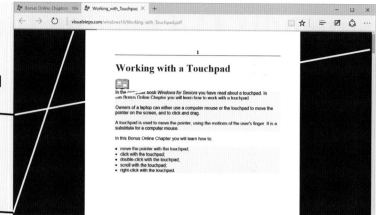

In *section 4.7 Printing a Web Page* you have learned how to print a web page. You can print a PDF file the same way. You can also save the document to your computer. This way you can open it at a later on.

☞ **Right-click the document**

☞ **Click** Save as

The *Documents* folder is opened by default:

To save the document:

☞ **Click** Save

The document will be saved in the *Documents* folder.

You can work through this bonus chapter in the same ways as you worked through the
chapters in the book. After you have finished reading, printing or saving the file, you can close *Edge*.

☞ **Close** *Edge* ✎¹

Appendix D. Opening the Instructional Videos

There are a number of instructional videos available on the website that accompanies this book. In this appendix you can read how to open and view these videos.

☞ **Open *Edge*** ♘♘³

☞ **Open the www.visualsteps.nl/windows10 web page** ♘♘²⁷

You will see the website that accompanies this book:

⊕ **Click**

Instructional videos

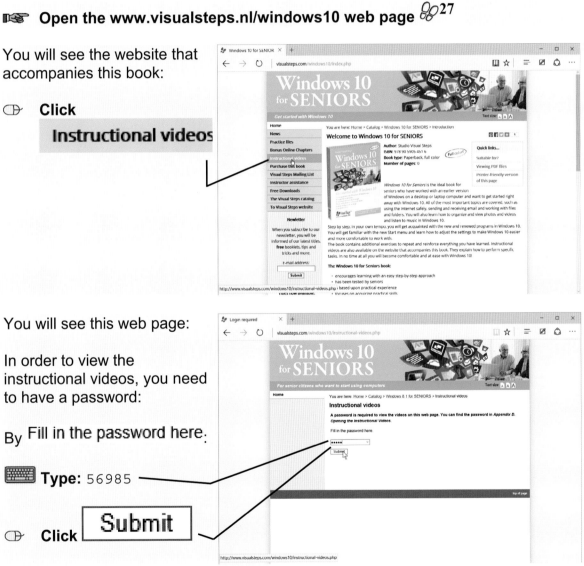

You will see this web page:

In order to view the instructional videos, you need to have a password:

By **Fill in the password here.**:

⌨ **Type:** 56985

⊕ **Click** **Submit**

You will see several
instructional videos:

This is what you do if you
want to watch a video:

- **If necessary, drag the
  scroll box downwards
  a bit**

- **By the desired video,
  click** ▶

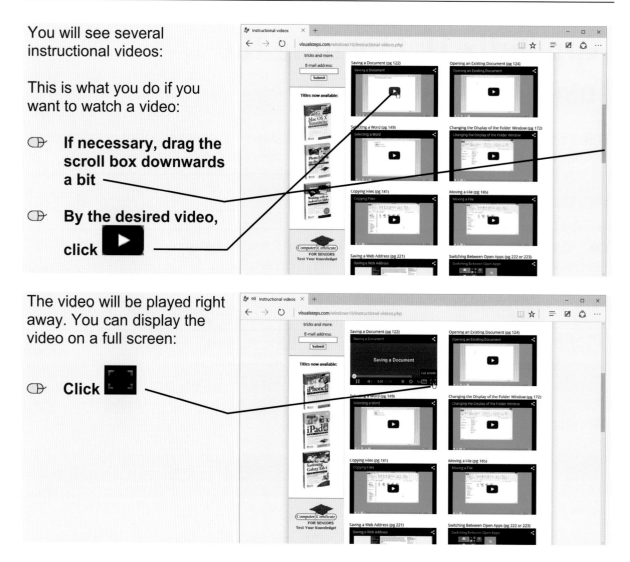

The video will be played right
away. You can display the
video on a full screen:

- **Click** ⛶

You may see an additional bar at the bottom of the screen. You can close this bar:

- **Click** ✕

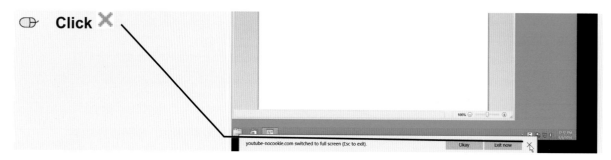

The video quality may not be optimized. You can adjust the quality or resolution as follows:

In the bottom right corner of the screen:

☞ **Click** ⚙ ────

☞ **If necessary, click** ▼
by **Quality**

☞ **If necessary, click**
720p ᴴᴰ

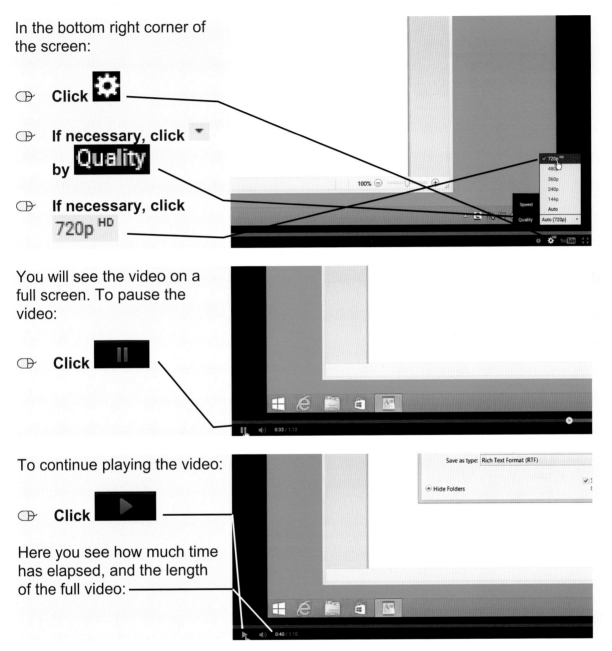

You will see the video on a full screen. To pause the video:

☞ **Click** ⏸

To continue playing the video:

☞ **Click** ▶

Here you see how much time has elapsed, and the length of the full video: ────

If you want to jump forward:

⊕ **Drag**  **to the right** ——

To go backward, you do the opposite. Drag to the left.

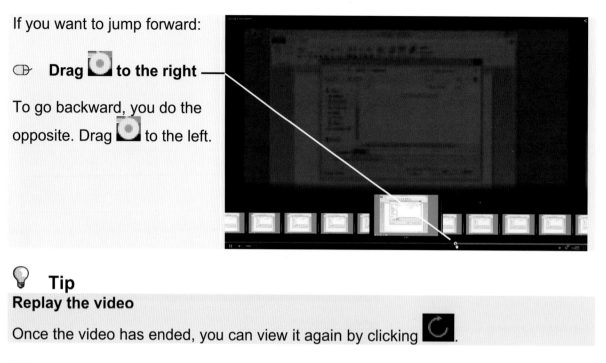

💡 **Tip**

Replay the video

Once the video has ended, you can view it again by clicking.

When the video has finished playing, you can close the full screen display:

⌨️ **Press** **Esc**

You can open the other instructional videos in the same way.

☞ **Close** *Edge* 👣[1]

Appendix E. Index